COMBAT JOURNAL

(Part 3 of 4)
"A Soldier's Journey To Hell"

by

John J. McBrearty

Lieutenant Colonel, U.S. Army (Retired)
Amazon Best Selling Author
In Iraq War History

Dedication

I want future generations to understand what we went through in Operation Iraqi Freedom.

I want to honor the 1,000 soldiers I deployed with.

I want to honor the five soldiers who never returned home to their loved ones.

I write these pages for you and your legacy as well as mine.

"In shaa Allah"

("God willing" in Arabic.)

John J. McBrearty

Operation Iraqi Freedom

4 May 2004

"Sometimes a man befriends his worst enemies in order to achieve victory over those enemies."

John J. McBrearty, Iraq 2004

CONTENTS

COMBAT JOURNAL

(Part 3 of 4)

"A Soldier's Journey To Hell"

The reason for writing this **COMBAT JOURNAL**. JM

Carol M Highsmith Archive Library of Congress Prints and Photographs Division

Introduction

We left off from **COMBAT JOURNAL**, Part 2 of 4, with our unit's first KIA (killed in action). The death of the battalion's first soldier weighs heavily on the unit, and particularly on the Battalion Executive Officer, Major Darby Hillcrest. Darby is faced with overwhelming odds stacked against him, not to mention his almost impossible Commanding Officer.

In **COMBAT JOURNAL** Part 3 of 4, we will witness continued decisive combat operations and, unfortunately, more death. Major Hillcrest gets a long-awaited reprieve from the war effort and visits home on an R&R trip. However, that trip home is quite short-lived as he returns to the "Belly of the Beast," and before you know it, Darby is back in the thick of things.

NOTES FROM THE AUTHOR

1. A point of clarification: it is grammatically correct to spell out terms in succession and then put the acronym followed by (parentheses). For example, medical treatment facility (MTF). However, sometimes I will also refer to the acronym first and spell it out secondly, as is a common practice in military circles: FOB (forward operating base). I also recommend glancing over the Glossary of Military Terms before plunging into this **COMBAT JOURNAL**. The glossary can be found in the back of the book.

2. *NOTE FROM AUTHOR: Italicized writings are often my observations upon editing this gargantuan four-part* **COMBAT JOURNAL**. *This journal series consists of over 1,200 pages of dialogue, photos, and media accounts of my two-year adventure. I decided to provide some 2023 commentary as appropriate, and that is in the italicized writings.*

3. Disclaimer. Historical concepts, race, terminology, and references used in my sources could now sometimes be deemed offensive, discriminatory, and politically incorrect. I in no way embrace such concepts or intend to use such terms as insults. However, I believe that we must preserve our historical roots and make our documentation as truthful as possible. *(Hey, I guess that qualifies me as an official "History Geek"?) LOL*

4. Both military time (1900) and civilian time (7 p.m.) will be used interchangeably. *Why do you ask?* I had a lot on my mind at the time, so just get used to it!

5. Photo disclaimer. Some of the photographs in the **COMBAT JOURNAL** book series are not up to industry standards, but most are to standard. The reason for this is that the photos were taken in the middle of the combat zone, in 120-degree heat and extremely harsh conditions. Some photos were even taken through night vision devices. I chose to keep these photos in the book series because they are an accurate representation of real combat.

6. The following disclaimer went out with all correspondence that I had with media outlets, family, and friends, informing them that any correspondence between us was fair game for my forthcoming book series, **COMBAT JOURNAL**. "<u>**LEGAL NOTE**</u>: **Any information that I send to the media could possibly be contained in my**

forthcoming books about my experiences on this deployment to Iraq. Although a news agency might copyright their respective stories on my deployment, I reserve the right to reproduce those news stories and correspondence in my forthcoming books. - John J. McBrearty, 7-12-2004."

7. MORE NOTES FROM AUTHOR: For those 1,000 soldiers of the Army National Guard whom I deployed with and any family or friends that might read this **COMBAT JOURNAL**, *I want to clarify that all characters in this publication are fictitious. Any similarities to living persons are strictly coincidental.*

8. This journal is narrated by our fictitious main character, Major Darby Hillcrest, the Armor Battalion's Executive Officer (BXO). Lt. Colonel John J. McBrearty, U.S. Army (Retired), is the author of the book series.

9. Although the events portrayed in this book series are based on events that followed 9/11, this literature is categorized as historical fiction.

Enjoy!

JM

Army Values

"LDRSHIP"

Loyalty

Duty

Respect

Selfless Service

Honor

Integrity

Personal Courage

Why on earth is this author starting off his manuscript with Army Values? I felt that it is an important point of reference for my readership. The nucleus of leadership revolves around the seven Army Values. In fact, I wrote an entire publication based on the numerous **LEADERSHIP LESSONS** *learned from the* **COMBAT JOURNAL** *book series. That leadership book will be available on Amazon upon the release of* **COMBAT JOURNAL** *(4 of 4). JM*

Our Cast of Characters

*NOTE FROM AUTHOR: I give a detailed biography of the main players in **COMBAT JOURNAL** (Part 1 of 4). Please refer to that previous volume if you require more information about our cast.*

Lieutenant Colonel Larry Slacker is the Commanding Officer (CO) of the Armor Battalion. LTC Slacker has a short temper, and he frequently humiliates his subordinates in public. The soldiers within his command hate him, and his staff officers hate him even more. Slacker is our COL Klink from the sitcom, "Hogan's Heroes."

Major Darby Hillcrest is the Battalion Executive Officer (BXO) and second in charge of the battalion. He is the book's narrator and main character. Hillcrest is an Active Guard Reservist (AGR) or full-time National Guard Officer and is happily married with two kids.

Hillcrest is 43 years old, of stocky build (ex-football player type), and quite athletic. A likable and handsome officer and a gentleman, Hillcrest has the leadership abilities to pull the unit through the roughest of times despite their commanding officer. Hillcrest is our COL Hogan from the television sitcom "Hogan's Heros."

This book is his story.

Command Sergeant Major Marcus Hunts is the senior enlisted soldier in the battalion. He is the quintessential non-commissioned officer (NCO), a true professional in every aspect of the word.

Captain (Promotable) Clave Rickets is the S3 Operations Officer and was promoted to Major in Iraq. Large in stature, he is an Infantry Officer who knows tactics and likes to bark out orders, often overpowering. He is addicted to playing X-Box.

Captain Ronald Randerson is the S1 Personnel Officer and mild-mannered. Randerson is often the brunt of LTC Slacker's criticisms and always in public. A Barney Fife type.

First Lieutenant Don Ridges is originally from the east coast and has a pronounced accent to prove it. Ridges majored in computer science in college and normally works in the computer field. He is a computer geek.

Captain Larry Castellano is the Battalion Maintenance Officer. Castellano is a stereotypical Italian who likes to talk with his hands and tends to yell a lot. This guy is very animated. Professionally he appears to be a buffoon. He reminds me of an Italian version of the late comedian Sam Kennison.

Captain Brandon Morehead is the S3 Air or Assistant Operations Officer. A capable and intelligent officer with a diverse vocabulary. He is quite lean in stature and appears to be very high-strung, as if maybe he has had one too many espressos.

Captain Will Cantez is the S4 Logistics Officer. Short and round in stature, he is built like a bowling ball. Cantez is the life of the party, always ready with a quick-witted line to bring a smile to everyone's face. An actor destined to play this officer in a movie, Danny DeVito. He also has issues with authority figures but does a good job despite his "shortcomings."

Brigadier General Kloster F. Killman is the Commanding Officer (CO) of the Brigade. He is of Filipino descent and has a pronounced accent. *(We can't understand a darn word he says!)* "War is Hell," and Killman made things worse for us, "Killman is killing us-man!"

Colonel Fred Brimstone is the Deputy Brigade Commander. He is a "crusty old Colonel," as they say. He physically looks and sounds like Fred Flintstone, no lie! This man growls when he talks.

Lieutenant Colonel Kabat is the Brigade Chief of Staff (COS) or Executive Officer (XO). Slacker and Kabat hate each other. This guy is a real backstabber!

Lieutenant Colonel Wayne Café' is the battalion commander without a command. He was commander of the Engineers, but that battalion was elected to be the "replacement" battalion for the other units. He has an explosive temper. Café' was in limbo, and when LTC Kabat was relieved, BG Kilman selected Cafe' to step in. Despite his imperfections, he did an adequate job as XO.

Chaplain Billy Farrell (Major) is the Battalion Chaplain. This is a revered and highly respected position. Chaplains must be ordained ministers with master's level education at a minimum. The Chaplain is a soft-spoken gentleman of much intellect. Farrell is a chronic snorer and could wake the dead!

Captain Saul Ryker is the HHC commander. He is normally a schoolteacher and should stick to that profession as he has little future as a leader in the military. Another Barney Fife type.

First Sergeant Jim Chord is built like an ex-football player. He is a smooth operator who talks a big game but delivers little. This guy reminds me of a used car salesman who always makes quota but who might blow his money and commissions by gambling, drinking, or whores. He got caught with his hand in the cookie jar and was brought up on sexual misconduct charges, relieved of his position, and taken off the deployment. A real piece of work!

Sergeant Major Westminster is the Operations Sergeant Major and is the second highest-ranking enlisted soldier in the battalion. He is built like a former football player, which lends himself to being a bit intimidating. Cynical and cocky would best describe this man. Every word out of his mouth is a complaint about how "f____ed up" things are.

Sergeant First Class Dwellers is a worthless excuse of a soldier. He is afraid of his own shadow and won't leave the wire (encampment) for anything short of a direct order. Most of the Battalion hates this guy's guts! A real "buddy fucker!" (Sorry for the language, but get ready for a bumpy ride on the following pages with this guy!) We later find out that Dwellers was a snitch for the inadequate Battalion Commander. A real prick!

Joining us later through the mobilization process:

Major Killerman, PA, is one of three Physician Assistants assigned to us for the deployment. M. Killerman is a Psychiatric PA and has no trauma experience (what a find for us in a combat zone!) He loves to talk and doesn't know when to shut up. A perfectly useless individual. Go Army!

Captain Irwindale, MD, The Army learned from its mistakes in Desert Storm and now only deploys doctors on shorter deployments of three months and gives them $50K bonuses. Not too shabby for another guy who has no trauma experience. LTC Slacker hates this guy and constantly makes fun of him. A tall, hulking fellow, seemingly harmless, and enjoys sleeping.

First Lieutenant Loretta Youngham is one of us, just like another "Joe," as we call it in the Army (a term of endearment for enlisted soldiers). One of the guys, this chick, is tough and very cool. She understands Army medicine and will let you know it. Youngham likes to talk, and talk, and talk; if you are the unfortunate bastard who she locks in on, you could be there listening for hours; good luck!

Colonel Quate Nosey was the former G3 of Corps Support Command (COSCOM). He was relieved of his duties there and sent here during the OIF I/II surge and when the main supply routes (MSRs) were clogged up with logistical traffic. The epidemy of a worthless governmental employee.

Lieutenant Colonel Emma Milling is the Commander of the Combat Support Battalion-"PROVISIONAL" (CSBp). Provisional means that the unit was created from nothing and is temporary. This is a fancy title for nothing other than a figurehead. One word to describe her: _worthless!_ She has a battalion staff consisting of nine NCOs and Officers who are assigned the mayor's duties at Combat Support Center (CSC) Scania. Anything she touches falls apart and turns to "crapola." She has no leadership abilities, and I would not follow her to the latrine (toilet). Everyone on the post hates her guts. A movie character who would personify her would be the Wicked Witch of the East from "The Wizard of Oz."

Her motto: "Do as I say, not as I do!"

Sergeant Major Moans is LTC Milling's Sergeant Major and acts as her shadow and bodyguard? All this part-time (Reserve) logistician cares about is the uniformity of the camp soldiers' uniforms. Moans is a large, intimidating-looking figure. He does not have a clue about anything outside the gates of his safe and secure in Camp Scania. We can sum things up with him in three words: A big buffoon.

Major Freakins is LTC's Executive Officer and a career logistician. She probably wonders how she got stuck working for the likes of LTC Milling.

She is a smart, nice woman and a hard worker. She is a ray of sunshine for her band of nitwits.

Major Smythe is LTC's Operations Officer and, like COL Nosey, is a career logistician who also doesn't have a clue about the fight that is going on outside the secure base camp, Scania. Quite the pompous ass.

First Sergeant Crowne is LTC Milling's First Sergeant and is another loser put out to pasture at CSC Scania. Fired from her actual initial assignment in Iraq, she too was sent to Scania, where she could hopefully do no harm and get no one killed. She pretends to work in the logistics field. A real piece of work!

Sergeant First Class I. Careless is another loser on the LTC Milling's team. A full-time Reservist and functional illiterate who, if he had a brain, would be dangerous. Careless has been charged three different times for sexual misconduct, so lock up your wives and daughters, as this guy has been known to hang out in the local park with nothing on but a trench coat!

Specialist Dole is a single mother of two from the mid-west. Somehow, she must have pissed someone off and gotten assigned to the mayor's cell for duty. She is a young blond female who is *"Looking for Mr. Goodbar."* Rumor has it that she flashed her tits for all the boys during her 4-day pass? Stay clear of this one, guys; she is pretty wild and looking for her next child support financier.

Wives:

Annette Hillcrest is the wife of the Battalion Executive Officer, MAJ Darby Hillcrest. An attractive 40-year-old schoolteacher and former ballet dancer. During the mobilization, Annette had to do the paperwork for the purchase of their new home, sell their existing home, move out of their existing home, move into the new home, raise their 2 1/2-year-old son Junior, and work full time, oh yes and handle her husband's investments and legal affairs. This mobilization could not have come at the worst time. This woman is a saint and not bad on the eyes!

Carmon Dwellers is the Battalion Family Support Coordinator and wife of SFC Dwellers, the personnel NCO for the Battalion. Carmon is a no-

nonsense type of person who, unfortunately, can rub some of the wives the wrong way. How she ended up with a loser like SFC Dwellers is anybody's guess because she is a nice person and attractive (everything her husband ain't!)

NOTE FROM AUTHOR: Saving the best for last. JM

Sherry Termagants is the older sister of Major Hillcrest, and she lives on the East Coast. As demonstrated by her actions, Sherry does not approve of our country's efforts in the global war on terrorism. She certainly does not support her brother and his participation in the war in Iraq and has cut off all ties with her family and him. The demise of their relationship weighs heavily on Major Hillcrest and his family. However, you cannot rationalize with the un-rational. The Hollywood actress that comes to mind that would resemble Sherry? Glen Closes' character in "Fatal Attraction." Scary!

Michael Termagants is Sherry's husband and brother-in-law of Major Hillcrest. Michael and Sherry are two peas in a pod. He is an enabler for his unscrupulous wife. Michael reminds me of a white-collar gangster that you see in the movies. But this guy is not in a movie. He is real-life evil.

First Act: More Death

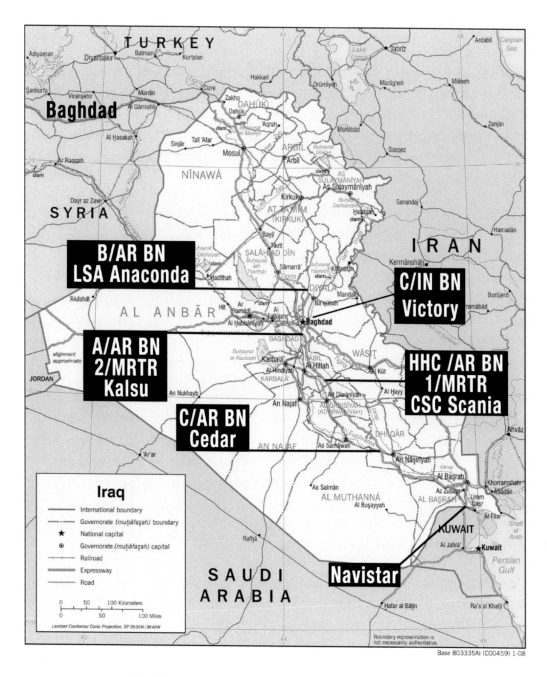

Iraq Country map with Armor Battalion unit locations.
Map by John J. McBrearty. Source: The World Factbook, CIA Maps.

26 May 04

Going to bed, there were sounds of small arms firing here and there. We believe it might have been Iraqi on Iraqi or the Poles near our area of responsibility.

27 May 04

LTC Slacker addresses MAJ Hillcrest in a forceful manner: I hear you are hiring locals to fill our sandbags? And having the 300th ASG fund it with CERP money? And why don't I know about it?" Hillcrest replies, "Sir, you weren't here yesterday. I was taking the initiative. And I don't know anything about the 300th ASG funding; I am funding this myself." Slacker yells, "It is stupid. Cancel the mission immediately!"

Cantez said this about the situation that he had just observed: "Sir, Slacker called this mission off because it wasn't his idea, and he didn't want you to get credit for something good." Unfortunately, I think CPT Cantez summed things up quite accurately. Herein lies the problem with Slacker, and could prove to be the catalyst to his eventual demise. We are talking about the SAFETY of our soldiers, and his ego has gotten in the way. Ego is more important to Slacker than our soldiers' SAFETY? I am banging my head against the wall. I would talk to Slacker about considering changing his decision, but also, unfortunately, that would be pointless as well.

Constant struggles with the fucking LA Paper reporter again. He has already written and published articles about SPC U.'s death. It is currently posted on the LA Paper National Guard Support website. He also mass-emailed the article to everyone and their brother, and we, the military, don't even have official confirmation of NOK (Next of Kin) notification. Even Slacker admitted that he made a mistake by informing California Leadership of the event. (What was he thinking?)

It is amazing to me to read the newspaper's email to CPT Laylock (Brigade Public Affairs Officer), as they think that they are doing us, the National Guard, a great service by having a website devoted to our deployment. They stated that they had devoted hundreds of hours of work, money, time, and effort to support us? Whoever asked them to start a website anyway? Certainly not us! Fuck that jacked-up reporter and his newspaper and their exaggerated tales of woe.

I am currently writing a condolence letter for LTC Slacker to send to the deceased soldier's family. When a service member is KIA (Killed in Action), we immediately turn off all means of communication to our respective FOB locations. This includes telephone and, of course, the Internet. The last thing that we want is for our soldiers to get the word out to the public before the family is officially notified. Military officials must have the opportunity to conduct proper NOK (Next of Kin) notification before word gets out to the public. The Army goes to great lengths to train its service members in the proper procedures and protocols necessary if the unfortunate occurs.

We still haven't lifted the communications ban on the post, and soldiers are squawking. CPT Castellano even asked Slacker to lift the restriction, and thank goodness Slacker said no.

We are totally exasperated. At morning chow, Slacker came in and joined me and 1SG Randerson. Not a word was hardly spoken. The atmosphere is ominous. Grief is the common emotion of the day.

I received press release statements from our home state and brigade, but unfortunately, both had inaccuracies in them. I emailed the state with my recommendations and called LTC Rosales. Hopefully, they will take my advice with the releases.

COALITION PRESS INFORMATION CENTER
BAGHDAD, Iraq
May 27, 2004

Release

Soldier Killed by Mortar Attack

BALAD, Iraq – A Brigade Combat Team soldier assigned to Armor Battalion Task Force was killed on May 25 when a mortar round landed on his sleeping tent. Additionally, nine soldiers were also injured in the incident, and eight were taken to a military hospital.

The injured soldiers were evacuated to the 31st Combat Support Hospital, Baghdad.

The names of the soldiers are being withheld pending notification of next of kin.

The incident is under investigation.

The LA Paper ran the story:

'My Son Was Not Going to Let Someone Else Die in His Place'

NOTE: This story came out on the 26th of May, and the soldier was KIA on the 25th? This poor young man's body is still warm, and the LA Paper is reporting it to the masses. This is just wrong! Unfortunately, it is because LTC Slacker informed the Division back in the States literally at the time of the event. This was a fatal mistake; I wish he had listened to me.

28 May 04

I am numb.

I wrote my wife a letter to break the news to her about the death of SPC U. and our other casualties:

From the desk of:
MAJOR Hillcrest
TO: Annette (aka: Woman of My Dreams)
SUBJECT: Situation Report
DATE: May 28, 2004

Dear Annette,

I don't want you to be worried about me, but I have to inform you that we sustained our first death due to hostile fire. The details can be found on the LA Paper website or possibly in the local papers. Several of our units have been under attack, and we have also sustained multiple casualties. This was the second worst experience of my life, next to losing my parents. Life has taken on a whole new meaning for all of us over here.

I don't want you to be alarmed and worrying. Things like this happen in war. What I will tell you is that we are taking EVERY precaution to prevent further friendly bloodshed or death. We have increased many measures of our offensive and defensive operations and done direct coordination with the local Sheikhs, Tribal Leaders, and other coalition units in our area.

Please don't worry about me. I wear my protective undervest everywhere, and I always carry my weapon, even to the shower. I also carry two weapons, whereas almost all others only have one assigned weapon. I always carry a side arm as well as my rifle. We have hardened our sleeping tents with heavy sandbags. We had several soldiers' lives saved the other night from just having adequate sandbag coverage of their tent. I truly believe that we are doing everything we can to survive this battle.

I am sorry about your difficulties with the move, house, etc. I recommend that you immediately get Junior out of your bed and into his own cot. That will be a bad habit that will be hard to break if he gets used to it. And trust me, when I get back home, three will be a crowd, *if you know what I mean.*

I am also sorry for not calling or emailing more often. With our current demise, it just wasn't in the cards. Please pass on to all family members on all sides of our family that I apologies for not keeping up with emails and thank yous for the numerous care packages, emails, and letters that they all have so graciously sent. I will try to write a letter and email it to all.

God bless.

Your husband

*NOTE FROM AUTHOR: Needless to say, I am in tears every time I read this letter to my wife. I only hope that in future book signings, my readers won't expect me to cite passages like this one because I won't be able to hold it together. I remember this event like it happened yesterday. To conclude, I must address "survivor's guilt." I will discuss this topic in much greater detail in my follow-on volumes of **American History, A Veteran's Perspective**. Survivor's guilt is what I experience every time I read about this soldier and our other soldier's deaths. It can be quite debilitating.*

From the desk of:
MAJOR Hillcrest
TO: The Families of Armor Battalion
SUBJECT: Specialist U.
DATE: May 28, 2004

It is with heartfelt regret that I have to inform you about our first death due to hostile fire. Life has taken on a whole new meaning for all of us in the Armor Battalion. I wish to express to the families of all our battalion members that we are taking EVERY precaution to prevent further bloodshed or death to our soldiers. We have increased many measures of our offensive and defensive operations and continue to have direct coordination with the local Sheikhs, Tribal Leaders, and other coalition units in our area. Your continued support of your soldiers in the field is greatly appreciated.

SPC U. was accomplished in martial arts and baseball. He joined the Army National Guard on June 9, 2003. Specialist U. was sent to D Company, 119th at Fort Benning, Georgia, for basic training. Upon completion of basic training, Specialist U. was assigned to Armor Battalion as an Infantryman. His current assignment is Company A, Armor Battalion.

Specialist U. fought with his squad in two previous engagements. On one mission, he detained six individuals and was the Platoon Leaders' RTO. Specialist U. held his military occupational specialty of being an infantryman to the highest standards, both mentally and physically, so much so that he had the Infantry crossed rifles tattooed over his heart.

He is survived by his father, mother, one brother and two younger sisters, and the loving memories of his family and friends.

Additional information regarding the Armor Battalion's deployment can be obtained at www.xyz.gov. For any media inquiries in the future, we strongly encourage you to first contact the Office of the Adjutant General's Public Affairs Office.

Sincerely,

MAJ Hillcrest

XO, Armor Battalion

29 May 04

I can't bring myself to write. Such trivial bull shit with the fucking Mayor's staff, particularly LTC Milling. The issue that COL Nosey raised from our attack is placing the BDOC (base defense operations center), or HHC HQs co-located with our operations and intelligence staff, as well as the MP's TOC, in the hardened building structure that is currently shared with the Mayors Cell. That makes perfect sense from a force protection standpoint. At 1400, we got the Armor Battalion staff with the mayor's cell staff in the conference room to staff the moving of various personnel to accommodate the Commander's intent. What a cluster fuck! COL Nosey gave LTC Milling the authority to make decisions as to moving staff and units into and out of the big, hardened HQ building. COL Nosey told the Armor Battalion staff that he wanted the BDOC to switch office space with the mayor's staff. The mayor's staff are obviously not happy with that choice. We attempted to wargame various other courses of action; however, she refused to move out of their office space. A middle road was achieved, whereas both sides (Castellano of the BDOC and the Mayor's staff) agreed to give up one of their closets for him to use as an office and move his staff into the conference room. I refused to accept that as an answer, and CPT Moans, the MP LNO for the MP Battalion (active-duty MPs), agreed with me totally. He and I concede that for force protection and command and control purposes, the BDOC needs to occupy the mayor's cell offices. This makes the most sense for survivability and control. The mayor's staff are secondary in mission to ours of force protection.

CSC Scania, Iraq BDOC (Base Defense Operations Center).

Following this cluster fuck, I hoofed it over to LTC Slacker's tent, where I found him sleeping in his rack (finally something that he is actually good at!) I woke him up and informed him of the situation and how Nosey told the mayor's staff one thing and us another. SGM Moans got extremely upset when I brought up the issue of having them move out of their offices. I reminded LTC Slacker that we need to focus on one thing and prioritize one thing: to get our boys home in one piece, and nothing should get in the way of that intent. He certainly agreed as we made our way towards his office. I reminded him that CPT Moans has the most experience around here, is an active-duty combat arms officer, and agrees with me totally. I stated that we are not here to "work together" with one another or to be politically correct. All that matters is surviving. The logisticians don't have a clue about force protection or combat operations. When the 504th was here, they utilized the entire building for their BN staff and BDOC combined. The problem we have is that the CSB staff got here three weeks before us and moved into their offices. The real problem here is that we have one too many battalions staff sections on the ground. In reality, a senior NCO like an E7 or E8 could handle the responsibilities of the camp Mayor. At FOB Kalsu, MSG Villa (who was fired from the 1SG position of A Co.) serves in the capacity of mayor. At CSC Scania, we have a newly promoted Lieutenant Colonel from the Army Reserve Logistical Corps and her staff as the mayor. Overkill? You bet your ass. It is a waste of a military officer; however, several of her staff members do show signs of competency. About half of her staff are either active Army logisticians or full-time technicians who support the Army Reserves.

I don't remember if I wrote about the night of the attack and the day after. COL Nosey came into the TOC sometime after our mortar attack. The lights were all out as we were practicing light discipline. He started asking a million questions about the QRF (quick reaction force), questions like, "Why was the QRF late, what about a secondary QRF why were they late?" I answered him at the top of my lungs; "All QRFs are out and were on time. We even have additional QRFs from the MPs, so please let us get back to work and leave us alone!!!!!!" All my staff looked on in amazement. I turned away from the COL and stomped towards the exit door. I gave the door a horrendously forceful karate kick to open it. The force was such that it pulled the door's hardware out of the wall! The sound was thunderous, talk about a dramatic exit! The next day CPT Morehead said jokingly in front of Slacker and the staff, "Boy you should have seen the XO last night, he earned my respect with how he dealt with Nosey." I said, "well sir, I chewed out two Colonels in one day, how about that?" Everyone laughed. Slacker even liked hearing this as he hates Millings guts with a passion and Nosey is not on the top of his friends list either. Later that day, Sergeant Major Hunts said that I definitely earned my combat pay and did the right thing.

30 May 04

Sunday. I slept in for about an hour and a half, yes that is about as exciting as it gets here (extra sleep). 1LT Artera, CPT Cantez and I jumped into our PT gear and dawned our Kevlar helmets (you must wear a helmet when traveling in a military vehicle). With our personal weapons in hand, we drove in a HMMWV to the sandbag filling area in "the yard" on the other side of post. We proceeded to fill numerous sandbags. This is the fourth time this week that I have worked on sandbags. It is about the most labor-intensive thing you can do. I am thoroughly drained from the experience. It didn't help doing it in the sunny heat of the day either. It is interesting to note that the local "Hadjie's" (how we refer to Iraqis) are hired daily as laborers and there was a team of roughly six of them near us. They are supervised by a KBR (Kellogg, Crown and Root, Inc. - a company owned by Haliburton). What is interesting to me is that on the fourth day doing this within the last six days, every time that we saw the Hadjie's working detail, they were laying around sleeping in the shade? We made our sandbags at different times each time we worked. We also were able to scam two extra pallet loads of sandbags that the Hadjie's made (hey, you do what you got to do in this environment!)

Sandbag working party with LNs (Local Nationals), CSC Scania, Iraq.

The workmanship was crappy at best. Our bags are almost completely full, which makes them quite heavy to pick up. The Hadjie's bags were all literally ½ full and half as heavy. We did our one pallet which gave us in total, three pallets of sandbags. We had a KBR forklift driver deliver two of the pallets for us to our tent and we drove one pallet in our jeep. We hardened our tent with the additional sandbags enhancing the entrance and improving our bunker (a defensive fortification).

Reflecting on the week, the biggest thing that I can't get off my mind is Slacker. On the morning of the day that he went to Kalsu for SPC U.'s memorial service, he came into my office, and several NCOs were present. Slacker was ranting and raving about how he didn't even want to go to Kalsu and that everyone needed to stop their sniveling about SPC U. and get back to work. No one said anything, but we all nervously looked at each other as if we were saying with our eyes, "Did he just say what I think he said?" He was so callus, curt, and downright disrespectful of our fallen comrade. I think he is trying to put up a tough front and scare everyone back into the business of war, but the technique isn't working. All I could think of, and I bet you anything that the other soldiers were thinking the same as me. Will he be saying that shit about me if I die? That is what we have to look forward to? I can't get Slacker's unemotional reaction to SPC U. out of my mind. It is all I think about: morning, noon, and night. I don't get him.

I attended Church after finishing a day of sandbagging, and boy am I bushed! I guess that I have become the unofficial Eucharist Minister for the Catholic Lay Services. I actually enjoy the whole process. Fortunately, the Chaplain does the preaching part (homily), and he is really well versed in the Bible with doctorate-level education. Following the service, I spoke with Chaplain Grazier for a while. We talked about the occurrences of the last week, losing three soldiers. I said that God called on SPC U. for a purpose, a great purpose. I believe that he was taken from us in order to save lives. His death has changed the way we all do business and how we now look at our lives here in Iraq.

Today I received two care packages, one from Annette and one from her brother who is a successful physician on the East Coast. He is married and has two daughters and one son. My brother-in-law is easily the most down to earth, unpretentious doctor that you will ever find. They are so thoughtful their care package included Philadelphia Tastykakes, a favorite of mine and just about all Philadelphians.

31 May 04

Memorial Day. Today is like no other Memorial Day in my life as it has taken on a whole new meaning for me.

We had a meeting in the morning, the 0900 BUB, which consisted of COL Nosey running buckshot over all of us. The meeting started out with his 10-minute introduction about how he is in charge and all that good shit. The meeting lasted 1 hour and 20 minutes, about 45 minutes too long. Following the meeting, the staff and commanders were released, and the

S3's of the post stayed and presented their respective COA Briefings to Nosey; Slacker was also present. What a cluster fuck, (I think I already said that). I see through Nosey as a smooth operator, it could actually be a requirement to make 06 (full-bird Colonel)? CPT Moans and I were the only ones in the MDMP process that disagreed to the recommended COA. He and I recommended swapping out the mayor's cell totally with the HHC BDOC, as far as office space.

My reasoning was the following:

1. Part of the evaluation criteria was "harmonious working environment" or "tenant harmony", my argument was that you can't quantify these criteria and it shouldn't be used. Besides, who cares if units or tenants don't like the outcome of the office space move, the military isn't a democracy, although we defend America's democracy.

2. The 504th (the unit that we replaced), had their entire battalion staff, to include the BDOC here under this one roof. With the history of the enemy's weaponry and actions, they don't have the firepower to take out the whole building, so we can accept some risk of a co-located command building.

3. This is the most important issue of all, survivability. Based on the activities on the evening of our attack this week, it is clear that a centrally located command structure is a must and the mayor's staff, although important in their own right, they have almost no play in force protection and survivability. COL Nosey allowed me to present my opinions, which were fully supported by CPT Moans, but Nosey went with the politically correct vote and sided with the recommended COA. HHC BDOC will occupy the S1 area, displacing the admin, legal and medical staff to HHC's previously occupied trailer and CPT Castellano will occupy MAJ Smythe's old office, of which it is currently empty. I lost this fight, but at least I was heard and was allowed to voice my opinion. Until I am the commander, that is all I can ask for. Also, I think too that all in the room respect the fact that I spoke up, even though they might not have agreed, but at least I showed the balls to not go along with the crowd if I didn't agree. Let them think what they like; I do what I do and say what I say because I think it is right. My gut says this. Oh well, on to the next battle.

It is a blistering hot day, over 108 degrees.

1830 The base conducted a Memorial Day picnic type of event along with a talent show. I say type of event because the extent of the cookout was that steaks, burgers and chicken were cooked on an outside grill and brought into the mess hall for eating. The talent show was pretty good stuff. I got suckered into participating and our act was up first. We did a skit from the old Dating Game Show.

Memorial Day picnic 2004 at CSC Scania, Iraq.

1 June 04

It is really June already? Wow, that is all I can say. The time is just flying away! This morning, I had a productive meeting with the CA (Civil Affairs) Team Chief (TC) for MND (Multi-National Division) Southeast Iraq. In the meeting were me, CA TC, 1LT Fernandez, our S5 Civil Affairs Officer, and 1LT Youngham, our Medical Services Officer (MAJ Freakins was MIA, which was concerning). The CA TC discussed the MEDCAP program in detail. MEDCAP stands for Medical Civic Action Program and is a method by which we provide humanitarian assistance to the Iraqis. He also discussed CERP funds (Commanders Emergency Response Program), which are also another means of resourcing additional humanitarian and civil assistance.

We just had two fast movers jet their way by us at a very low altitude. You can only experience that sound at a military air base or an air show. It is uplifting to hear those sounds as it gives us all a sense of security and empowerment.

At breakfast, I joined a table full of our various battalion members. LTC Slacker was seated across from the CA TC, and boy, Slacker was on a roll! I thought it was hilarious because SGM Westminster said to me in a low tone, "Same old stories, just a different audience." I couldn't help but laugh because Slacker's old "when I worked at the Division Headquarters" stories are getting very old for all of us.

Later that evening, LTC Slacker took a "select" few of the staff with him to Sheikh Hatim Al Jarian's home for dinner. He had the CA team join him (of course). This Colonel has a history with the National Guard in our state and knows many of the players. Cantez and I figure that Slacker was trying to impress him because of his California affiliation. Slacker never even mentioned the dinner to me, not once. Only a few staff were included. Following his last dinner at the Sheikh's home, he said that I could go on the next venture there. I guess he forgot. I sure feel left out of things when Slacker is involved.

We had an illumination 120mm mortar go off at 2115, which also gave us a sense of security.

2 June 04

Meetings all morning, what a (you guessed it) cluster fuck! 0900 COL Nosey again opens with the "I am in charge speech." Then Nosey precedes for 10 minutes, discussing radio chatter on Motorola handheld talk about radios. There is an underground radio network that converses on none other than channel 69. As the channel might imply, the conversations are like that of a Tom Lykus or Howard Stern type of radio show and are sexually based. Nosey wants to ban all these radios in the camp because of it.

CPT Lance, the Field Artillery turned Military Police Provisional, mentioned in the meeting that his soldiers had spotted an E7 in a John

Deer "Gator" (a small all-terrain lawn mower type of vehicle) taking sandbags off some of the tents in the LSA (living support area).

Sandbags are in place for the protection of living quarters for soldiers, CSC Scania, Iraq.

This confirmed my suspicion that we had about two rows of sandbags missing from our tent. I stated, "Well, let's narrow it down. What units have access to a Gator?" LTC Milling quickly jumped in defensively, "Well, we have a Gator, but lend it out to other units." That is bullshit; I posed the question because, like a good lawyer, we all knew the answer. I even saw SFC Careless driving the Gator around yesterday. Later, LTC Milling defended the sandbag issue further, stating that her Sergeant Major directed taking any bags in excess of the required height off of tents and giving them to tents that had little or no bags. This met with a wave of controversy because it was never previously discussed, and nobody agreed to this. Millings said that it was put out in the mayor's meeting last night and inferred that some units weren't in attendance. This must be the dumbest idea that I have seen to date. We, the guys in my tent and many other tents busted our asses to improve our living quarters safety, only to have some lamebrains come along and take our comfort zone away?

Without our approval? If I had seen this taking place, I would have done what we refer to in the military as the horizontal butt stroke to the head with my rifle butt.

This meeting lasted over an hour, and it was brutal. COL Nosey is losing our collective respect very quickly. The follow-up meeting was our weekly camp meeting with all the non-military tenants of the camp. This was a further extension of the earlier goat rope. One issue that came up was the movement of the DSN (defense service number-telephones) tent to the LSA (Living Support Area). MAJ Smythe, with the CSB, immediately responded that this was a bad idea because the soldiers that use the DSN phones are mostly the transient tenants, and we don't need that additional traffic in our living area. Nosey simply said bullshit to that idea and that all soldiers are to have equal access to everything on the post. I had to speak up with my concurrence with MAJ Smythe. I pointed out the fact that we are mitigating the problem now, such as soldier-on-soldier crime, theft, rape, etc., by not putting the phone tent in our living area. The living area is not secure. The tents don't have locks, and female tents are spread throughout. Slacker even mentioned in the meeting that Nosey was just making all the decisions and not stuffing anything. Later, Morehead, Ridges, and I had quite a joke from that comment as I said, "Boy, that's the pot calling the kettle black!" As mentioned earlier, Slacker did just that when he got over here in this big, old, horrible sandbox. He didn't staff anything as we had trained; he just made all decisions and micromanaged everything! Now, the shoe is on the other foot since he isn't in charge anymore, and he absolutely hates it.

Another issue that Nosey decided on, without discussing it with our staff, was to relocate the basketball and volleyball courts next to the MWR tents. They hadn't actually been built yet but have the green light to do so. Nosey said to tear down the three tents next to the MWR and put them there. He said that the soldiers would just have to double up the living arrangements. This, too, met with stern opposition from all as we are pretty cramped on space as it is. This is a fucking nut roll! At this point in time, I really see a SITCOM in the making. These characters are so strong even a gifted writer couldn't have dreamt them up. Here are the characters: Slacker-egomaniac, micromanager, dictator. Millings -so incompetent that if she had a brain, she would be dangerous, Nosey - a Regular Army Logistician who got fired from his G3 assignment while working for the big boys and sent here to do his time in country as there was nowhere else to put him. Nosey has an active-duty mentality, is very rigid, and rarely thinks outside of the box. He and Milling would rather have workers do camp beautification projects rather than force protection projects the week following our mortar attack? Force protection projects would include sandbagging living quarters, offices, and bunkers. There is also talk that all these Colonels are chicken shit. Other players in this SITCOM include the staff sections of the two battalions (heck, you hardly need one full staff to run this place). An interesting note: All of the CSB staff, as well as COL Nosey, are African Americans. MAJ Rickets told me on his last trip down here that in the logistics MOS (military occupational specialty), there is a proportionately large population of African Americans. Rickets is far from prejudiced as his wife is African American. I cannot confirm or deny his assertions.

Today, I couldn't take the stomach cramps and diarrhea anymore and visited the TMC (troop medical clinic).

Medical facility at CSC Scania, Iraq.

3 June 04

Only one meeting in the morning. COL Nosey, LTC Milling, MAJ Freakins, I, and SGT Freedom were in attendance. We covered the base expansion project that we are going to pitch this Saturday. The meeting was somewhat uneventful. The mayor's cell staff are getting very frustrated with Nosey because he does things his way, regardless of their input. It is all comical to me. I also informed Nosey about my media background and mentioned that we might want to do a story on him.

Today, I reviewed admin paperwork for CPT Randerson and burnt up (burn pits) a bunch of classified documents that I had locked up in my filing cabinet. I spent the afternoon cleaning my weapons as tomorrow I will be driving down to Talill and Cedar for Saturday's meeting, and I want to ensure that my weapons will fire properly if needed.

Today, we had quite a bit of aviation flying overhead. We also had a Blackhawk land in the trucking yard.

Nighttime close air support over CSC Scania, Iraq.

The moonlight is at full illumination, and you can see for miles at night. The weather is still pretty hot, but not as hot as the past three days. This is the last day before the MP's departure. I gave MAJ Tim O'Reilly a copy of his fallen soldier's video that I shot and edited. He was very appreciative.

Mohammed brought me currency today; the Iraqi dinar is now worth 144 per 100 American dollars. I bought $500 worth of it in the hopes of making some money for the exchange later in the year. If the value goes up like I think it will, I might even buy more currency.

Iraq dinar (currency).

Today, CPT Crader came down with his crew to pick up their mail. I spoke with him a bit about SPC U.'s death and other things surrounding the attack. Crader isn't happy about the changes in the family support situation in the States and doesn't want an election of new family support volunteers.

I am taking antibiotics again for G.I. problems. It is a ramped problem over here.

4 June 04

Convoyed from Scania to Tallil Airfield. We bunked in transient tents, very dusty, dirty, and full of crawly things. We had pizza at the Italian base and hit the PX (post exchange) for some class 6 stockage (personal items like health and hygiene products, snacks, etc. (refer to glossary for classes of supply). *It is interesting to note that at the Italian base here in the Tallil area, the soldiers are allowed to drink beer and wine with their meals in their military mess halls.*

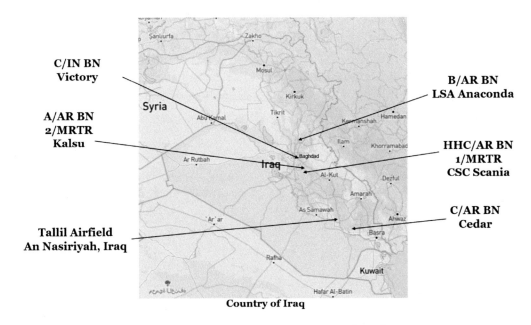

C/IN BN
Victory

A/AR BN
2/MRTR
Kalsu

B/AR BN
LSA Anaconda

HHC/AR BN
1/MRTR
CSC Scania

C/AR BN
Cedar

Tallil Airfield
An Nasiriyah, Iraq

Syria

Iraq

Kuwait

Country of Iraq

Tallil Airfield is located near Camp Cedar, Iraq. Map by John J. McBrearty.
Source: © OpenStreetMap (data is available under the Open Database License)

5 June 04

The big meeting was at 1000 and lasted about two hours. COL Randoms, the COSCOM Commander, was present. She is a middle-aged Signal Officer who stands about 4'10." COL Reese, the Artillery Brigade Commander assigned to force protection at Cedar, was present. Our C Co. works under him at Cedar.

The City of Ur with Abraham's original home in the foreground and the Ziggurat in the background. Photo source U.S. Army, in the public domain.

Visited the City of Ur. We went on a tour with tour guide Dhaif Muhsen. We took many pictures and visited Abraham's original home and birthplace. At the Tallil PX, I bought a mountain bicycle for exercise in the future. CPT Ryker and CPT Smythe from brigade saw my bike and bought one for themselves. Ryker is our liaison officer at Brigade HQ in Anaconda, and Smythe, along with MAJ Lukes of the Brigade S4, also visited us in Tallil/Cedar and Scania. They are a good bunch of guys.

6 June 04

0630 Convoyed from Cedar II to Scania. Arrived at Scania around 1030. Slacker was big-time pissed, stating that the 3-day trip was a waste of time. He was just in an awful mood. I say give us a break and allow us to get off post once in a while.

1330 meeting with COL Nosey about interpreter accountability.

7 June 04

0900 BUB with COL Nosey, I filled in for LTC Slacker (again!) No major issues. Nosey was harping about interpreter accountability. Apparently, the "Good Idea Fairys," aka LTC Milling's mayor's cell, invited the

Brigade's S5 NCOIC to our camp to assist with CA liaisons with the locals (where was this support two months ago when we first arrived at Scania?) Also, no prior mention or coordination with this individual was made with the Armor Battalion and or its S5 staff? Hidden agendas? I'd say LTC Milling and her methods will get soldiers killed and hurt with this type of business. Here is an excerpt from our S5, LT Fernandez's recent report; note that the Tuesday and Saturday council meetings were held by LTC Milling, and she never communicated any of this to us for the past two months?

The S5 section was made aware of city council meetings held on Tuesdays and Saturdays. SFC Miatke, MP BN, was one of the people assigned to Scania and did CMO (Civil Military Operations) work prior to the Armor Battalion's arrival. He is here in Scania to help give information about the area to aid with CMO operations. SFC Miatke escorted the S5 to the city council meeting and introduced the S5 to some of the local nationals he worked with.

3. Issues.

a. Issue # 1: Lack of Preparation for Providing Information.

(1) Discussion. SFC Miatke offered assistance with information. Unfortunately, there were no written records that he could offer. He stated that he had given documentation to 1LT Hensel, who did the RIP (Relief in Place) with the Armor Battalion. 1LT Hensel gave some information that he gathered and typed from memory and handwritten notes, but there were no chronological records. What SFC Miatke was able to offer was introductions to key people he worked with in the AO.

I am sure that Miatke did wonderful things while he was here, but unfortunately, there is no written record of it, and no area assessment was conducted. What we have accomplished to date is that we have done extensive research into the local communities by conducting a multitude of meetings and follow-on meetings with every local village and town in our area of responsibility. This was done so that we could systematically assess their current situation and identify their needs. From this background data, we will list, budget, and assess a priority of work for funding and eventual execution, hence meeting the desired end state of our coalition's main effort and objective, winning the hearts and minds of the Iraqi populace, and creating a better quality of life for them, eventually putting the control of their country back into their own hands.

On another note, our BDOC has reported and confirmed that SFC Miatke took an HMMWV out to a local village at around 2030 (8:30 pm) one evening by himself, with no escorts, and met with a dozen local nationals. This is an absolute no/go for any American or coalition soldier, as it poses a great risk to them and our forces. I will recommend to LTC Slacker/LTC Milling /COL Nosey that UCMJ action be taken with this "do-gooder" soldier.

Nosey is concerned about the interpreters because, through this Miatke character, he received a tip from one of the interpreters: the same guys that mortared us last week are going to hit us again 15 days from last Thursday. Again, our BDOC folks, CA folks, and S2 folks don't see any credence to the threat; again, Nosey is working with bogus information, with an end result of bullshit. Milling and Nosey are dangerous; we must protect our soldiers from them.

Fear. I should address fear. At times, I have been overcome with it. It is embarrassing but true. Sometimes, I find myself getting almost claustrophobic, even short of breath. It could be the anticipation, "When will it come?" "When will they hit us again? Will today be my day? Will I ever see my daughter Nina's wedding day? Will I be allowed to raise my son Junior? Will I ever be able to make passionate love to my enamored wife, Annette? Will I ever be able to hold my wife and tell her how much she means to me? Will I be able to tell my wife that I love her, just one more time?" These are the questions that race through my mind when this fear erupts. If I get scared, it usually occurs at night. We get hit by our mortar attacks at night, so it could be psychosomatic. I sometimes retrace my steps from the night of the 25th of May 2004. I have found that my actions, although possibly brave (or stupid), weren't as efficient as they could have been. Rather than running around making sure LTC Slacker was safe and informed, I should have taken cover with my IBA and weapon. I guess that you can't put a price tag on loyalty. SPC U. was killed as he was attempting to assist LN's (Local Nationals) into a bunker. That could have easily been me. When we were taking fire, all I could think about was keeping my commander safe.

8 June 04

Another day in the jungle, unfortunately or fortunately, in this combat environment, the pace isn't always "balls to the wall." Days like today can get on your nerves. In other words, it isn't a busy day with meetings or attacks and the like, so it gives the leadership like LTC Slacker time to get into everyone's business. Frankly, he is bored. Here is my example: yesterday, I directed CPT Randerson (S1 Personnel Officer) to have SFC Dwellers drive down with his NCO SGT Ragitan and pick up the mail at the Tallil Air Base. As you might remember, Ragitan, on his last trip down there, lost his weapon and didn't even know its serial number. On this past weekend's trip to Tallil, SSG Kanister had one ten-ton HMMET Cargo truck to pick up class II and IV supplies, as well as mail. CPT Lance and his MPs also picked up a small truckload and trailer load of mail for CSC Scania. There was so much mail that Kanister didn't have room to pick up his parts. I directed the S1 that from now on, they would drive their own 10-ton truck down with SSG Kanister for the sole purpose of picking up and dropping off mail. I directed that SFC Dwellers go on the first trip down to Tallil with SGT Ragitan so he could get a firsthand understanding of the scope of the mail situation and lead Ragitan by hand through the process.

Let me tell you about SFC Dwellers. He is a poor excuse for a former Marine. Dwellers is an AGR (Active Guard Reserve-full timer) Guardsman who makes the least amount of effort humanly possible. He is technically knowledgeable and uses that to his advantage to bullshit his way out of work and responsibilities. You will never, never hear this individual admit to any wrongdoing. Dwellers is an NCO who is reminiscent of the NCO gangster mentioned in the previous **COMBAT JOURNAL**, Part 1 of 4. A leadership philosophy of intimidation, extortion, and nothing short of criminal behavior (gangster). Fortunately, most of the key NCO leadership that were in the battalion when that NCO ruled the nest are gone; 1SG Chord currently pending discharge and criminal charges for sexual misconduct, 1SG Villa was relieved of his position with A Co., the HHC 1SG was relieved (forget his name), and the B Co. 1SG was replaced by a MSG, the battalion Master Gunner (tanker), and the C Co. 1SG out of Apple Valley retired. Quite a track record for these gents. However, Dwellers remains, and that insane gangster mentality still persists.

Dwellers put up a fight to go on this trip, as was expected. Last night, he telephoned me wanting an explanation, and I simply told him to speak with CPT Randerson about it. He later came into my office and informed me that he was instructed by the BC to never leave this post without his authorization. I told him, tough shit, you are going to render his NCO leadership to his subordinates. Knowing Dwellers for the slithering snake that he is, I telephoned the BDOC to see if Slacker and his crew had arrived back from their trip to Hilla/Babylon. As I figured, they had probably been back a whole five minutes. I knew what that meant, that Dwellers would have the BC and or CSM cornered, telling them that Hillcrest was directing him to go to Tallil for no good reason. I immediately grabbed my weapon and went to the BC's trailer, and as I expected, Dwellers was in there discussing the trip with Slacker. As unpredictable as it sounds, Slacker didn't object to Dwellers making the trip. I almost couldn't believe it. Slacker is the type of guy who is so insecure with himself that he typically would override my decision just to undermine my authority and remind everyone that he was the #1 and was making ALL decisions. (Are we getting cynical here? You bet your ass we are!)

Well, back to where I started in this discussion, it is around 0930 or so, and I am knee-deep into reviewing a superb training program for public affairs that was prepared by the 5th Special Forces Group and Slacker stomps in. He addresses the issue of sending Dwellers to Tallil as being a bad idea and says that he doesn't need to know the whole mail big picture. I told Slacker that it was a staff function and that I thought the staff needed to know the whole picture of the complexities of our mail program, as well as the needed mentorship of SGT Ragitan for losing his weapon and not even knowing his weapon's serial number. I said that these are NCO issues and that Dwellers is the senior NCO, and it is his responsibility. Why is Slacker questioning and overriding how I conduct business with my staff? Slacker has absolutely no leadership skills whatsoever. He has undermined just about everything I have said or done since Ft. Lewis, I and the rest of the staff are just fed up with this asshole. It is no wonder that he must sleep with his weapon (in his bed) and has to have a personal bodyguard with him 24/7. Slacker is smart enough to know that he is such a fucking dick that his life is in greater danger from his own troops than it is to enemy action. This is really quite sad. I sometimes want to go to General Killman and just ask for a ticket out to get away from Slacker because he is impossible to work with. Ask him for reassignment to the Brigade Staff, Kalsu, Cedar, anything but away from Slacker. But I don't do that because I truly feel that I am here for a reason, and that reason is largely due to the fact that Slacker has so many shortcomings and that CSM Hunts and I are his voice of reason that pick up the slack for Slacker's shortcomings. I feel that it is in the best interest of our soldiers that I stay and put up with his bullshit.

Earlier this morning, the topic of retention came up in a conversation with CPT Randerson, 1LT Tonic, and me. As is typical with most Guard officers, Tonic is at 18 years of good service as does CPT Randerson. They both have a lot of previous enlisted time, and that is how a junior officer would end up with so many good years for retirement. (A good year of service for a reserve component retirement requires 50 retirement points.) Tonic says he is planning on retiring, and Randerson stated that he is staying around. I mentioned that following the deployment, I still had another 8 years to do for my active-duty retirement and that if I didn't get promoted to Lieutenant Colonel when I got back or shortly thereafter, I would quit the full-time AGR program and just ride out my M-Day or weekend warrior retirement. I mentioned that I had enough civilian opportunities knocking at my door to make an adequate living and that finances wouldn't be a problem and possibly even work from my home. My issue was that this 18-month deployment for the AGRs was really a 2-year deployment because of all the work that we had to do before the mobilization. In addition, we had our initial alert at the outbreak of the war in March 2003. Most of the pre-mobilization work then was done exclusively by the AGR soldiers. My wife remembers me working until 1000pm every night and not getting any weekends off. Again, my issue was time away from my family had taken its toll and that I'd probably see another mobilization within my remaining years with the Guard. We will cross the career bridge once this goat rope is over.

Prior to my interruption from Slacker that totally pissed me off and "de-motivated" me, I was gainfully productive researching a course of instruction for public affairs. We are getting an LA Paper embed next week, and I wanted the battalion's leadership to brush up on the dealings with the press. Slacker put a screeching halt to this productivity, so here I am, directing my efforts towards my journal. This is my only escape from tough times here. There is no shoulder to cry on, no wife, no girlfriend, no Priest, and not even any other Majors around. This journal is it for me!

1628

I spent this afternoon fine-tuning my press release for the battalion and sending it to several of our local newspapers. I read a little from a history book about Ancient Mesopotamia. I find the whole subject fascinating since I now live here and have visited several historical sights.

Today, the mayor's cell "do-gooders" held a sandbag contest in order to get sandbags around the Chapel and MWR tents. I found out about this only one day prior to the event, so I just wrote it off as another "good idea fairies" from the mayor's cell folks. They had limited participation, which included CPT Morehead and four other Armor Battalion members. They actually made quite a bit of progress with the tent hardening. Again, sandbags and tent hardening are a sore subject with me since my tent had sandbags taken from it by the mayor cell idiots!

I really miss my wife today. I got an email from her and haven't stopped thinking of her since. I wish I had more pictures of her.

8 June 04

19:00

It was one of those days.

9 June 04

Tomorrow is my father's birthday, and I am not looking forward to it. I miss him so...

Today was a good day. Slacker was in a good mood, and that permeated throughout the staff, as well as the rank and file. I caught a glimpse from our local paper that ran a story on us:

"Guard Hangs Tough Despite Attacks."

Iraq: One local National Guard soldier died, and 10 others were injured in a mortar assault.

The May 25 mortar attacks that killed one soldier and wounded 10 others from our local National Guard unit in Iraq was a reminder of the reality of war, its second-in-command said Tuesday.

"The death of a soldier hit us really hard," said Maj. Darby Hillcrest, the executive officer of the Armor Battalion.

Hillcrest, in an interview from his location south of Baghdad, discussed how his National Guard unit has dealt with mortars, missions, Iraqis, and life since reaching the Middle East in March.

The May 25 mortar attacks that killed one soldier and wounded 10 others from a San Bernardino-based National Guard unit in Iraq was a reminder of the reality of war, its second-in-command said Tuesday.

"The death of a soldier hit us really hard," said Maj. Darby Hillcrest, executive officer of the Armor Battalion.

Hillcrest, in an interview from his location south of Baghdad, discussed how his California Army National Guard unit has dealt with mortars, missions, Iraqis, and life since reaching the Middle East in March.

"The death of our soldier caused all of us to do some reflection," Hillcrest said. "It heightened our sense of awareness of our surroundings."

Despite the mortar attacks, Hillcrest stressed that the battalion commander did not want family members to worry. The unit underwent realistic training at Fort Irwin before leaving for the Middle East.

"We're on par with any active-duty unit, bar none," said Hillcrest.

Hillcrest stated that unit soldiers patrol around the clock, but most of the unit's work focuses on humanitarian assistance projects ranging from medical care and water filtration to road projects and school renovation. He said the unit has a positive relationship with local Shiite leaders.

"We work hand-in-hand with the locals," he said. "If a bad guy comes in the area, they will tip us off."

Hillcrest said the morale among soldiers is high. They have access to phones and the Internet, he said. The soldiers live in groups of up to a dozen in air-conditioned tents. Outside temperatures often reach 120 degrees.

The battalion is spread among four locations, three south of Baghdad and one north of the city, he said. Security concerns prevent him from being more specific.

The unit, according to a press release, is equipped with armored Humvees that have reinforced steel-plating, bullet-proof windshields, and machine guns or grenade launchers.

Hillcrest said soldiers must contend with ambushes, car bombs, and mortar attacks, but the unit's experiences are not as intense as the images Americans see on television.

"We are so far removed from Abu Ghraib," Hillcrest said, referring to the prisoner-abuse scandal. "It's a different world from us."

The soldiers are aware that the Army might keep them in Iraq longer than their initial one-year tour, he said.

"It's eight to nine months away. We will cross that bridge when we get to it," he said of a possible extension. "At this point, all of us will accept our fate. There isn't much we can do about it."

Hillcrest's battalion of more than 750 citizen soldiers is normally headquartered in Southern California. The battalion was called to active duty last year and merged into the Enhanced Separate Armor Brigade with the Washington Army National Guard.

End of story.

Issues:

0900 BUB with Nosey.

1330 Meeting with Nosey & mayors' cell.

Had lunch with CPT Steve Crader, 1SG Rangston, who was very quiet and hardly said a word for his entire visit.

Visited the Hadjie mart and spent some $ since it was closed yesterday; I splurged on some computer speakers.

Slacker ferret is dying? Slacker an animal lover? Who knew? By the way, what in God's name is a ferret?

Mailed package home.

That's it for today!

10 June 2004

Today is my dad's birthday; I haven't been looking forward to this day at all. I miss that old guy terribly. Today, I also found out from my wife that my mother-in-law must undergo some very serious surgery on June 28th. Life is flying by childbirths, participation in war, illness, and death. Our family has experienced all the above (and all in the last year!) All I know is that more and more, I have had a much greater appreciation for LIFE. I have learned how precious it really is. I think that most of us just wander through life, living day to day, without thinking of the "big picture" and or the results of our actions and decisions here and now. Maybe I am getting philosophical, but when you look at a day like today, if you are even remotely compassionate, you can't help but philosophize and reflect on times gone by.

My Father was quite a remarkable man, to say the least. I will attach his epitaph written by the East Coast newspaper published at the time of his death. It was actually written by me with the assistance of one of my dad's most trusted friends and professional colleagues.

Darby Hillcrest, Ph.D.

Dr. Darby Hillcrest passed away peacefully on Sunday, May 25, 2003, at a medical care facility in Pennsylvania. Dr. Hillcrest was happily married to his wife for 48 years. Dr. Hillcrest is the loving Father of Sherry Termagants and son Major Darby Hillcrest, U.S. Army.

Dr. Hillcrest was the brother of the late Edward Hillcrest, the late Marie (Hillcrest), and the late Teresa (Hillcrest). Dr. Hillcrest is also survived by his 5 Grandchildren: Cousin #1, Cousin #2, Cousin #3, Nina, and Junior.

Dr. Hillcrest was a longtime member of the Catholic Church and was an altar boy in his youth.

Dr. Hillcrest was a combat veteran of WWII. He served on B-17s and fought proudly as a member of the Army Air Corps in the African and Italian theaters of war. Upon returning home from the war, Dr. Hillcrest enrolled in university utilizing the G.I. Bill. He completed his BS, MA, and Ph.D. in clinical psychology. Following his university studies, he met his wife, a Registered Nurse, while they both worked at a Psychiatric hospital. Dr. Hillcrest taught psychology at several universities and maintained a successful private practice that included psychotherapy, biofeedback, group therapy, and supervision.

As a college professor, he greatly influenced, mentored, and shaped the careers of numerous clinical psychologists. His interests included behavioral approaches to treating patients, value orientations and the creation of a scale to measure values, existential phenomenology, and virtue ethics. He was widely published in these areas of interest, and he developed an outstanding reputation as both an academic and applied psychologist. Dr. Hillcrest also worked and later retired as a Medical Research Scientist at a State Hospital where he pioneered drug and alcohol rehabilitation programs. Dr. Hillcrest served as a consultant to many other psychiatric hospitals and agencies in the East Coast area and was active in leadership positions in many professional organizations. He was the chairman of the Ethics

Committee of the Society of Clinical Psychologists for many years, and he was awarded the Lifetime Achievement Award in Ethics. In Dr. Hillcrest's senior years, he particularly cherished the time he spent with his son, his daughter, and his five grandchildren.

Dr. Hillcrest led a prosperous and successful life that was focused on his life's passion, helping others. He ventured into a field that was quite literally in its infancy. He has made a noble and profound impact on his profession by helping thousands of students, psychologists, and patients over the years. He was a man of the highest moral values and integrity and had an impact on all who came in contact with him. He was the quintessential academic, a perfectionist who never let down his fellow man. He will be greatly missed, as he was truly a blessed individual.

NOTE FROM AUTHOR: What can I say about my father? I am what I am what I am, largely due to my dear father's influence in my life. He represents the quintessential kindhearted gentleman who always puts the needs of his fellow man before his own.

Donkey shooting incident A Co.? Are you serious? Is this a modern-day "Hogan's Heroes" (SITCOM from the 1970s), or what? More to follow. MAJ Hillcrest has just been appointed as the investigating officer of an incident involving A Co. soldiers shooting and killing a donkey in cold blood. I am not making this stuff up, ladies and gentlemen. I told Cantez, "I have now hit the pentacle of my career, investigating officer for the shooting of a donkey."

11 June 04

3 Memorial Services in two weeks, shit! The MP Battalion lost 8 Soldiers in the time that we were here. Fuck.

Diarrhea again!

Today, I broke new ground with COL Nosey and his LTC Milling. In our 0900 BUB, rather than bringing up an issue in front of the big group, I stated that I could discuss it with the two Colonels after the meeting. I did, and it worked out great. I explained to them that our southern checkpoint still didn't have shade for the soldiers. We talked over the issue, and the result will be that KBR is constructing a new shade setup similar to the northern checkpoint.

For the first time, LTC Slacker went out with the S5 folks to be shown our area of operations. *We have been here almost three months now, and he is just now getting out and about???* Well, at least he is doing it now. We think it is to get away from COL Nosey and his morning meetings.

In another Einsteinian maneuver, LT Youngham went out to some school with her medical friends and gave out stuff to the kids. That's great, but they didn't tell a soul about this. We could have come along and taken pictures and written a story about it. Additionally, we could have also provided her with the proper FORCEPRO (force protection). That afternoon, I wanted to talk to her about that, along with another medical matter, but she was nowhere to be found. I will have to talk to her about that, too.

I wrote a loving email to my wife that I knew she would like as it was full of "how I feel" stuff that women like to hear. But now I really mean it!

I attended ANOTHER memorial service today for another fallen soldier.

12 June 04

Really miss my wife. I wish I could hold her body next to mine. I won't elaborate as that wouldn't fit the genre of my memoirs here.

A Blackhawk just flew by pretty low. The COSCOM Commander is due to visit today; maybe it was her bird? She is a short, stocky broad, around 50 or so, and I kidded CPT Cantez that we were going to try and set him up on a blind date with her since they both had height challenges in common.

LTC Slacker has directed me to visit FOB Kalsu for a few days to conduct the investigation of a shooting. SGT Corales, our Legal NCO, is on the ground doing the initial work. I am not looking forward to the visit as Kalsu is our "hot spot" for enemy activity. It is where SPC U. was killed, and 10 other Soldiers were injured last week. Hopefully, it won't be my turn.

Slacker took a crew over to Shiekh Hatim's house for dinner but failed to mention it to me? Very strange? He even included Maurice, the KBR security supervisor, a civilian contractor? To add insult to injury, several days later, he attempted to placate me AGAIN on this issue, "Oh John, next time we'll take you to the Sheikh's palace for dinner." What the fuck is it with this asshole???? He has the habit of after he fucks up or says something bad to someone or chews us out, he'll come up to us later and try to smooth it over like it is all okay now. You will see this pattern of behavior time and time again. Well, it is not okay, and it is not just me saying this; many others have mentioned this tactic of Slacker and have identified it as bullshit.

Since this not inviting the BXO to the big Shiekh's house with Slacker has happened several times, I am left to conclude that there must be an underlying reason. He likes to be "the man" always, so is it that he doesn't want to share the limelight with another field grade officer? Who knows? Perhaps we will never know? Slacker certainly is a mystery to us all.

Going to FOB Kalsu tomorrow, so if there aren't any more entries in my journal, I didn't make it back.

Thanks for listening.

Darby Hillcrest

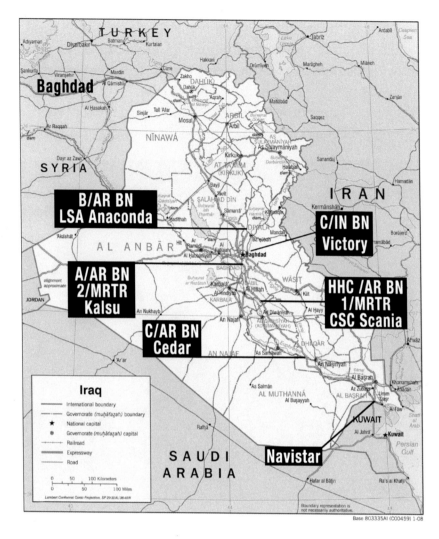

FOB Kalsu is in the heart of the deadly Suni Triangle, Iraq. Map by John J. McBrearty. Source: The World Factbook, CIA Maps.

13 June 04

I took a convoy north, exited the 16A off-ramp, and visited FOB Kalsu. Conducted a 15-6 Informal Investigation into the "Donkey Incident." Despite the unusual circumstances that brought me to Kalsu, I was quite glad to visit A Co. and all the Armor Battalion soldiers there. I have to admit, I was very apprehensive about the trip. Less than two weeks ago, they were hit with some 19 or so mortars in a single attack that resulted in 3 dead and over 10 wounded. Yes, I was scared to make this trip.

Getting to Kalsu was an experience in itself. I had to make the arrangements for joining in on a northbound convoy that had already been planned for early in the morning. I had two HMMWVs with a total of four soldiers, which included me, going on the trip. I dug out maps and plotted my course the day before. I made sure my driver, SPC Stephens (a very squared-away young man who had previous active-duty time with the 82nd Airborne Division), knew how to get the Blue Force Tracker (BFT) computer system turned on and operational prior to the trip.

Blue Force Tracker computer screen.

The BFT has a global positioning system in it that reads where you are from a satellite. It has a computer screen, much like what you might see in a police car. We got on a convoy that headed to BIAP (Bagdad International Airport -formerly Sadam Hussein Airport). I informed the MPs who were escorting the KBR convoy that we would be peeling off at 16A, which is an off-ramp of MSR Tampa, at about the halfway point to BIAP from Scania. As we ventured north, I constantly tracked our grid coordinates with the GPS, BFT, and my good old map. Once we were approaching 16A, I radioed the MPs and my other vehicle, or "Victor" as we call it, and informed them of our exodus from the convoy. The MPs replied, "Roger, good luck and be careful." We took the loop off the freeway, not much different than those freeways back in America. I was getting more nervous as this was my first time visiting Kalsu, and none of the other soldiers were with me; SPC Stephens, SSG (commo nco), and

SGT Alonzo knew exactly how to get there. What I noticed from about the halfway point to Kalsu was that there was a lot more civilian activity in this area. In the central and northern portions of Iraq, civilians were prohibited from using the MSRs, but the side streets were quite crowded. This is a much different atmosphere than down in the Scania area, where you see many civilians utilizing MSR Tampa. Upon exiting the freeway, I couldn't help but notice the high volume of surface street traffic there was. This is not necessarily a good thing. Where there are Iraqis, there is danger for American soldiers.

We eventually found our way to the entrance of the camp. The guard at the gate knew SPC Stephens, and they exchanged pleasantries with one another. We ventured several hundred meters through a maze of bunkers and armed American soldiers standing security. Noticeable and comforting to see was the brigade's patch on each of the soldiers' left shoulder. After the maze of obstacles, we came up to a crossroads. This juncture had a "Welcome to Kalsu" sign that explained the meaning behind the name of the camp, as well as two intimidating Soviet-made artillery pieces. We turned right and, after a short distance, ended up at A Company's TOC (tactical command post).

My first impression of the camp was its size; it seemed quite compact to me. To the left as you entered were the mighty M1A1 Abrams tanks of the 1st Armored Division, as well as some Armored Cavalry units. A Co. took up the right part of the post (northern & western portion). A Company shared a TOC building with an MP unit that was stationed out of Kalsu, not much different than the MP units at Scania. A Company lived in numerous tents that weren't far from the TOC. Most of the officers either had their own GP Small tent (general purpose tent) or shared it with one other person. The tents were fairly spacious for a single individual. The enlisted soldiers had larger tents but had several soldiers in a tent. Overall, the living conditions were much more spacious than in Scania, where some tents had up to ten occupants. I presently share a tent with four other officers, and we all are pretty cramped.

There is an old dining facility where the soldiers eat, but the food is prepared in an outside mobile kitchen called an MKT. At Kalsu, you have "real Army cooks" cooking "real Army chow" and not our contracted food as we have, which is quite common in most other facilities in theater. The best dinner I have had in country was actually the steak dinner that I had at Kalsu on my second night of visiting. I have to hand it to the Army cooks; they really know their business. (I later found out that one of the cooks was actually a gourmet chef who worked at a nice restaurant as his civilian job.)

I was greeted by Major Rickets. It was great seeing him with his new rank; however, on the first day of my visit, I saw that he was dressed in PT attire. Unfortunately for Rickets, most of his uniforms were ruined in the recent mortar attack. Rickets gave me the fifty-cent tour, which took all but about ten minutes. They put on a pot of Starbucks coffee for me, and then we talked, and we talked, and we talked. Poor Maj Rickets had many frustrations with the battalion and LTC Slacker. Little did he know that I had very similar frustrations with Slacker.

The news of the day was no water. The local Iraqi National who was contracted to truck in the freshwater for the camp was murdered the night before. This marked the second water contractor to have been killed. The previous had his hands cut off because he was helping the Americans. The three days that I spent at Kalsu became pretty nasty for me physically. I have gone without showers before, but in 120-degree heat, which is a different story. Luckily, before I came here, CPT Ridges, who had previously stayed here at Kalsu, advised me to bring plenty of baby wipes along for the ride. I did, and that is how a soldier showers in the field. That is a great way to describe Kalsu's field conditions. They have a shower set up, which pales in comparison to ours; it has running water but no porcelain toilets, only porta-potties. Overall, I saw a real hygiene challenge before my eyes.

Three different officers and NCOs told me where I was to sleep while at Kalsu, in the only basement of the complex and the safest place in the camp. It is the basement of the battalion aid station building. It wasn't air-conditioned, and I actually slept in my own pool of sweat, but I was safe. Maybe? On the second night, I was covered from head to toe with insect bites. It itched quite a lot and later in the week, I saw the Doc for it. Who knows what I might have contracted? I made sure to keep a copy of the medical report of my insect bites in case it manifested itself into something serious.

NOTE FROM AUTHOR: I am taking a moment to point out something here that is intended for any prospective or current military member of the armed forces. When you are young and healthy, you sometimes feel invincible to injury or disease. At least I am certainly guilty as charged of those assertions. However, it is important to note that MAJ Hillcrest makes it a point to document his medical incidents during his deployment and continued career. This can have a significant impact when a service member leaves the military and chooses to file a medical claim with the Veteran's Administration. The VA requires documentation of illness or injury related to military service prior to approving such claims. What this means to the Veteran is money! Tax-free money for your service-connected illnesses or injuries that you so rightly deserve. Document my friends! Document!

14 June 04

I stayed an extra day at Kalsu and escorted the LA Paper reporter around the camp.

The reporter was accompanied by CPT Laylock, Brigade PAO. He was a pretty good guy (particularly compared to the older jerk-off reporter back in Los Angeles), and I helped him get on board a patrol mission with A Co. He got some good story ideas and was grateful. I also tried to steer him toward SPC U.'s friends and Platoon Sergeant to get the straight scoop about this heroic soldier.

LA Paper reporter with a soldier at the approximate location where the battalion's first fatality occurred at FOB Kalsu, Iraq.

15 June 04

Return trip from FOB Kalsu to CSC Scania. Before we left, I took a moment and walked to the QRF vehicle staging parking lot and stood where SPC U. fell to his death. I prayed for him and for our soldier's safe return home from this deployment.

Upon my trip back to Scania, I was determined to make some kind of difference for our soldiers at Kalsu!

16 June 04

0900 Meeting with COL Nosey, the normal battle update briefing.

1330 Meeting with COL Nosey, this was the weekly planning meeting.

Quiet day, Slacker is gone. He went on a convoy to Anaconda for a meeting with BG Killman. The LA Paper reporter later returned with Slacker.

17 June 04

Slacker is still up north, thank God! I slept in an extra ½ hour yesterday and today; yes, I guess that I am going wild and letting loose! I haven't written much lately for several reasons; first, I have actually been out doing "stuff," and secondly, I didn't bring my computer on my Kalsu trip, and third, I need a break from it - writing, that is. I have so much bottled-up hostility these days. I guess that I am extremely upset with how our troops at Kalsu must live and that we have it so well off here in Scania. C Company in Cedar is also living high on the hog in a friggen "Hilton-esq" type of environment. B Co. is up at Anaconda along with, now get this, 20,000 other Soldiers/Airmen/Marines. You know that they have a good life support system set up there with that many people and numerous General Officers running amuck. I am sure that B Co. is seeing their share of action since they have their M1A1 Tanks with them. I hear that the tanks are such a deterrent that they don't end up having many enemy engagements. A funny thing to note about Anaconda is that it must be on the luxurious side of life here in Iraq as it is one of the destinations for soldiers like ours to take on a 3-day R&R pass.

I am mad that A Co. has such a crappy setup and is in a highly dangerous area of operations. Originally, LTC Slacker and most of the battalion staff were to be stationed there with only one company and maybe a battalion staff slice here at Scania. I guess Slacker liked what he saw here and decided to stay. Right now, A Co. is in a shit hole (that is an actual quote from MAJ Rickets) and needs help. I investigated the shooting up there on my visit to Kalsu, and I recommended that LTC Slacker go to Kalsu for an undetermined period of time to mentor the Company Commander as well as to fight to improve their infrastructure, civil affairs operations and other missions. He'll never go for it knowing Slacker, but he might send me up there to do HIS job.

When I returned to Scania, I had long talks with Slacker and later with CSM Hunts. Slacker didn't agree with my recommendation from the investigation (BIG SURPRISE THERE!) I recommended that the shooting of the animal (a donkey - yes, I literally had a hard time keeping a straight face during the interviews; my legal NCO, SGT Corales, is a former Marine, a bucking muscular fellow who has a very serious nature, and hearing him talk about donkey's, i.e., "When did you first see the donkey?" "Did you touch the donkey…etc…," the whole situation cracked me up.

The actual shooting incident fell within the ROE (rules of engagement) for theater operations. However, their conduct of cutting off the donkey's ears as a gift for their Company Commander was conduct unbecoming of a soldier, and they should be disciplined for that. Slacker is planning on firing the Company Commander, Platoon Leader, and Platoon Sergeant over the matter and sending them back home. I think this is overkill, and I wouldn't send anyone home until we all get to go home. Besides, this could be construed as an entitlement, going home and getting out of danger? Heck, Slacker would create an environment where the soldiers might think that if they conduct themselves egregiously, they, too, could be sent home! If he is dead set on firing these guys, I say give them staff assignments or something, but not a ticket home. I do think that the Company Commander isn't leading from the front and should be replaced. His first sergeant is a lazy pig (I call it as I see it).

Slacker also mentioned that he would make MAJ Rickets take over as the Company Commander and that he would send me there as the C2 commander of the post. This was all my original idea; I only had Slacker and some staff going there versus me. A Lieutenant Colonel could get a lot more done for them since they are OPCON (Operational Control) to the MP Brigade; you would have an LTC fighting for them versus a Major. Whatever happens, I would rather be there at Kalsu. Although it is a nasty place and highly dangerous, Kalsu is away from Slacker and the political, garrison bullshit of rear echelon commandos like LTC Milling and her sidekick Sergeant Major Moans as well as COL Quate Nosey, three has-beens put out to pasture here at Scania. *(I think we call that a run-on sentence?)* I really think that I could make a difference for our troops at Kalsu. I am pretty confident in our abilities to protect ourselves here in Scania. Hell, we have taken forces away from A Co. at Kalsu to do it (that made absolutely no sense to me at all, but I was overruled by guess who?)

I also recommended to Slacker that they need a CA (Civil Affairs) program up there at Kalsu in order to make peace with the locals, which will lessen the attacks on our soldiers and the camp. Over the last three months, LT

Fernandez has effectively developed our CA program here, and now it is up and running. All we need at this point is follow-up missions and requests for funding of projects that we have identified during our initial assessment of the area. The hard part is over here as I see it, and we should move our main CA efforts (ME-main effort) to Kalsu, i.e., LT Fernandez. I would leave LT Artera here to conduct the follow-on missions, contract negotiations, and project oversight. I doubt that Slacker will go for this, as Scania will be a textbook example of good civil/military operations.

We could have some big visibility from our civil/military operations here. Heck, someone might even write a book about it someday! JM

The bottom line is that we have sustained many casualties and our first KIA at Kalsu, and we must do more for our soldiers there. I feel that he, as a battalion (SLACKER), has turned his back on them, and I believe that they feel that way as well. Numerous soldiers at Kalsu voiced their complaints to me that they thought the battalion commander was afraid to come up and visit them. I also heard complaints that they haven't seen the Sergeant Major visit; in fact, the Brigade Sergeant Major has visited them more often than the Battalion Sergeant Major. To CSM Hunts' defense, the main reason he hasn't been able to visit is because Slacker doesn't let us leave. Hunts is a great Sergeant Major and would like nothing other than to be with his soldiers out in the field. Unfortunately, Slacker won't let CSM Hunts do Sergeant Major's work but rather keeps him close hold as his own personal bodyguard. It is ironic that he has the greatest fear of his own troops, vice the enemy. I almost feel sorry for Slacker.

So, I am HMFIC (head mother fucker in charge) while Slacker is away. It is a good feeling. Today, I had SFC Navarro take me in his HUMMV to the North and South checkpoints. I took many pictures of the barricades and shaded areas, as well as spoke with the soldiers. Just spending an hour and a half out there in my body armor and helmet, I must have sweat off several pounds. It is terribly hot in that sun. I could tell that the troops were glad to see me visit them. I hope to do that some more in the future.

18 June 04

Oh yes, another incident with the ever-so-infamous "Mayors Cell." May there ever be peace between us? Doubt it! I had Morehead brief me on our current ops (operations) in my office around 0815 or so. He mentioned that COL Nosey was not here and wouldn't be attending the 0900 meeting. I told him to continue to march as planned and that we would make it a "brief" meeting. (Would you call that a brief briefing?) At 0900, all units had their respective representatives in place, some twenty-five or so participants. At around 0904 or 0905 or so, I asked MAJ Smythe if LTC Milling was going to attend, and he said that he didn't know. I said, "Well then, let's get started." MAJ Smythe said to wait and see if anyone else would show up. I said no, that we were going to move ahead and get started, as I didn't want to waste anyone's time. MAJ Smythe again said no, we are not to start without them. I then said, "MAJ Smythe, I say we start now, and you may leave if you don't like that." Smythe left the room, and we started the meeting. At about 0920, we got to the last slides of the briefing. COL Nosey walked in, and we all stood up. He said to continue. LTC Milling, SGM Moans, and MAJ Smythe also followed into the room. I told COL Nosey that we were almost finished, and I could brief him up on what was missed after dismissing the others. He said fine. We were at the final 3 or 4 slides, and it was conveniently at the CSB (P-provisional) slide. LTC Milling started yelling, directing her hostility towards me about how we must wait to start the meetings for her, etc., etc. I interrupted by saying, "Mam, this isn't the forum for that discussion; if you would like, we can discuss it offline, you, me, and COL Nosey." She responded intensely, "You need to be aware of military courteously MAJOR! etc., etc." Tonic said that she said, "You need to check yourself, Major?" I don't know what that means and don't quite remember that, but she was pissed. COL Nosey interjected and stated that if he is late due to answering various commanders, we are to drive on without him. (I believe that is what I was doing?)

Later, MAJ Smythe got up and said his piece, "I am venting, but yada, yada, yada about how we must all work professionally together in a harmonious work environment, yadda, yada, yada...." Smythe is a smart guy and picked effective words, but I think he is barking up the wrong tree. He was trying to make my actions look bad (we combat arms folks think differently). Much later, at the conclusion of what has now turned into an hour-long meeting, I said my peace ever so briefly; "The last time I checked, we are in a WAR zone. Pointing at the MP Representatives and BDOC CDR, you all are out of the wire every day and know what is going on in the WAR. You are truly in harm's way every day. Others on this post are not leaving the wire and don't have a clue what is really going on in the

WAR. I am not going to SHOWBOAT here, that is all." COL Nosey concluded that again, in the future, continue with the meeting if he is late. I saw the look of "thank you" from several of my staff officers, CPT Ridges, CPT Morehead and 1LT Tonic. Following the meeting, CPT Ridges came up to me, shook my hand, and said thanks. CPT Morehead started laughing, stating, "Well, sir, you had us out of here in 20 minutes; good going." After a brief pee break, COL Nosey returned for a force protection update with me, CPT Moans (MP BTN LNO), and CPT Morehead.

I bumped into CSM Carr in the hallway; he returned from Anaconda and then Kalsu with our S4, LT Youngham, and the Brigade S4. They are working to improve conditions at Kalsu. I thanked him and offered him a cup of coffee from my office. I learned this practice from my deployment to Japan for Yama Sakura, a multi-national war exercise. The Japanese Army Officers always serve hot tea in their offices as ice breakers with other military officials and visitors. I learned this cordial hospitality practice from the Japanese and continued that practice successfully throughout my entire military career.

At noon chow, I sat with the Armor Battalion staff, and they all gave me a "that-a-boy" regarding this morning's meeting. I said that it was a "Hillcrest-ism" and that I wasn't looking to showboat or anything. The staff really got a kick out of the scene.

This evening, after chow, some of the Brigade staff stopped in. When they left, a bunch of us kidded and made fun of the day's events and each other. Included were LT Tonic, CPT Cantez, SFC Barnum, SSG Kanister, and me. This is how we often pass the time. Usually, Cantez and Tonic go at it with racial cuts on each other (they are Mexican and Japanese dudes). It is quite funny at times. The Japanese guy speaks in a Mexican accent, and the Mexican guy speaks in an Asian accent. Hysterical!

19 June 04

Here is a historical glimpse of where we stand internationally: efforts to transform Iraq into a stable, prosperous democracy are proceeding on four main tracks -- security, the establishment of a representative government, reconstruction and rapid return of service, and building a free-market economy. Falah al-Naqib, the interior minister, also warned that he might impose martial law to control "terrorist acts" after 41 people were killed in two car bombings on Thursday. The head of the United Nations electoral team in Baghdad announced the formation of Iraq's Independent Electoral Commission - the autonomous body that will guide the country towards polling set for January 2005.

Today was a quiet day. I hit the gym in the afternoon, showered, and dropped off laundry (do we see a recurring theme here?) I let the staff have a ½ day off if they wanted. In the late morning, Slacker popped his face in our office, I was shocked to see him as we thought he was going to be visiting Kalsu for a few days. He said, (CPT Cantez), "I want to see you!" We all knew what that meant, that he was on the hot seat. I told Cantez that I would join him to take the brunt of the pain (this is my typical M.O. that I developed early on in the deployment, supporting my staff). I was in PT gear because I visited sick call today to have them check out insect bites that were all over my body from the Kalsu trip. Slacker chewed out Cantez for not visiting B Co. while he was at Anaconda. He was right; he should have personally checked up on them.

After conversing with CSM Hunts, I wrote up an AAR (after-action report) from my Kalsu visit. They need help and additional battalion staff there, so based on Hunts' advice, I proposed sending the entire battalion staff there to Kalsu for a two-week period to conduct an assessment of the camp and area of operations. Of particular interest, I pointed out that there were currently little or no Civil Affairs missions being conducted and that we needed that to commence immediately. We will see what Slacker thinks.

20 June 04

Father's Day, here in Iraq, oh joy. Yep, I will be thinking about pop a lot today, and I will hit church at 1600. Extra prayers for my dad and father-in-law. This morning, CSM Hunts stopped in, and we had a nice exchange with CPT Cantez and SFC Barnum about funny things. CSM was kidding Cantez about getting supplies and the psychology of acquisitions. For example, we had FOO money to buy stuff, which was a hard road to get there. But now we finally have some liquid cash. We are using folding chairs for seats in our various offices, and many upper-echelon commands have luxurious office furniture. This is a small detail, but here is where the CSM was going with this, "CPT Cantez, here is the Psychology of being successful as a logistician: purchase a nice executive chair from the locals with FOO $ and give the chair to the Battalion Commander. You win him over and make him think that he is special as he is the only one to get a special chair. A week later, get chairs for the rest of us, but since you got it for the BC first, he thinks he is special." CSM Hunts is a very bright and insightful NCO. He also mentioned that Scania could be relocating in three to six months to Ad Diwaniyah, which is 18 clicks south of here and a highly volatile shit hole and home of the Almahdi Army. It is a very dangerous place. Oh, happy day!

21 June 04

I called home and spoke to Annette, Nina, Junior, and my father-in-law. I was glad to reach them all on Father's Day (yesterday for us here).

The 0900 meeting with COL Nosey was a flop. Over one hour and ten minutes of nothing but the same old issues revisited, a total waste of time. The force protection briefing followed, and that pushed us up to 1030. ½ the day has gone by, and nothing productive has been done! Slacker and the CSM took an early convoy up to Kalsu but didn't share that with any of the staff? I had no idea that he was going. I filled in for Slacker in the 0900 meeting: oh joy! Nosey mentioned that he would be gone on Wednesday, and I informed him that Slacker would also be gone. LTC Milling said joyfully, "Oh, I guess that leaves me in charge then." NOT. According to Army Field Manual 3-90 Tactics, the senior maneuver commander is placed in command of a base camp in a combat environment. Later I mentioned that to Slacker, and he responded, "Fuck her, she ain't in charge of shit!" My sentiments exactly!

22 June 04

My wife Annette's Birthday! Actually, it isn't the 22nd yet in Calif, but I am thinking of her all the same. I sent her a cool email yesterday. Here is a clip:

21 June 04

Hi Annette,

Thanks for the nice Father's Day email.

Tomorrow is your birthday, and I wish you a Happy Birthday!

I wish that I could be there. I was surfing the web and came across a critique of a campy student film that we were involved in. I thought you would get a kick out of how they described you:

"Every one of the girls in the film looks like she just graduated from modeling school......this is the kind of movie whose idea of a "nerdy" girl is a blonde bombshell with glasses, a baggy sweater, and put-up hair."

So, the reviewer thinks you are a graduate of modeling school and a BLOND BOMBSHELL! Not too bad, girlfriend!

See, you always had it; you still have it, and you always will!

I will always love you.

HAPPY BIRTHDAY (tomorrow)

Your Husband

Annette really appreciated the thoughtful gesture, and I think that she actually got a kick out of reading about herself from a film critique. When you get over 40, you will take any kind of boost to your ego like that. Annette was always pretty hot and still is!

Today is slow, thank goodness! Slacker left early with the Sergeant Major to visit C Co. in Cedar and would like to take the tourist visit to the City of Ur and the Tallil Airfield. The trip is a long and arduous one, but will do him some good to get away from here. It definitely lowers our stress level quite a bit when he leaves. Also, he returns in a better mood than when he left (possibly because he is returning to his comfort zone).

Yesterday, he said something that I thought was interesting. He said that he was mad that troops were saying "that it took a soldier to die before

Slacker would leave his post and go out and visit his soldiers throughout Iraq." I have to say that I think it is quite ironic. All I can say is that if the shoe fits....... Between the Sergeant Major and I, I think that we are accomplishing our mission; to get Slacker off this post and visit our other units. Between the CSM and me, we are finally getting that accomplished. It has taken 3 months, several enemy attacks, wounded soldiers, and even dead soldiers to make it a reality, but I am glad that it has finally come to fruition.

MAJOR Wanda Freakins did a good job of putting out the first Scania newspaper. She didn't ask for help, although she knew that I had some journalism background, as was mentioned by CPT Laylock, our Brigade Public Affairs Officer. Laylock told me that Freakins was hurting for material and asked if I could help her out. I asked Freakins if she needed stories. She responded, "Are they time-sensitive?" As if, "If they are, there just isn't time and forget it!" I was a bit taken aback by her response, knowing what it is like to be on a deadline; an editor will look for any lifeline that is thrown at them. I did give her a copy of an article that I wrote for the Brigade's monthly newspaper. The story was about one of our Medics performing the Heimlich maneuver in the chow hall. I was very surprised that she actually used my stuff in the paper. Well, part of my stuff, at least. Of the original 437 words and two pictures, she chose to edit out 285 words and printed the article with a total of 152 words and one picture? What the fuck? I will mention to Freakins that she did a great job with the paper and maybe later mention that it isn't proper to edit so much from a writer's original story? This isn't the LA Paper! Also, there was some big space given to some real bull shit, but that is my opinion. For now, it is back to the business of warfare.

A traveling bazaar that is associated with our AAFES (Army & Air Force Exchange Service) visited our camp today. I picked up some killer stereo speakers for my computer. It contains a large subwoofer and two smaller tweeter-type speakers. It sounds great! It set me back $55., and the same setup in the USA might run me $125-$150.

The LA Paper article came out, and I think they did a bang-up job with it; published on June 21, 2002:

THE GUARD GOES TO WAR

Untimely Death Rattles Fellow Soldiers

L.A. Newspaper, June 21, 2002

23 June 04

DEATH again! I guess that I am developing coping skills; I listened to my new stereo speakers at high volume most of the day. We got word that two more soldiers from California were KIA yesterday. 2LT T. and SPC M. were of A Co. Engineers and were killed in an ambush on their patrol yesterday. Also, from A Co. was an injury sustained by another soldier. This is tough, very tough. Several of our Engineers in our unit knew these individuals and are taking it pretty hard. I got an email this morning from the family support rep, Carmon. They knew instantaneously about the KIA's, which has us all worried.

Today were meetings as always on Wednesdays. I cried a little today when a certain song came on. I borrowed a classical music CD from CPT Cantez, and "Alleluia" by the Mormon Tabernacle Quire came on. It was one of my father's favorite songs, and he played it in our home often. I miss that old guy so much! I know that he is looking over my shoulder every step of the way over here. Thanks, Dad!

Today, I received an email from Meggy. She asked if she could share my emails with the alumni association of my former High School and reproduce them. I said certainly and emailed her another newspaper article. I am glad that there is some interest in our mission from back east; maybe someday my sister might read about it in the local papers? I feel sorry for her to miss such an event in our family's lives. Just today, I received a beautiful card for Father's Day from my nieces on Annette's side of the family, but nothing from my sister's kids?

24 June 04

Death toll as of last week: 828 U.S. service members have died; 609 of them died as a result of hostile action, and 219 died of non-hostile causes. Since 1 May 03, when the President declared that major combat operations in Iraq had ended, 690 U.S. service personnel were killed, 500 as a result of hostile action, and 190 due to non-hostile actions. (Major combat actions ended? Does the enemy know about this?)

Today, I saw images of SPC M. and LT T., and it hit home. I recognized M. very well. I remember him as a positive guy up at Ft. Lewis and NTC. Sucks, both guys were 34 years of age, and M. was married and a father of two.

Also, last week, three soldiers were killed at Camp Anaconda (near the city of Balad), where our Brigade Headquarters and B Co. are stationed.

Today, A Co. visited on their weekly mail run. CPT Crader and MAJ Rickets were with them, and Rickets is staying for a few days. He and I talked about the issues that Kalsu has and how LTC Slacker is overlooking our recommendations for whatever reason- we are bewildered?

Last night, I stayed up late and wrote the following essay for the Brigade newspaper.

*(AUTHOR'S NOTE: This essay can also be found in **COMBAT ESSAYS**, American History, A Veteran's Perspective, Volume II).*

"Our Trip to Ur"

A Day in the Life of an Armor Battalion Soldier

(3rd edition in a series of essays)

by

MAJOR Darby Hillcrest

23 June 2004

The thermometer reached a scorching 120 degrees Fahrenheit, so no one dared venture anywhere without their water bottle in hand as members of our higher headquarters (Brigade) and our Armor Battalion braved the sweltering weather to visit the Sumerian City of Ur, the ancient city of Mesopotamia. The ruins of the City of Ur are conveniently located adjacent to the Tallil Airfield in Southern

Iraq. "Over here, it's Abraham's house!" shouted Major Lukes, S4 (Logistics Officer) for the Brigade. SSG Kanister (S4 NCO, Armor Battalion) followed as Major Lukes led 1LT Youngham (Medical Officer, Armor Battalion) to the rebuilt home of the profit Abraham. They, along with other members of the brigade and battalion staff, enjoyed a quick tour of the Ur ruins between logistical meetings at Cedar II and Tallil Airfield. Local Iraqi national Mr. Dhaif Muhsen served as a conversant tour guide to this distinguished group of American soldiers. In perfect English, he told them, "I have been featured on CNN, The History Channel, and PBS."

Ur was the principal center of worship of the Sumerian Moon God Nanna and his Babylonian equivalent, Sin. The massive ziggurat for this deity, one of the best preserved in Iraq, stands about 21 meters (about 70 feet) above the desert and dominates the flat countryside. The biblical name, Ur of the Chaldees, refers to the Chaldeans who settled in the area about 900 BC. The Book of Genesis (see 11:27-32) describes Ur as the starting point of the migration westward to Palestine of the family of Abraham about 1900 BC. Ur is believed by many to be the birthplace of the prophet Abraham.

The Mesopotamian City of Ur is famous for a multitude of reasons, among which it is presently one of the oldest cities ever inhabited in the world. Ages before the rise of the Egyptian, Greek, or Roman empires, it was here that the wheel was invented and the first mathematical system developed. Here, the first poetry was written, notably the Epic of Gilgamesh, a classic of ancient literature.

The first village settlement in and around Ur was founded (circa 4000 BC) by the so-called Ubaidian inhabitants of Sumer. Before 2800 BC, Ur became one of the most prosperous Sumerian city-states. The ruins of Ur were found and first excavated around 1854 or 1855 by the British and later by the University of Pennsylvania. In addition to excavating the ziggurat core, they partly uncovered the ziggurat of Nanna. The British Museum commenced excavations in the early 20th century here and at neighboring Tell.

The expedition unearthed the entire temple area at Ur and parts of the residential and commercial quarters of the city. The most spectacular discovery was that of the Royal Cemetery, dating from about 2600 BC and containing art treasures of gold, silver, bronze, and precious stones.

Early cities such as Ur existed by 3500 BC. They were called temple towns because they were built around the temple (ziggurat) of the local god. The temples were eventually built up on towers called ziggurats (holy mountains), which had ramps or staircases winding up around the exterior. There, the god visited Earth, and the priests climbed to its top to worship. Public buildings and marketplaces were built around these shrines. The temple towns later grew into city-states, which are considered the basis of the first true civilizations. At a time when only the most rudimentary forms of transportation and communication were available, the city-state was the most governable type of human settlement. Of gargantuan proportions, the ziggurat mirrored that of an Egyptian pyramid. However, it is now known that they were not burial chambers like the pyramids of Egypt, nor were they for human sacrifice like the Aztec pyramids of Mexico. Various theories have surfaced over the years that suggest that they were a nostalgic re-creation of the mountains the original settlers had left, an attempt to raise the city's god above the material life of the streets below, or even an attempt to reach closer to heaven.

The City of Ur is situated between the Tigris and Euphrates rivers. This area was known in ancient days as Mesopotamia (Greek for "between the rivers") where the lower reaches of this plain, beginning near the point where the two rivers nearly converge, was called Babylonia. Babylonia, in turn, encompassed two geographical areas—Akkad in the north and Sumer, the delta of this river system, in the south. All of the Sumerian cities were built beside rivers, either on the Tigris or Euphrates. The city rose, its brown brick walls held together with a black tar type of substance that is clearly visible today.

During Ur's supremacy (about 2150 to 2050 BC), Sumerian culture reached its highest development. Shortly thereafter, the cities lost their independence forever, and gradually, the Sumerians completely disappeared as a people. Their language, however, lived on as *the* language of culture. Their writing, their business organization, their scientific knowledge, and their laws and mythology spread westward by the Babylonians and Assyrians.

Visiting the ruins of Ur and its enormous ziggurat was an arduous task for our Brigade and Armor Battalion staff members. Venturing through the ruins of Ur proved quite a challenge in the near-120-degree heat. "We had to climb down this long shaft to get into a burial site," remembers 1LT Youngham. No matter how you look at it, this hurried trip through the ruins of Ur, for the fortunate staff members of the Armor Battalion and Brigade Headquarters will forever be recalled as the opportunity of a lifetime.

End of essay.

The Ziggurat, City of Ur, Iraq (2004).

NOTE FROM AUTHOR: Here is the latest report from the LA Paper regarding the death of our fellow CA NG Soldiers: June 24, 2004 (2 More California Guardsmen Killed in Iraq). The newspaper did not answer my many requests to reprint their article. So, despite their lame protocols, and as a courtesy to my readers, I am mentioning it for your future review if you so desire.

25 June 04

I can't believe that June is about over. I realized something last night. I used to take my laptop to my "hooch" at night, but about six weeks ago, I stopped doing that and started locking it up in my office. I am curious to know if there has been a noticeable change in writing style as a result? I think that during the day, as I am writing now, I tend to be a bit more on edge and possibly rushed at times. At night I am more relaxed and might tend to do more venting. Just a question to ponder.

I opened an email from my wife; she sent an informative email to my three Nieces: Cousin #1, Cousin #2, and Cousin #3. It is unfortunate that their mother, my sister Sherry, won't allow our families to communicate? I call it white trash syndrome; Sherry has all the qualifications for a Jerry Springer episode.

0951 Just returned from another nonproductive meeting. COL Nosey is still gone; LTC Milling was also absent, leaving LTC Slacker as "the man." Oh boy. The meeting was coming to a close, and I had a comment at the end. MAJ Smythe noted that the Combat Stress Team was now on board and would be putting out a schedule with their office hours. I commented that the term office hours troubles me as we are in a war zone that is 24/7. Does the enemy keep office hours? I asked if there was to be an on-call person. Slacker jumped all over me, stating that they will have office hours. I said softly, "What if the soldier has a crisis at home, off hours, stuff happens..." Slacker continues yelling at me, "These motherfuckers aren't to be waking up the stress team in the middle of the night every time their pussy hurts!!!!" I said under my breath, but loud enough for him and him only to hear me, "Whatever, sir." Following the meeting, he tried to make up with me by explaining himself. I didn't buy it. You just humiliated me in front of 25 people, and now, privately, you want to make it all better. No, not just no, but fuck no! This is Slacker's MO (modus operandi), his methodology of dealing with other human beings. This is an example of why WE hate his fucken guts so much and DON'T respect him. Humiliate us in public, praise us privately. When I was trained by the world-renowned U. S. Marine Corps and later by the U. S. Army, what I was taught was to praise in public and reprimand in private! I must talk to him about this. But more as an ODP (officer development program). I will tell him that if he wants to look like an "a-hole" in front of others, that is his business, but I would refrain from that type of treatment of his staff in public. He has 24/7 to fuck with us, chew us out, or do whatever he wants with us. We are in an audience situation for one hour three times a week, and that is not the time to beat up his staff in public and demonstrate to the world that you don't have unity of command within your organization. You would think, with soldiers dying every other week, that we would have bigger fights to fight and bigger issues to deal with. Slacker must learn that if he is going to treat his XO in this manner, his XO won't take it lying down.

Slacker and I had a long talk, and we patched things up. I think he is getting a little better at listening and even respecting what I have to say. He admitted that he was wrong to fly off the handle at Phil (CPT Cantez) and me. He thanked me for bringing it to his attention. I emphasized the point that we, as the Armor Battalion, need to have a strong front and can't show any dissent in ranks or problems in public. People need to know that if they mess with any Armor Battalion member, they are taking us all on as we are a united front, a tight unit, and a together unit.

(Maybe they don't teach this approach to leadership in the Army's officer training but the Marine Corps sure as hell did!)

26 June 04

Another heart-to-heart, but this time at CPT Craders request. Included were LTC Slacker, me, MAJ Rickets, and CPT Crader. We held the meeting in my office trailer after kicking CPT Cantez out. The lights were out, leaving a cooling atmosphere from ambient light emanating through my window. Crader had a beef with Rickets over a treating and demeaning email that he received from Rickets. To make a short story out of a long-winded situation that took the good part of the morning to talk through, Rickets was very pissed off at a failed telephone conversation he had with Crader that concerned a mortar mission planned based on actionable intelligence. Rickets threaten to recommend his removal, etc., etc. A lot of harbored animosity and hostility was aired and discussed. The LTC and I used us as examples of how we talk through problems (yeah, right!) Anyway, it was a very productive meeting with all of us on the same page, particularly Crader and Rickets, who must work together 24/7.

Following the meeting, we shared a scrumptious lunch provided by several of our Civil Affairs Interpreters. The dish served is called Dolma and is considered a delicacy in Iraq. It was absolutely delicious! The dish is served in a big pot, the type that you would serve: a big serving of spaghetti or a big casserole. The dish includes stuffed potatoes, peppers, and tomatoes with various vegetables and rice. As in typical Iraqi cuisine, you eat with your hands, putting some of the dishes on a pita type of bread. Absolutely delicious!

Crader doesn't partake in the local cuisine, so I joined him at the chow hall. I won't let a visitor to our base from one of our fellow units eat alone if I can help it. We had a nice chat about service here in Iraq, NG, careers, and overall operations. I escorted him to the barber as the barber at Kalsu quit because of the recent murder of the local and national workers on the post.

27 June 04

Sunday, I slept in. Cantez woke me up (that is a switch!); "The Lion came in looking for you this morning, and he told me to get out of PT gear!" I replied, "Fuck him, you can't work 365 days in a row!" After brushing my teeth and shaving, I dressed and made it into my office. I checked my emails, none from anyone but one or two from our battalion, not too many from outside the battalion on weekends. See a trend here? Slacker informed me that Ranger Boy had returned from his pass. Slacker chewed him out and asked for documentation regarding his bumped flights (canceled flights). Ranger Boy responded that his integrity shouldn't be in question; Slacker said that it already is. I concur with Slacker this time.

Slacker, Hunts, Crader, and Lieutenants; Mates, Ronsen, and O'Shannon flew out on a Blackhawk to Camp Anaconda for LT T.'s memorial service, which will be tomorrow afternoon. I videotaped their take-off.

Rickets last day here and there is more talk of A Co. relocating here to Scania. Overall, it was a slow day. I helped as the lay leader for Catholic services, which lifted my spirits and gave me some sense of escapism. This afternoon, I took a moment out and watched "House on Haunted Hill" with Vincent Price. I enjoy those B movies.

28 June 04

10:26

This will be a day for the history books, as the TOA (transfer of authority) took place this morning. The TOA was done covertly this morning at 10:26 am, as advertised on the 30th of June, for security reasons; anti-coalition groups were reported to be planning a string of car bombs and other mayhem to disrupt the transfer. Paul Bremer handed a sheaf of documents to Chief Justice Midhat Mahmoud, thus formally transferring sovereignty to an Iraqi government. I applaud American Intelligence's efforts with their decision, as tension is currently very high. All MSRs (main supply routes) are closed from here north to Baghdad. Our S2 informed me that all military traffic in and out of Najaf is presently forbidden. We closed the Smythe Gate (rear gate) and the Hadjie market also for security reasons.

19:31

I just came from a link-up with the Stryker Company that is here in the yard with CPT Morehead. I thought it would be prudent to have some coordination in case of an attack, and CPT Morehead agreed. We walked the lot and eventually met up with the Stryker leadership, CSM Strom, and CPT Bloom. We informed them that we had intelligence that activity was going to go down hard in Baghdad tonight and that we had some actionable intelligence here that a VBIED (vehicle-born improvised explosive device) would be striking us at our Smythe gate entrance (earlier, we shut down the Hadjie Market as a precaution). CPT Morehead asked them if they could man two OPs (observation posts) on the north end of camp as they have enhanced night vision capability, like that of our M1A1 Abrams MBT (main battle tank). My thinking was two-fold; first, the presence of Stryker's defending our camp sends out a message loud and clear, and secondly, with their night vision capability, it would greatly enhance our preventive measures for an enemy attack. CSM Strom was adamant about not doing any additional missions unless his Squadron Commander ordered it. He said that they had to get up at 03:00 for a 04:30 departure north. CPT Bloom was more receptive but sided with the CSM. I then suggested that if we sounded our siren, they could react to preplanned positions. They agreed to that. CPT Morehead made sure we would all be on the correct frequency so we could communicate. We will see.

I telephoned home, speaking to my in-laws this evening and morning for them, Monday, June 28, 2004. My mother-in-law is undergoing surgery today, and I wished her luck with the procedure.

This morning, CPT Castellano became disrespectful and belligerent with me during our force protection briefing with COL Nosey, CPT Moans, CPT Lance, CPT Morehead, and me. I told him to report to me in my office following the meeting. He stormed out of the briefing in a belligerent manner. I consequently wrote up a DA (Department of the Army) FORM 4856 General Counseling Form, citing his disrespectful and unprofessional behavior. I instructed him that he needs to be able to control his temper better and that we cannot and will not have Armor Battalion staff bickering or fighting in front of other individuals who aren't in our Battalion. Castellano didn't like getting counseled; heck, no one does, but he took his lumps and left.

Tonight is about as close to knowing that the enemy is going to strike as it gets. My feelings are not of apprehension but rather of responsibility. Are all our soldiers and tenants ready if it comes? Will our QRF (quick reaction force) be quick enough to respond? Will our towers be able to spot the flash of mortar fire? We will see.

29 June 04

Today is the day after Iraqi sovereignty was declared. I wish I had my laptop with me last night so I could accurately describe the emotions that were running through my head all night, and yes, it was a sleepless night! For starters, the MND put out that a change was to occur with the day-to-day convoy operations; of course, this is our bread and butter here at CSC Scania. Convoys are not to move out under the cover of darkness at night. So, the sounds of the camp were quite voluminous due to the high volume of tenants.

Convoys in staging yard at CSC Scania, Iraq.

The Hadjie trucks traveling up and down the MSR, in and out of our staging and fueling yard, made for a night of a lot of commotion. This certainly added to the tension of the current event that took place that day, as well as the actionable intelligence that we received that a VBIED might be headed for our own gates. 2100, 2200, 2300, 2400, 0100, 0130..... time just ticked away, and no one in our tent slept a wink. This morning, I let CPT Cantez and 1LT Artera sleep in as I made it in to work at our normal time, 0800. In the mess hall, we now have military television programming, and sometimes, we get news from the states. We watched a glimpse of what was being broadcast all over the world. THIS IS THE FIRST TELEVISION PROGRAMMING THAT I HAVE VIEWED SINCE WE STARTED THE DEPLOYMENT, NOVEMBER 15, 2003. (IT IS NOW THE END OF JUNE!)

For God and country, my friends!

I would say that last night was the third most restless night's sleep that I have endured. The worst night's sleep was the night following the May 25, 2004, mortar attack on Scania. The second worst night's sleep was my first night's sleep at FOB Kalsu, a short time following their May 25, 2004, fatal mortar attack. And then there was last night, I would say that it ranked right up there with the others. The feeling of helplessness was present, as we all knew, particularly those who viewed the results of the Kalsu Mortar attack that killed SPC U. and injured ten other soldiers; you can prepare all you want, you can stack the most sandbags and wear two body armor vests, but if a mortar or rocket lands with a direct hit on your tent or even your bunker, it is all over. That is God's will. That is how you feel when you are lying on your rack at night on one of these crucial evenings, somewhat helpless. I took as many precautionary measures as I could: retraced my steps in the dark to our bunker (a week and a half ago, I did this and smashed my face into a pallet that was serving as our bunker's roof, holding up additional sandbags for overhead cover-I still have two gashes in my nose and face from that fiasco), swept the dust out from under my bed as that is the first place that I would go if an inbound mortar were to be inbound, positioned my body armor and Kevlar helmet right next to my bed where I could reach it as I dove for the floor, and put my second chance vest next to the pillow area of my bed so I could grab that quickly as well. But if a direct hit comes, so be it. I can honestly say that I have done everything in my power that I could to protect myself and my men from harm. I can also say that I have corrected any negatives in my life. So, if it is my time to exit this wonderful planet, I will do so with a clear conscience. It comforts me to no end knowing that I have a young son to carry on with my name and life. My daughter, of course, is quite important as well, and I know that she will be a very successful, happy, mature woman with a great life ahead of her. Additionally, my wife would probably be the most impacted if my demise were to occur, and for that, I would be extremely saddened. She is a faithful "trooper" of a wife who, when God created her, broke the mold! Probably, my only unresolved issue is with that of my sister. But I don't have any regrets or remorse, just sadness that she had to turn against me and my family for the sake of her own greed. For that, I truly feel sorry for her.

Well, it has been almost two hours since I started documenting my "night from hell," and I should get back to work (I was interrupted by LT Tonic regarding a communications issue). Slacker called me from LSA Anaconda, stating that his flight for today was canceled. He had some administrative issues to cover, but nothing significant.

15:15

Some very strange turn of events today with our infamous "Mayors Cell," as in the last hour, COL Nosey and LTC Milling entered my office (this is a first). It is funny to watch people's reactions; CPT Cantez and SFC Barnum hopped up and left not a minute after their entrance; pretty funny. Milling had her typical sour-puss face emanating; "why am I here in this man's

93

office?" COL Nosey seemed frustrated about getting the run-a-round regarding duties and responsibilities on the camp. He said that he asked the mayor's cell about something, and they said it wasn't their lane, talk to Armor Battalion, etc. He pointed out the example of the motor pool, "Who is responsible for it?" he asked. I simply responded that I didn't really know, although, in my mind, I knew there was discussion with CW2 Cliffs handling the issue. I talked about that a bit, and I mentioned his name. I tried to call him, but he wasn't in his office. COL Nosey picked up my putter and hit a few balls into the putting cup. Milling mentioned something about taking some lessons, and I used that as an icebreaker; "Oh, did you take golf lessons, mam?" She replies, "Yes, but I found it boring." I then went on about my start in golf at the course at Los Alamitos, where Tiger Woods got his start. I must have struck a nerve with COL Nosey and after Milling left because we talked golf for a while.

After Nosey left, I telephoned SGT Freedom to discuss the golf project getting resurrected. Here is another observation of these S5 Soldiers: I call them, and LT Fernandez answers and says that SGT Freedom is in a meeting with MWR. I said to put him on the phone; let me see here folks, a Major is calling to speak to a Sergeant, and he is too busy to come to the phone? Do you see my point here? I think I could put two and two together, I guessed that the pretty lady from the MWR department was probably with the guys and was driving them wild. The head of MWR is one of two "regular girls" here on post who aren't military; they are civilian employees, and they are just like the women back at home, if you catch my drift. They ain't too bad looken' and they don't have the military attitude going on. Talk about a diamond in the rough; guys tend not to be themselves in these situations, and even more so here in the combat zone of Iraq.

I had to dispel this assumption for myself, so knowing that they were all coffee drinkers, I took what was left of my pot and ventured to their trailer next door. 1LT Artera and SPC Todd welcomed a fresh cup of my Starbucks. The oddity enough, here is MAJ Freakins (XO of the mayor's cell) in their office and in conversation with the S5, 1LT Fernandez. MAJ Smythe (Operations Officer for the Mayor's cell) was also in the trailer but seated looking through a magazine and appeared to be bored. I don't trust the mayor's cell! I like and can trust MAJ Freakins, but not who she works for. My suspicions? That they are up to something.

Oddly enough, the MWR lady made an unusual comment to me; "you are very persistent." I guess she was referring to my telephone call to SGT Freedom. Oh well, get over it, sweaty! You ain't all that to me, just because SGT Freedom is "gaga" over you, like many others here, I ain't! (My parents wouldn't approve of my use of "ain't," but that is how I feel at the moment.)

Picture SGT Freedom, a pencil neck geek, former Air Force Captain who worked in Civil Engineering for several years in the Air Force. Why he left and became a Sergeant in the National Guard is somewhat of a mystery to us. He is doing a kick-ass job as a project engineer for us, but he is a fucking geek! Typical for an Air Force puke, he is also a backstabber, and he talks way too much! He, as well as the other S5 staff, are far too friendly, way too friendly, with the Iraqis and the Interpreters for my taste. Caution, my good soldier, caution. Freedom is a two-time looser with women and could be on his third wife? He is a smart guy, but I worry about him and don't trust him.

SGT Bourdon is the other NCO working for the S5 section, and I don't trust him either. Like Freedom, Bourdon is educated with a degree in Archeology? What do you do with that? He wrote up an article for the base paper about him "saving the birds." Some owls were living in the old cement factory that we tore down, and he adopted them. Eight out of nine birds died, and he arranged to have the surviving bird shipped to an animal facility in Kuwait. His animal husbandry is honorable, but frankly, folks, I couldn't give a shit! Dood, we are in a friggen war zone! Birds? WTF! I guess there is a real need for stories around here, as his was such a hit that it was also run in the brigade monthly newspaper. Not to sound caulis, but I don't get it? Back to Bourdon, he is having an extremely close relationship with a Specialist Dole, a young blond-haired, blue-eyed Midwestern girl and unmarried mother of two little toddlers (refer to Cast of Characters). I have made it a point not to get into discussing male/female relationships up to this point of our deployment, but enough is enough, and I can't hold out any longer (by the time I am done with this deployment in 9 months or so, I'll probably have a spin-off book on this topic alone!) Honestly, there haven't been that many women in our lives of this deployment. We are a combat arms unit, and other than with aviation, the Army doesn't put females in those positions; hence no women with us. Even at Ft. Lewis and Ft. Irwin, we didn't have much interaction with the females in the brigade. The females are primarily in the Combat Support Battalion, Brigade Headquarters, which includes the MPs. In any event, the only women we see here are female soldiers, mostly assigned to the MP (military police) units. There are a few in the medical and maintenance units here as well. The civilian females are from the KBR crew, and as I mentioned, there are only two that are young and pretty. The rest are older, way older, and there aren't many of them. You will never see an Iraqi woman anywhere. If I am convoying to Tallil or Kalsu, I always get a picture of them if I see them in the fields working because we never see them. They wear the black Barka (similar to a hijab) from head to toe, and you can only usually see their eyes. The Iraqi culture keeps the women hidden from outsiders and only seen by their families or clans. So that is my story about women here. Pornography, yes, they have it here. You can buy it at the "Hadjie" market on CDs, yes, CDs, not DVDs because it is cheaper that way. For around $4.00 (USA dollars), you can get a one-hour CD. The material was obtained from pornographic satellite programming from France. It is pretty nasty stuff that you won't typically find in America. Some guys at other locations have their own satellite programming hooked into their tents and might be able to access adult programming. We don't have those opportunities here in Scania. I am trying to get AFN (armed forces network) in our office area in order to keep up with world news.

16:30

Here is a perspective from the home front, compliments of Mrs. Annette Hillcrest.

> I listened to this special on CNN about a Marine unit that was returning. They went on and on about the family support they have on the base. They talked about the different programs that they have and how the wives also help each other on base. Then they went on to ask the wives how they managed to have their husbands away for 6 months. I thought 6 months, and they were going on and on how hard this must have been for them. Not only were they only gone for 6 months, but they had all this help and support. All we have is a computer letter once a month, maybe, and scheduled activities once every month and a half. No one in the neighborhood to help, and our husband has gone for 1 ½

years, but with you, it is close to 2 years of unavailability because of the pre-deployment phase. Crazy.

Here is my response.

> The family support issue that you brought up is a valid one. It is also even more reason that you should be documenting your days in a diary or journal or something. You will someday really regret that you didn't. I am telling you, you could publish your experience, be it that the National Guard Family Support System is broken and in need of dire repair.

21:44

I just wrote brief letters to the following: Annette & the family, a college friend, other family friends, several cousins, Annette's aunt, uncle, and parents. Annette got me some stationary that had the American flag on the front prior to our deployment, and since the 4th of July is around the corner, I will use them now. Thanks, Annette! I also sent my buddy Luke a backup disk of my writings.

Tonight at 23:05, we will be conducting mortar firing. I plan on videotaping the event. Tonight, we hear the convoys rolling out, not a usual sound here at night. It makes for raising the tension up a few notches as we hear bumps in the night, and it makes us jumpy.

120 mm Mortar night illumination mission, CSC Scania, Iraq.

Today was supposed to be the transfer of authority to the Iraqi interim government, although it took place unexpectedly on the 28th, we are still preparing for hostilities today, tonight and over the next week particularly. We are ready.

10:00

The following essay was also featured in **COMBAT ESSAYS**, American History, A Veteran's Perspective, Volume II.

Inspired by this milestone in world history, I wrote the following.

A Day in the Life of an Armor Battalion Soldier

(4th in a series of essays)
by
MAJOR Darby Hillcrest
June 30, 2004

Letter to the Editor from the front lines,

In a letter written by the National Guard Adjutant General to the families, friends, and members, the General sent a well-versed message of sympathy for our two recently fallen heroes: Second Lieutenant T. and Specialist M. The letter mentioned that as of to date, the State has lost a total of seven (7) Soldiers as a result of conflict in Iraq: 25 seriously wounded and 75 with less serious wounds. The General's message was clear: to never forget our fallen comrades and to never forget why we serve to defend freedom. The price of freedom is rising.

As much as I dislike being in the combat zone of Iraq in lieu of being with my loving family in Southern California, I am proud to be involved in our nation's quest for the expansion of human rights and liberties. Having grown up in an environment that could be considered somewhat privileged, I have found that it is often commonplace to take our amenities and our rights for granted. After experiencing combat operations in this theater of war, I will forever be changed both as a man and as an American. I hope to return to America as a better person and as a crusader for the improvement of the human condition for all citizens of this remarkable planet. If we are only on this great earth for a microcosm of time, I have learned that each and every moment of our time, as well as each and every relationship, is exceedingly valuable to the point of unfathomable proportions. Some Vietnam generational vernaculars included "love the one you're with." After our experiences in Iraq, I have found that there is a lot of wisdom in that colloquial. I would venture to say that most, if not all, of the California National Guard soldiers currently deployed in Iraq have developed a new and enlightened respect and love for our country, our families, and our friends.

Please keep the faith and "keep the home fires burning."

Respectfully,

Major John J. Hillcrest
Executive Officer
Armor Battalion

Central South Iraq.

(Major Hillcrest, age 44, is a full-time military officer who resides in Southern, CA with his family: wife - Annette, daughter - Nina, and son Junior)

17:46

I just spent the last ½ hour or so looking at news websites that had stories about our two recent fallen comrades. I am really shaken up right now. Seeing SPC M.'s image in the paper it is too much to bear. There was a story run about how his mother allowed the press to cover his remains' arrival at the Sacramento, CA airport. I must applaud her efforts, as SPC M.'s death wasn't in vain. I am glad that Mrs. M. is taking measures to get the truth out to the American public that American soldiers are dying in Iraq on a daily basis, and the American public has a right to know.

There is a wonderful website at MSNBC News that contains a photojournalist's coverage of various funeral services held for fallen military personnel from operations in Iraq. It is quite touching as this photographer really captured the essence and magnitude of the situation. I sent MSNBC an email simply saying thank you, Maj Hillcrest, Central South Iraq.

I am very sad today. Looking at the images of our fallen soldiers and reading about their memorials and their families, I am really sad. God bless them; they will be missed. God, if you are listening, please don't let me join them. Little Junior is a rabble-rouser and needs his dad home to straighten him out and raise him properly. Nina needs to have her father give her hand away in marriage someday. Oh God, how I want to get home in one piece. Out. (Out is a military term meaning the end of conversation.)

NOTE FROM AUTHOR: Folks, I cannot read this stuff without getting choked up. I am sorry.

1 July 04

LTC Slacker returned on an early morning helicopter ride from LSA Anaconda. I heard some birds fly in before sunrise, and I knew that it was probably him and our crew. He was in his typical agitated mood as he greeted the staff as they arrived at work. "Where's Artera and Freedom!" Slacker clamored. I replied, "They should be in their offices, sir; I will look into it." This is a typical response to Slacker and his explosions. Actually, a little bit earlier, I sent a runner to go and wake up Artera and Cantez as I heard Slacker had arrived. When you have a battalion staff covering down what is really a company-size mission, things like punctuality, I suppose, take on a higher degree of importance to the commander. We play the game to shut him up. Personally, I prefer how things are run at Kalsu, low stress for the minutia bullshit like being at your desk on time in the morning and in proper uniform.

Today, I wrote a lot and produced several letters. I also put out some fires here and there and had a civil affairs update brief. The first piece is for our family support monthly newsletter.

> I would like to take this opportunity to thank you for the wonderful support that you have shown our deployed soldiers. With our celebration of independence upon us, this is a good opportunity for us all to reflect on the meaning and purpose of our unit's current mission: to defend freedom. We should all feel a sense of pride to be involved in our nation's quest for the expansion of human rights and civil liberties.

> Unfortunately, the quest for freedom has come at the ultimate price for some of our soldiers, Specialist U., Specialist M., and 2LT T. These Soldiers and their families will forever be in our prayers. We will never forget our fallen comrades, and we must never forget why we serve - to defend freedom for our fellow man/woman.

> This chapter of the history books is being written in the blood, sweat, and tears of not only our soldiers but with that of their families and friends as well. Without YOUR support, our unit could not succeed in its mission. Thank you from the bottom of our hearts for all your love and support.

MAJ John J. Hillcrest

Executive Officer

Armor Battalion

I also successfully contacted the local newspaper where I grew up. I thought that they might want a story about a local boy who is serving in Iraq. July 4th is only three days away. I sent them my letter to the editor piece, an updated battalion news release, and several pictures. If no story ran, that is okay by me. I guess I want a story out there back home so my fellow 25th-year high school reunion buddies can read it, as well as my sister and her family. I have virtually no means of communicating with them. They couldn't avoid the newspaper if it ran. In the pages were discussions about our fallen comrades, mortality, and duty here in Iraq.

I ate dinner late this evening, and I barely made it in before they closed for the night. We now have armed forces news playing on television sets in the DFAC. Saddam Hussein was featured as his trial was kicking off. When I see his image on the TV for me, it is like seeing Satan himself. He is the reason for our loss of three American soldiers from the great state of California. He is the reason for us having to bury LT T., SPC M., and SPC U. That is what I think of when I see Saddam Hussein. I have a hatred that builds up like I can't describe.

This evening, there was a breathtaking sunset and a full moon. I captured several pictures of the full moon. Last night, we conducted mortar illumination fire, and I captured it on digital video with my Sony Cyber-shot by shooting into my NODs (night observation device). The images are of a green tint and pretty clear for shooting in total darkness.

Photo taken through NODs (night observation devices) at night on MSR Tampa, CSC Scania,

Tonight, I am pretty worn out. I guess from not sleeping too well this week with the transfer of sovereignty and the shift of convoys operating at night versus the daytime.

It got to be pretty late when LT Artera came into my office. He informed me that he had some soda and offered some to me. We proceeded to the rooftop of the mayor's building, where we sometimes smoked a cigar or two and bolted down a few ice-cold sodas. It was nice, and the moon was fully illuminated. At around 0200, our Mortar Section fired off a few rounds. I awoke quickly to hear, "Incoming! Incoming!" I, of course, knew that it was friendly fire outgoing, as did most of the camp. There is a distinct difference between the sounds of incoming and outgoing, and you never forget that difference once you have experienced both.

2 July 04

The 4th is approaching, and we are taking precautions for an attack on our camp. Intelligence reports that VBIEDs would be the most likely scenario. Two and a half hours of wasted time in meetings this morning with COL Nosey at the helm. Can you say cluster fuck? Slacker was at the end of his rope, and he leached out, attacking the mayor's cell for various idiotic actions that they have participated in, such as cutting the wires of a satellite system of one of our interpreters without talking to him first? Will they ever cease to amaze me with their stupidity? If LTC Milling had half a brain, she would be dangerous!

Well, that blew the entire morning, and to go that long without a drink of water in this environment is dangerous and not the least bit healthy. I felt my sinuses acting up today and was on the verge of a cold coming on, so I actually hit the rack this afternoon for an hour-and-a-half nap. This was a first!

Following the lengthy battle update brief, we do the force protection brief. All the Armor Battalion staff are against COL Nosey's desire to close the Hadjie Mart and clamp things down for security purposes, all but me. I sided with him on this one, and Slacker didn't like that a bit. He chewed me out in front of the group because I told him that I didn't agree with him that there is no imminent danger here at the camp with the 4th of July and the transfer of authority this week; however, theater-wide intelligence says different. Nosey believes this, and so do I. When it comes to the safety of our soldiers, I won't roll over for Slacker or anyone else until I am at least heard. I don't care if they don't want to hear it; if I think in my gut that my way is better or safer for our soldiers, they are going to hear me out! Following the meeting, Slacker called me to the side, outside the building, and he made his normal apology for yelling at me. I didn't let it bother me at all this time. I remembered something that I had just read from the Bob Woodward book; he cited an interview with General Tommy Franks. Franks tells of how he and Mr. Rumsfeld didn't necessarily get along at first and butted heads. Franks mentioned that part of one's success in the military is having the ability to adapt to a multitude of diverse supervisors, bosses, or commanders. He said that adaptability is a big part of being successful. I remembered that and didn't let Slacker get to me. It worked! Thanks, General Franks.

Big picture: the Army will call up 5,600 soldiers in the Individual Ready Reserve beginning July 6, 2004. The Army needs soldiers as drivers, automated logistical specialists, light-wheeled vehicle mechanics, administrative specialists and combat engineers, cooks, carpenters and masonry specialists, petroleum supply specialists, and cable system installer-maintainers. In the officer ranks the specialties are concentrated in the combat service support branches. Soldiers usually enter the IRR after finishing the active-duty portion of their enlistment. Army General

George Casey became the senior U.S. military commander in Iraq, taking over the reins from Army Lt. Gen. Ricardo Cantez. Casey, who'd previously served in the Pentagon as the Army's vice chief of staff, now commands 160,000 US and coalition troops that make up Multinational Forces Iraq.

21:18

Talk about funny; SFC Barnum just walked in and informed us that the mayor's cell, Sergeant Major Moans, was zip-tied inside his tent. That is a riot! Zip ties are what we use to handcuff the Iraqi's hands behind their backs when or if they are arrested or detained. Also, the mayor's staff and COL Nosey had their telephone and computer wires cut. We are told that the mayor's staff cut the satellite system wires of one of our interpreters and wouldn't allow the FA (MP provisional) unit to have satellite systems in their tents. The mayor's staff have just pissed off everyone with the stupidest decisions I have ever seen. They are dangerous!

3 July 04

Today is a good day. We haven't been shot at or mortared in a while, and I received more care packages today than any other day in theater. Seven packages! My previous record for a single day was five. However, three of these seven were from orders that I placed online, which I don't think really counts towards the record. Here is the lineup of packages; you might be thinking, "Who cares about your stupid packages?" Believe me, this is a very big deal for us here in this God-forsaken place! Today's packages were from two from Amazon with books that I purchased- two screenwriting books and one book about writing a book (how appropriate), two big packages from my wife that contained many items that I needed - deodorant, toothpaste, candy, and pillows! Yes, no more having to prop up my dirty laundry bag to read at night! I also received a package from my in-laws with goodies and several magazines, and lastly, my box of bike parts arrived. I am so glad that I ordered a pair of riding gloves as they are the same type of gloves as the shooting gloves that I purchased at Ft. Lewis and are perfect for the hot summer months here. We do two mail pickups a week from Tallil Airfield, and our mail sometimes gets backed up there, which is why we will sometimes get a large number on a given day.

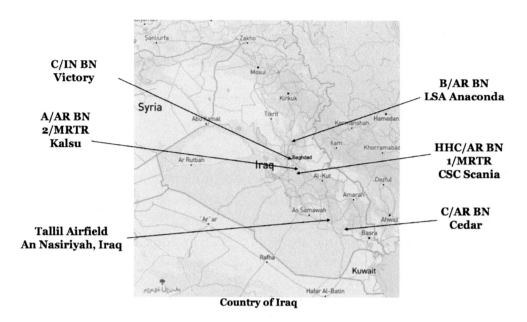

C/IN BN
Victory

A/AR BN
2/MRTR
Kalsu

B/AR BN
LSA Anaconda

HHC/AR BN
1/MRTR
CSC Scania

C/AR BN
Cedar

Tallil Airfield
An Nasiriyah, Iraq

Country of Iraq

Tallil Airfield is south of CSC Scania and just north of Camp Cedar. Map by John J. McBrearty.
Source: © OpenStreetMap (data is available under the Open Database License)

I received the nicest letter that I think I have ever received from anybody. A former postal employee of mine wrote to me from his retirement pad in Southern, CA. Dick was a career letter carrier for the U.S. Postal Service and worked with me for about a year or so as I had a brief stint in their management circles prior to going into the full-time National Guard workforce. I don't like to even admit to having worked at the Post Office as it quite literally was the worst experience of my life! Honestly, it was worse than coming here to Iraq and getting shot at on your first day of combat! Every horror story that you might have ever heard about the postal service is true, at least for me. The postal environment that I was exposed to stifled intellect frowned upon initiative, and forbade compassion of any sort! Come to think of it, I think that Slacker missed his calling; he would fit right in their management style (or lack thereof)!

Here is some of what Dick had to say.

> "Greetings from a former hostage of Ayatollah She-Devil, Dick, route 4001...I have no idea what 'the bitch' does now.... our gripes about She-Devil seem universal, several employees have postal nightmares...sounds like post-traumatic stress syndrome to me."

She-Devil was that psychotic postmaster that we worked for. She was a person of little character and wasn't capable of leading an employee to the bathroom, let alone sorting or carrying mail. Rumor has it that she has been sued by several former employees for anything from harassment to misconduct to impartiality. As a result, the postal service put her out to pasture somewhere. Similar to the MOB, the Postal Service does not fire their CAPOS (MOB Captains) (aka Post Masters); they just put them somewhere else. I truly hope that She-Devil has gotten some mental health treatment. She-Devil and my sister would probably get along quite well together. Hell, for that matter, they would all probably get along quite well with Slacker!

Dick continues.

> "My wife and I have enjoyed following your Army career. I am really impressed. Also, I am a bit concerned for your welfare. I had no idea of your rank. I had the greatest respect for our XO on my Navy Destroyer. You have a great deal of responsibility, which I am sure you handle well. You were one of the very few who showed any decency, concern, or compassion for your employees. I am indebted for that. We know that you are not there for the money. You must be there for our country. We say a quiet prayer when we see the planes from the March base fly over us. May God bless us all."

Needless to say, I am speechless.

Another fine thing happened today: I was seated near MAJ Smythe and MAJ Freakins in the chow hall. The one and only COL Nosey comes by, and we exchange a few words about a soldier who shot himself in the foot last night. CPT Rourke walked by, and I noticed his patch was that of the CSC, which is headquartered in Los Alamitos, California. I asked him if he was from California, and he said that his unit was but that he was from Philadelphia. I almost fell off my chair. It turns out that he is from the suburbs of southeastern Pennsylvania, very close to where I grew up. I later stopped in his office to find out more about his background. Talk about a small world; he obtained his BA from Princeton and his MBA from Drexel. We shared Pennsylvania stories for a good half hour or so in his MCT (movement control team) office. His unit controls the movement of the convoys up and down the MSR (main supply routes). His operation is a 24/7 business and is pretty hectic. I suggested that he and I submit a story about us to our hometown. He agreed.

This morning, I thought it was going to be another rough ride. I am at my desk along with CPT Cantez, SSG Kanister, and CSM Hunts visiting. Slacker busted in, yelling at me, "Dwellers is coming back today; make it happen!" He turned and stormed out? I told the CSM that he couldn't be undermining my orders to people without asking me about the issue or reasoning. I wasn't going to take this and proceeded to go and find him. By this time, Slacker was in the BDOC, checking his email and conversing with CPT Morehead. What I had to discuss was important, and I wanted to speak with him alone. I went and got a cup of coffee out of my office and kept checking his office for his return. In about half an hour, he returned, and in his office were Master Sergeant Moocheff and CSM Hunts. Hunts saw me come in and knew what was up. He signaled to Moocheff to get "out of dodge." I approached Slacker. Slacker directed me to his computer screen to show pictures of his house remodeling project. Slacker is a very smart guy, and he probably saw the NCOs leaving and probably figured that I was there to talk some serious business. He knows that I don't like him to yell at me in front of soldiers. He diverted my attention to small talk about his house. After what seemed like an eternity, I got to the point. He again apologized for his gruff actions. I told him that I wasn't so much concerned with that, just that I gave a directive to have Dwellers go to Kalsu to develop and mentor SPC Kacrader, who was having many challenges. I talked it over with him, and I believe it was a misunderstanding with CPT Randerson in the middle. I explained the multitude of reasons for Dwellers to spend time at Kalsu; 1) Mentor Kacrader -reports from Rickets that he is a piece of shit that only works when he wants to, and that is only 10% of the time. 2) To show A Co. that the battalion is supporting them and having a battalion presence there. 3) To get Dwellers out of his "office pogue" complacency and get him in touch with the real war zone and threat outside of the seemingly safe walls of the Scania compound. I further elaborated on my philosophy of having each staff officer, and NCO leave the wire at least once a week on a patrol, guard tower, or convoy in order to keep them in the game of warfare and to lose the false sense of complacency. I also told Slacker that I wanted to manage the staff as I saw fit, as that is the duty and responsibility of an Executive Officer. Slacker understood and thought that I was making perfect sense. He said that he wouldn't interfere. I later thanked the CSM for giving us the space to air our differences. Hunts is a true professional, and I like and respect him immensely.

I received an email from my wife Annette today. She attended LT T.'s funeral, and here is her report.

3 July 04

Dear Darby,

Today was a very emotional day, and there is so much to say, actually more than I have the strength to write. I will tell you someday.

I attended the funeral in Compton, rode the motorcade, and attended the burial in Riverside. As the coffin was in the hearse, I placed my hand on Lt. T.'s flag-draped coffin and spoke words as to rest in peace from Major Darby Hillcrest and the Hillcrest family. Both events were very well attended. The ceremony at the cemetery was full of military honors, presentation, and respect. There were so many people at both events, but I could not see one person that I recognized. There was only one man that I remember from one of the balls, but he did not approach me.

I came close to being in a serious accident going to the cemetery as I was driving in the motorcade. A car traveling in the opposite direction lost control on Van Buren Boulevard and began spinning around many times and skidding right toward me in front of the driver's side (right where I was). It stopped just inches from my car. The police that were orchestrating the motorcade came running. I had to pull over and catch up with the motorcade because my body would not stop shaking for about 10 minutes. I feel that I came so close to death or serious injury. My life was definitely spared today.

I hope all is well. I hope that you are all safe and things are OK. PS If you have the SPC M. family's address, that would be great. I will send both families a card.

Love, Annette

God bless LT T., SPC M., and SPC U; may they never be forgotten.

4 July 2004

Happy Independence Day! Well, this holiday came roaring in like a lion! Last night, I left the office around 9 p.m. or so. I took my new pillows to my "hooch" (tent) and enthusiastically set them up on my bunk. This is as motivating as it gets! I settled into my new comfort zone and commenced reading my current self-imposed reading assignment, "The Commanders," by Bob Woodward (one of my favorite authors). This was a required reading when I attended Command and General Staff College (prerequisite military education for consideration for promotion to LTC and COL). After about two and a half hours of reading, the staff duty officer 2LT O'Shannon (a very light-skinned African American man who is a Military Intelligence Officer assigned as the Scout Platoon Leader) busted into my tent, informing me that LTC Slacker was found face down in the latrines, that he fell and was passed out. I jumped up, put on my PT (physical training) gear, and headed immediately for the MTC (medical treatment facility). I actually got there before Slacker arrived. Eventually, the military ambulance arrived. CSM Hunts was in the back with Slacker and a medic. Slacker was on a stretcher, strapped in. He was not coherent and had an IV in him. I just about shit, thinking he had a stroke or broke some ribs falling or something terrible had happened to him. I felt the weight of the entire world on my shoulders at this moment. One thing Slacker does is talk. He talks a lot. He wasn't talking and wasn't even awake; I just knew it was serious. We all carried him into the MTC, and the PAs (physician's assistants), CPT Morgan, and CPT Andrews were there to treat him. They hooked heart monitors up to him and took his vitals. Eventually, 1LT Younghams, our Medical Platoon Leader, arrived, as did CPT Castellano, our BDOC Commander. SGM Westminster later joined in the excitement. Once Slacker started coming to, our concerns were lessened. He took a total of four bags of IV. Apparently, he had been throwing up and, had diarrhea and was extremely dehydrated. Eventually, he was talking, and the crew started cracking jokes. Westminster said, "Hillcrest is out here ready to take over for you, sir!" I said, "Yea, Westminster, I am already sewing on Lieutenant Colonel rank on my collar." Everyone laughed.

One by one, the curiosity seekers left. CSM Hunts and I stayed with Slacker until about 02:00; then, we walked him home. It was a long night. The PAs told the Colonel to take a few days off.

Could this be a foreshadowing of things to come for Slacker?

This morning, we received a SECRET FRAGO (fragmentary order) directly from MNCI (Multi-National Corps Iraq) instructing us that we are to cut a platoon loose from A Co., Armor Battalion at KALSU and send them to the Camp Bucca prison near the Kuwaiti/Iraqi border. They will have a force protection mission to allow the current FORCEPRO (Force Protection) platoon of MPs to shift into the prison for additional support needed for a surge of prisoners from the Abu Ghraib prison in Baghdad.

5 July 04

Another holiday came and went without incident. I spoke with Annette, Nina, and even Junior last night. That made my day. Little Junior said he saw Spiderman on "television." I have never heard him say that big of a word before. He is a crack-up.

Business as usual, 09:00 meeting with all the same players, including LTC Milling and SGM Moans, who returned yesterday from their monthly planning meeting at Tallil Airfield. Oh joy, Milling is back! The meeting was pretty uneventful and actually pretty quick. It adjourned after only 40 minutes or so (a new record!) The force protection was a lot longer than it should have been. COL Nosey was on a roll about having the QRF (quick reaction force) doing more visible patrols (within the wire!) After heated discussions, we ventured into the next topic, which was brought up by 1LT Olouski, who was filling in for CPT Castellano, who, like the Colonel, was out with a stomach virus. Olouski communicated that Ali and the vendors at the "Hadjie Market" were very upset at the closing of the market for two days over the 4th of July weekend. He stated that they lose $3,000.00 a day when it shuts down. What I am trying to figure out is why Castellano and Olouski are so worried about this.

6 July 04

Lunch with S5 section.

Went with rovers (soldiers on roving patrols) on night patrol.

Armor Battalion on roving patrols at night. Photo taken through NVGs (Night Vision Goggles).

7 July 04

It is funny that I did the least writing the day I had the most to report. The lunch excursion we conducted yesterday, I can sum up with my AAR (after action review) that I counseled 1LT Fernandez with:

Here is an example of a trip report that we utilized in Iraq:

SUBJECT: Trip Report for a trip to Al-Jawadia

1. Summary. We attended a lunch with a prominent local in Al-Jawadia named Halim Kadem Radi to support host-nation relations and discuss local issues.

2. General. The lunch went well, and all parties present were pleased to meet, exchange cultural understanding, and build relationships. We enjoyed the meal together and discussed social topics and specific issues on road repair, vehicle bridges, and the local school. Attendees included Maj Hillcrest BXO, CPT Cantez S4, CPT Olson TMC, 1LT Tarasewicz, and the S5 staff.

3. Issues.

a. Issue # 1: Road Repair

(1) Discussion. The main road into Al-Jawadia runs along a freshwater canal east and west. This road needs repair to improve traffic ability during rainy seasons and reduce dust to enhance visibility and safety year-round. The minimum improvement would be grading, laying etch, and gravel, further improving the road.

(2) Recommendation. This can be added to the project list and prioritized accordingly. Improvement of the road will service the entire village and improve safety and traffic ability.

b. Issue # 2: Vehicle Bridge

(1) Discussion. Two vehicle ridges along this canal allow traffic across the canal. These ridges service the entire village. The eastern bridge needs repair.

(2) Recommendation. SGT Freedom and I can survey the bridge and the road, get the necessary grids, and determine the level of repair needed. This will be added to the project list after the survey.

c. Issue # 3: Local School

(1) Discussion. The school in Al-Jawadia was repaired. Repairs focused on the facilities inside the structure to provide functioning toilets. The structure that houses the toilets, however, still needs some minor repair.

(2) Recommendation. SGT Freedom and I can survey the school toilets and determine the need for this work. This may be added to the project list and given low priority.

4. Enclosure 1 is the BXO's AAR comments for this mission.

5. Conclusion. The POC is the undersigned at DSN......

Enclosure: FERNANDEZ

As 1LT, IN

S5

Enclosure 1

BXO AAR comments.

1. As a Civil Affairs mission, I would categorize this event as successful for the following reasons: all participants made it back to base camp without any major incidents. The needs of the public were identified and addressed for follow-up actions by the S5. Goodwill medical assistance was rendered to us by CSC Scania's Physician Assistant, CPT Olson, and an overall atmosphere of camaraderie and friendly relationships improved.

2. As a military operation, I looked to the American Heritage Dictionary for help. The one word to summarize this military operation is cavalier: CAREFREE AND NONCHALANT. As a mission, this event was an abomination. I have derived this analysis for the following reasons:

a. The S5 mission missed its SP (start point) by 40 minutes.

b. NO PCI (pre-combat inspections) and NO PMCS (preventive maintenance checks and services on equipment and vehicles) were conducted prior to the execution of the mission.

   c. Vehicles were not properly dispatched.

   d. Vehicles were out of gas prior to leaving for this mission.

e. The vehicle that the BXO road in ran out of fuel, was out of power steering fluid, and the brakes squeaked.

f. At the destination, one of our vehicle's batteries blew up, deadlining the vehicle, which required a maintenance retrieval mission to be executed (additional security needed).

   g. Not all vehicles had maps of AO.

h. No safety briefing was conducted prior to the mission.

i. No AAR was conducted at the conclusion of the mission.

j. No talking points or purpose of the mission were discussed in any detail with the participants.

k. No self-recovery cables or straps were on any vehicles on this mission.

l. The Officer in Charge got lost on the way to the destination. (NOTE: The destination was not more than 3-4 clicks (a click is approximately one kilometer, 1,000 meters, or 0.6214 miles) from the camp; however, it took over 40 minutes to get to the destination? This conduct isn't acceptable during training at NTC, and certainly is not to be tolerated in a theater of war where American soldier's lives are at risk.)

m. The overall leadership climate of the S5 section is in question. The section seems to operate more like a "good old boys club" rather than a military organization. Although the S5 section has developed many good working relationships with the local Iraqi populace, they must keep their eye on the ball and remember that they are still in a hostile environment to never let their guard down and to not take their working relationships to the personal level.

3. Recommendations:

a. NCOs of the S5 section need to start doing NCO business. I am directing NCODP training to be conducted by this section immediately. This training will be dictated by Command Sergeant Major Hunts.

b. Officers of the S5 section need to start doing Officer business. I am directing ODP training to be conducted immediately by this section. This training should include mounted or dismounted land navigation, PCI's and PMCS. This training will be designed and supervised by S3 Air, CPT Morehead.

c. Increased situational awareness must be a priority for this section. The BXO will be conducting bi-monthly assessments of S5 operations.

d. Trip tickets for the section will be filled out and turned into the BDOC prior to any mission off post. See CPT Morehead for details and format. The trip ticket includes a map of the AO traveled, radio frequencies, and a personnel manifest. END OF REPORT

(All I can say is good grief!)

I received quite a few emails from my wife, Annette, over the last two or three days. These are personal family issues that might not have much relevance here; however, I will say that issues at home really do impact our performance here on the front lines. It can take your head out of the game when you are worried about the home front. I try not to let it affect me, but it does. COL Nosey said the other day that after the sixth or seventh month here, it really starts to take a toll on a soldier. He is probably right. There is a great sense of frustration at not being able to help with family and home problems from here. There is a feeling of helplessness. I really don't know what I would do if I had a wife that I couldn't trust. I have accumulated some minor wealth *(I will reiterate minor wealth-LOL)* from investments, savings, and prudent retirement plans. If my wife wanted to, she could literally wipe me out. I feel so grateful for having the woman that I have. I thank God several times a day for her, my kids, and for the wisdom and sound judgment that keeps our soldiers alive.

Roving patrol in Central Southern Iraq.

The night patrol was probably the most exciting thing that I have done since I have been here. It is an infantry/MP type of mission to cruise our area of operations in HUMMV gun trucks, just looking for trouble or anything out of the ordinary. At night, we set up several random vehicle checkpoints. Much like our border patrol checkpoints in California, they stop each car on a given road, check out the contents of their vehicles, and inquire who the people are and where they are going. I was amazed at how well the roving patrol soldiers were received by the locals. The Iraqis waved at us when we drove by. The largest town closest to us is Ash Shumali, with a population of approximately 5,000. The town has a main drag flanked by many stores and restaurants, not much different than our small towns at home. The blocks behind the main road are apartment complexes, and further behind the apartments are houses and, eventually, farmland. Downtown, there is a police station, city hall, and a gas station. We pulled up to a restaurant and ate shish kabob and soda pop. We ate outside on a patio and were well received by the locals. My curiosity got the best of me, and I toured the inside of the restaurant. The front entrance was entirely open, unlike enclosed restaurants in America. The floor was a hard surface, possibly tile. The structure was made of cheap concrete that was painted over. To the right of the entrance was a window. Behind the window was the kitchen, which was fairly spartan. I poked my head in and startled an older Iraqi woman. She was dressed in the typical black burka. As you make your way into the restaurant, to the left, there is a back room, unfurnished, with only little mats on the floor. That is a Mosk for Islamic prayer. Out the back door was a courtyard. On the other side of the courtyard was a row of single bathrooms. The bathrooms consisted of a small room similar to an outhouse. There was a porcelain device on the floor in the middle of the small room. This was the toilet. It was like a porcelain drain. There was a small garden hose for hygiene cleansing, quite different from our American customs.

We traveled mostly in blackout drives, utilizing night vision devices to see. They work extremely well and make it easy to sneak up on someone at night. The lunch event started at about 1230, and we returned at about 1630. I left with the rovers at around 1730 and stayed with them until midnight. It made for a very long day as I was wearing body armor and Kevlar the whole time. Boy, do you sweat up a storm wearing that equipment? When I got back, I was still pretty hyped up from adrenalin. I telephoned my wife, who was somewhat surprised to get a call at that late time. I would equate the roving patrol to a ride along with your local police force or sheriff's deputy back at home. It was a very similar situation. You are always at the ready and on edge. The gun crew that I was with is a good example of what the National Guard brings to the table here in Operation Iraqi Freedom; the driver was a Specialist and a police officer for his day job, and the Vehicle Commander was an SSG who is also a police officer but with a different agency, and the team leader/machine gunner was SFC Barnum who is an AGR (active guard reserve) soldier with over twelve years of active duty Army Infantry experience. This crew is about as good as they get. Currently, in Operation Iraqi Freedom, the Reserves and National Guard make up 61% of the forces in theater. This, in its own right, is a historically significant fact.

9 July 04

This is the morning following the evening of the big PX caper. Apparently, our PX was robbed last night of over $10k worth of electronic devices, DVDs, DVD players, digital cameras, etc. A shakedown of the camp was conducted, but nothing was found. It was probably transient tenants here in Scania who are long gone with the loot by now.

PX (Post Exchange) at CSC Scania, Iraq.

Today, I wrote a postcard to my brother-in-law's mother, thanking her for sending me a wonderful care package. It was full of many pricey goodies that included a bunch of stuff from Trader Joe's. Yesterday, I sent postcards to my cousin in Wisconsin (my Mother's Nephew) and my aunt and uncle in North Carolina (my mother's brother and his wife.) Also, today, I received a nice email from one of my High School friends who later became a psychologist. She saw my writing in the local newspaper, and here is what she wrote:

9 July 04

Dear Darby,

I picked up three copies of the local paper (7/9/04) and will gladly mail them off to you. Your article was great to read and very informative. You are remarkably focused and articulate. I would like to enclose some other "goodies" in the package, but I have no idea what you might need/enjoy. I just read an article in Newsweek that said that soldiers in Iraq love receiving Kool-Aid and a particular type of Carefree chewing gum. I cannot imagine how you are tolerating the heat! Please let me know what else I can include to brighten your day.

We were on vacation in the Yucatan portion of Mexico over July 4th. We did a lot of exploring and had an excellent time. The beaches, ocean, and snorkeling were wonderful. We met some old friends from San Diego there. The kids, of course, had a blast. Will you be able to meet up with your family on some type of leave in the near future? I certainly hope so. The job you are doing is just incredible and sounds very exhausting.

Again, let me know what else I can include, and I will mail off a package as soon as I hear back from you. I have your address. Sincerely,

Your bud from Algebra class.

The paper printed essay Chapter 1 from the **COMBAT ESSAYS**, American History, A Veteran's Perspective, Volume II book. The essay is entitled: "A Day in the Life of an Armor Battalion Soldier."

Today, I concluded an investigation of one of our officers that we believe was in violation of his integrity. This officer (who will remain nameless here) went on his R & R (rest & relaxation) trip to Qatar, an island country south of Kuwait. The R & R time is four days, with a day of travel at each end of the trip, totaling six days off duty. This officer returned after twelve days off duty, and his excuse was that his flights kept getting canceled. After my investigation with the air operations and passenger terminal staff at Qatar and Tallil, it was discovered that there were several flights that the Lieutenant could have gotten on. I recommended a letter of reprimand for basically lying to his Commanding Officer and Executive Officer, which is a real no/no in the military. I also recommended that his forthcoming promotion be held up until after the deployment. Slacker concurred with my findings and recommendations. The officer is doing a stellar job here for us and is recoverable. He just needs to grow up.

Big news last night: I was informed that my name was pulled out of the hat for taking leave. I didn't give it much thought, thinking that the senior leadership would not be able to go at all. I told my family from the beginning that it would never happen for a major, and they weren't expecting it. Well, I discussed it with Slacker and Hunts, and I told them that I wanted to give my leave to CPT Randerson because he and his wife just had a baby. Slacker said no, that I needed to get home, too, to see my family and that Randerson would have ample opportunity to get home later. Well, I didn't put up much more of a fight at that point. I almost started crying as it was the first time that I had ever thought of seeing my lovely wife and children. I was completely overwhelmed with emotions. My plan is to surprise them and just show up. Also, I don't want them to get their hopes up, as anything could change over here. Slacker also knew that Annette and the family needed to move into our new home and that the timing would be perfect for us. Slacker said that he planned on going home when his name came up.

For the third time this week, I lifted weights with CSM Hunts at the A Co. Field Artillery's (Military Police Provisional) company area. They have a weight set and bench on their patio. I got the idea to work out there because they had a leg extension bench, and I needed to build up strength in my leg that had the knee surgery. It gets quite hot lifting outside, but it also helps us get used to the heat. I think that I have found a lifting buddy. It is much easier to lift with a partner than by yourself.

10 July 04

Convoyed to Kalsu, SGT Corales drove. Two-gun trucks as escorts, no incidents on the way up. The main entrance of Kalsu was now closed, so we had to make our way all the way around the southeast side of the camp, almost doubling back parallel to the freeway. The new entrance is much more tactical with much more standoff distance in the case of VBIED (vehicle-born improvised explosive devise).

The camp has improved somewhat since my previous visit last month. There are several more porta-potties, and the ROWPU (reverse osmosis water filtration unit) has arrived and is operational. There were two bulldozers building up berms that surrounded the compound, and the biggest change was the absence of the 200–300-foot communication towers in the camp.

We proceeded into camp, and I made my way to CPT Bordham's tent and stowed my gear there. He was in the rack (sleeping) when I knocked on his door. I picked his tent to bed down for the night as I knew he had a satellite dish in his quarters. I then knocked on MAJ Rickets' tent and woke him up; it was now around 10:30 or so. With the strong possibility of

A Co. moving down to CSC Scania with us, they will miss the opportunities to sleep in as they do now.

I later met a doctor who was the National Guard's State Surgeon, who is here for his three-month rotation with us. He is a LTC and seemed very cool. He said that he was the only physician in the state who was an actual surgeon.

I started my investigation into a shooting incident that occurred here on the seventh of July. The camp was conducting a battle drill to a camp attack and using live fire in conjunction with the drill. Apparently, the MPs overshot their intended targets and damaged a Local Nationals home, nearly killing some of its occupants.

13:40

I met with CPT Buyers of the MP Company to discuss the investigation. He was extremely rude and uncooperative. I will complain about his behavior to his Brigade Commander, as he is the Commander who assigned me to do the 15-6 investigation. CPT Buyers knows that his soldiers did the shooting of the weapons that impacted the Local Nationals' home and doesn't want an investigation into it implicating his men. He refused to cooperate. I will just put that in my findings of the report and recommend further investigation of the Company by this Brigade. Guys like Buyers give the MPs a bad rap. Even SGT Corales said that when you deal with legal issues involving law enforcement types, they are always the least cooperative. (Maybe it is like trying to medically treat a doctor; good luck with that!)

15:00 SGT Corales and I went out to visit the house that received damage in the live fire incident. The home was a spacious farm home that resembled that of the main residence in the movie, "Gone with the Wind." It was old and in need of some paint but quite spectacular. I venture to say that it must have been around 6,000 square feet, with a courtyard containing trees and plants in the middle of the home. The front had large pillars like the "Gone with the Wind" plantation home. The Iraqi family met us upon our arrival. They were all men, of course, as you never see Iraqi females anywhere in this part of Iraq. The culture is very conservative, and they are extremely protective of their women. We had our translator, "Sami," tell the Local Nationals of my intent to investigate

122

the circumstances around the shooting of their home. I made a tour of the area and took pictures of the impact areas. SGT Corales questioned witnesses at length. The temperature was a sweltering 120+ and humid. We were roasting in our body armor and Kevlar equipment. I felt pretty secure as we had a security team surrounding us. It resembled what you might see when the President of the United States walks around, and Secret Service Agents are maneuvering in and around his travels, protecting him. Upon our departure, I told the LNs that we were very sorry for the incident and that I was investigating it in order to get to the bottom of the situation and prevent it in the future. The LNs said that they want us safe because it makes them safe. We all shook hands and parted company. We left the Iraqis several cases of bottled water, of which they were quite grateful.

Upon our departure, we saw several cute kids, as you might see in any inner city. One little boy had not a stitch of clothes on, and the other children were all barefoot, as is often the case in Iraq. We gave them candy, and the children were elated.

20:50

SGT Corales and I are still working on the investigation. Three USMC Cobra helicopters just landed in the FOB. That is like music to our ears, the sounds of security and a projection of power. The Marines are bringing a whole new dimension to the force protection of this base. I have a much better feeling now about the security of our soldiers here at KALSU. Our guys are also to be congratulated as, from beefing up their patrols and presence in the surrounding community, there haven't been any significant attacks on the compound. Today, we received the FRAGO (fragmentary order) from (MNCI Multinational Corps Iraq) stating that the USMC unit here would be taking C2 (command and control) of the FOB Kalsu and that in a few weeks, our BCT (Brigade Combat Team) would be taking over control of A Co., Armor Battalion. This is a good thing all around. We are sending one platoon from A Co. down south to do the force protection mission at a prison on the Kuwait border, and we are hoping that the balance of the company will be sent to CSC Scania to make up for our manning shortcomings. I saw CSM Carr today here at KALSU, and he told me that the Brigade would be pulling all the tracked vehicle mechanics from us and redistributing them throughout the brigade. I would suspect that they will also be taking some more soldiers from us as well.

At KALSU, it is hot, very HOT! KALSU does not have air-conditioning in every building like Scania has. Also, the AC units at KALSU do not muster up the power that ours do at Scania. Consequently, you are always sticky, real sticky, while here at KALSU. When you walk around anywhere, you perspire, and I mean really perspire. When we returned from our mission outside of the wire, my entire uniform was soaked from head to toe. This is just the way things are for us here. You just deal with it as you don't really have a choice.

Tonight, it is quiet, very different from the last time I visited. I hope to get a shower in their nasty shower facility and watch some satellite television with CPT Bordham. I hope to wrap things up here tomorrow and catch a 17:00 convoy down to Scania with the platoon that is pulling out of here.

11 July 02

A Co. is working on their TOA (transfer of authority) briefing for the Marine Corps follow-on units here at KALSU. I continued working on my investigation. It was a difficult night's sleep as USMC Cobras were very active on missions in and out of the FOB. Also, I was sleeping in a tent that had been basically blown to hell, and back on the 25th of May, not more than several feet from our beloved comrade, SPC U., fell to his death; it was not so easy to fall asleep.

Major Hillcrest,

Hi. I am writing for the local newspaper in your hometown in Pennsylvania. You spoke to one of our editors about a week ago. First, let me say thank you for sending the essays, press releases, and pictures. I thought they were very interesting. It's not often I get to hear day-to-day details about the life of soldiers in Iraq, and it was nice to hear about some of the positive things that are happening on the ground aside from just the usual combat reports we see on TV. We ran one of your essays in the opinion section of the paper last week. For this week, I want to write a feature article about you and your unit. I was hoping you could answer a few questions for me. I know you are in a combat zone and may be too busy to give a lot of details, but anything you could offer would be great.

What made you want to join the military?

When I was a youth, I joined the U. S. Naval Sea Cadet Corps, Philadelphia Division. From these experiences as a young man, I found discipline, self-worth, and success. I applied this success to my day-to-day life, and it resulted in a dramatic improvement in my grades in school as well as my athletic endeavors. I received an ROTC scholarship offer in college as well as the choice to attend most of the universities in the country. Again, due to my early military experiences, doors were being opened for me. This, along with a sense of patriotism in wanting to serve my country, there was never a question about me serving in the military. I always felt that each of us (Americans) needs to serve our fellow man/woman and or our country in some capacity. I chose the military and have never regretted it for a moment. I now see the big picture and can see firsthand that my choices and decisions are now keeping American soldiers alive and improving the quality of life for thousands of Iraqi citizens. That is quite a rewarding feeling.

I enlisted in the Marine Corps Reserve while attending military school and attended drills at Willow Grove Naval Air Station. I eventually committed to the NROTC program and was commissioned as an Officer of Marines. I served close to four years of active duty in the USMC. My final duty assignment was a ground maneuver unit in 29 Palms, CA. From there, I went into civilian business for a while, only to be recruited into the National Guard. I currently work full-time as an Army Officer in the AGR (Active Guard Reserve) program. My experiences in the military have brought me to Iraq, Kuwait, Germany, Japan, and most states in the union.

My future plans include capturing my experiences by way of a book that I hope to get published following the deployment. My desire is to create a historical reference for future generations of historians. At the time of the deployment, I was working on my master's degree in American History.

My long-range plans include getting my **COMBAT JOURNAL** made into a feature motion picture.

Hillcrest quotes the late great acting teacher, Sanford Meisner:

"You have to live life in order to write about it." Consequently, I think that there is quite a story that I am experiencing that people will want to hear and see.

What kinds of differences between Iraqi schools and American education did you notice while working on refurbishing the school? Besides the final exams, did you notice any other similarities between American and Iraqi school kids?

The biggest thing that I have noticed about the Iraqi children and their schools is that they are no different than the children and the schools of the United States. I have seen so many cute children that you just want to give them a big hug. They are absolutely adorable and really love the American soldiers. We have a great sense of accomplishment seeing, for example, the children attending school in their newly refurbished classrooms. They constantly thank us for our efforts. It is so rewarding. Seeing a farmer's face lit up with joy as he now had water for his crops and the means of providing for his family and being productive in his village. That is also quite rewarding.

What was it like meeting with the village leaders? Did you learn anything about their culture that surprised you?

The initial impression was pretty overwhelming as I am not used to being treated like royalty or a VIP. The Tribal leaders and village leaders really go out of their way to make us feel welcome. They know that we want to assist with improving their way of life and the way of life for their people. They also know that we want peace for us and for them. I have learned that there are good and bad in every society and that the good far outweighs the bad. I have learned that the true followers of Islam are loving, kind people. The Baathists, Al Qaeda, and the like have twisted this religion around to meet their own objectives, needs, and agendas.

Cultural surprises? In the central south and southern regions, the people live very conservative, traditional Iraqi lives, similar to that of the 4th Century. They really live in the same manner in which the Profit Mohamed lived. The women are never seen by outsiders and wear black burqas from head to toe. I can't imagine wearing such an outfit in 120-degree heat! Although historically, Iraq has educated its women, here in the agricultural regions, I see much oppression. Other customs that are hard for our soldiers to grasp include the holding of hands of men and kissing of another man upon greeting. Other customs include never waving or shaking hands with your left hand and never showing LNs (local nationals) the bottoms of our feet. Iraqi food is fantastic, but it takes your system a bit of time to adjust to the bugs here. Soldiers are constantly plagued with dysentery (diarrhea).

Have you ever felt your life was in danger? Besides the religious services, what else do the soldiers do on your base to cope with the stress of being away from home in a dangerous place?

Life in danger? Try 24 hours a day, 7 days a week, 365 days out of the year, and from an enemy that is surrounding you at 360 degrees. No exaggeration; this is our life here. You are always on guard, 24/7. When you have seen your buddy die right in front of you, you know that you are in a dangerous place. Unfortunately, death is a daily event here (not necessarily all Americans dying, and not every day). This is our life as deployed servicemen/women in Iraq. I paraphrase this environment as; "A cross between Vietnam and the Wild, Wild West." No exaggeration at all; it is very dangerous! But we are the best-trained military in the history of civilization, and we know how to fight and survive. Also, keep in mind that for us and our unit, enemy contact is not constant, but the threat is. Just as important, the coalition forces know how to conduct civil affairs operations and are making incredible improvements for the Iraqi citizens. Thousands of Iraqi citizens now have electricity and running water that they didn't have before our arrival. Thousands of children have received inoculations that they wouldn't have received otherwise. Hundreds of thousands of Iraqi children are enjoying the benefits of a better education in our local village due to the coalition rebuilding efforts, similar to our Bahkan School project.

Back to the question of danger, you must develop coping skills; it is a matter of survival. Your survival instincts kick in and are in overdrive. When you are witness to death constantly, you learn to cope. You also learn how important your life and time are. You learn how important your family and friends are. Often, I have to ponder the question, "If it is my turn (to get hit - as I refer to getting killed), did I tell my wife that I loved her often enough? Did I tell her that when we last spoke? Did I tell my daughter how proud I was of her? Did I spend enough time with my son, Junior, prior to deployment?" Here in this environment, you find out what is really important to you in life because, quite frankly, you might not have a long life. These are the facts of life facing our American servicemen/women who are serving in Iraq, and we all think about them often. **I can't explain in sufficient detail how important it is for the American public to stand behind their deployed service members.** Our forefathers experienced these exact same situations and circumstances three hundred years ago as our country struggled through its beginning. Without communities pulling together, we would have never earned our freedom and become the United States that we are today. Our military operations are a direct result of the attacks on our Country on 09/11/01. That was our generation's Pearl Harbor, and we are part of the response to that attack. I pray for my fellow Americans not to lose sight of that fact. Now, in Iraq, as the military operations will eventually subside (someone, please tell that to the enemy that is shooting their mortar rounds at us), the focus of our efforts here is on the improvement of the quality of life for the Iraqi people. Everything from schools, road reconstruction, utility upgrades, improved security, empowerment of the Iraqi leadership/police/military, and health and hygiene improvements are all the focus of much of our current and future efforts here. We are here to promote freedom, democracy, and human liberties to a previously oppressed society.

To combat stress? I write and read a lot. Others lift weights and work out. And, of course, there are DVDs to watch. There is a combat stress team at our camp that encompasses mental health professionals who are there to listen to our problems if they arise. Getting a comforting email from home or a care package is about the best stress relievers that we have. Sometimes, those calls home or emails can also have an adverse effect, but that isn't very common. The support from the home front is about the best combat stress reliever for our soldiers (Hillcrest's opinion).

Are there any new developments or projects that you can tell us about since your last letter?

There are numerous improvement projects in our area of operation. Currently, we are completing four contracts that include rebuilding bridges, cleaning sweet water canals - resulting in numerous villages having the ability to farm and cultivate their land- and making road improvements. Future projects include the installation and repairs of water treatment plants, repairing a soccer field stadium (very big over here), repairing additional schools & roads to those schools, repairing water pumping stations, repairing road overpasses and village access roads, extending water services, repair of drainage canals, repair, and installation of power supplies, assisting with medical care improvements, and many more projects in our area.

It is worth noting that all these projects are within our immediate area of responsibility. To put things into perspective here, multiply these types of civil-military operations across Iraq with the hundreds of American and coalition military units here; you get the picture of the vast good that we are doing for the Iraqi people.

For our current projects in the completion phase this week:

Repairing the Access Bridge, Village of Al-Bahkan

1. Description. The purpose of this project is to repair the damaged bridge that serves as the main access to the village of Al-Bahkan across the Nahr Shakh River. The result is a highly durable 10-ton capacity bridge that will serve the public well, whether school children are traveling to school or local farmers are taking their

produce to market. The new and improved accessible bridges add to a greater quality of life for the local Iraqi residents.

Clean, sweet water canals of the Ibdaa-Gryaat River Basin so they are free of obstructions and vegetation to allow unhindered flow for freshwater access.

Results: The result of cleaning sweet water canals is multifaceted. Not only will the local farmers be able to prosper from growing more vegetables and crops, but inter-village rivalries over access to limited water availability have all but been eliminated as water is now available unilaterally without conditions.

Repair Culverts, Al-Bahkan Road

1. Description. The purpose of this project is to repair 17 culverts that cross the Al-Bahkan road to the town of Ash-Shumali. This will result in the unrestricted traffic flow of children getting to school, local commerce, and accessibility to medical emergency facilities.

MAJOR Darby Hillcrest is the second senior officer of the nearly 1,000 National soldiers currently deployed in support of Operation Iraqi Freedom. The results to date from Major Hillcrest's unit in the central south sector of Iraq have been significant. The area maintains a secure environment free from criminal retaliation, persecution, and intimidation. The Armor Battalion will continue to help the Iraqi people build not only schools but also a prosperous, secure, democratic nation where individual rights are protected.

NOTE: I don't want to alarm you, your readers, or my family and friends back on the East Coast, but as I finished writing the answers to your questions, we came under fire by way of a rocket attack. Here is the setting: I just made my way from the BDOC (base defense operations center) to my" hooch" (tent) that I am staying at one of our FOB's (forward operating base) KALSU in the central south sector of Iraq-we are currently in the infamous "Sunie Triangle" also known as the "Triangle of Death." I was sent here to conduct an investigation into a shooting incident that involved some damage to a Local National's property and possible injury (as one of the few Field Grade Officers in our area, I, unfortunately, get these types of taskings often, particularly if other officers are involved). The time was around 23:00 (11 p.m.), and it had been a very long day in temperatures of 120+ degrees. I had just sat down and taken off my heavy boots and sweaty fatigues when I heard a "thunk," followed by a whistling sound (similar to a sound effect in a cartoon or film). Then there was another "thunk." I hit the ground immediately, reaching for my body armor and helmet. There was another "thunk" that was again followed by another whistling sound. I had my suspicions it was rockets. My suspensions were validated when I stuck my head outside of the "hooch," looked to my left (west), and saw a green subdued flashlight running across a parking lot, the same exact location where Specialist U. fell to his death from a massive enemy mortar attack on the 25th of May 2004. I couldn't help but ask myself, "Was that some kind of sign from SPC U. warning me of the danger?" I looked to my right (east), and I saw a soldier wearing his body armor and helmet running in a southerly direction toward the BDOC. It was then that my suspicions were re-confirmed. I grabbed my M16-A2 rifle and ran as fast as my legs would carry me to the BDOC. On my way, some soldiers informed me that we were under a rocket attack, that the QRF (quick reaction force) had been dispatched, and that USMC (United States Marine Corps) attack Cobra helicopters were already airborne (that was quick! Love those Marines!). I arrived at the BDOC and was given an immediate BDA (battle damage assessment), which is an update on the situation. (In times like these, even though you might be in charge of the senior man, you must remind yourself to step back and allow the battle captains and NCOs, as well as the fire direction team, to do their jobs.) They already had a fix (identified location) of the rocket's impact area and were working on identifying the point of origin. (We own the night with our extraordinary night vision capabilities, and having those Cobras in our hip pocket was quite an advantage.) To compound matters, we had an inbound medivac (medical evacuation) helicopter coming to pick up an American soldier who had just been hit by an IED (improvised explosive devise) that was on the MSR (main supply route-or highways that the military use

131

to get around and move logistics), just to the north of camp. The soldier had extensive wounds to his face, but they were deemed not life-threatening by the medical staff at the medical aid station. Eventually, there was another rocket fired at our compound; however, we sustained no casualties. And so, the night went on. After several hours of assessing the situation, implementing a reaction plan, and conducting an informal AAR (after action review with the other tenant units of the camp), all seemed to quiet down. I eventually did get to my "hootch" and bedded down for a few hours. Yes, even after having your adrenalin pumping in overdrive from an enemy attack, you still make yourself sleep when you can get it over here. That is the way of life here. Again, **not every day is like today,** and I certainly don't want to alarm family and friends, but when the enemy attacks, no matter how minor or grandiose and elaborate, the bottom line is that they are trying to kill you and your men. That is the difference between being in a combat zone and training; the bullets are quite real.

I can't relate to how tough it must have been for the Vietnam Vets or even the Korean War or WWII Vets. I can only imagine how horrible some of their experiences were with similar situations to ours this evening. I would venture to say that they all had things a lot worse off than we did. But I do believe that we all share a common bond that is hard to put into words. We and our families have lived through the process of paying a very high price for our freedom. From the bottom of my heart, I have to thank my family and friends who have supported us, and I extend my sincere gratitude to all of them. That support is what gives me the strength to weather the storms as we had this evening. Some have chosen not to be supportive, and my feelings on that are as follows: I am so glad that we, as Americans, have the opportunity and freedom to make those choices.

MAJOR Hillcrest-Out.

LEGAL NOTE: Any information that I send to the media could quite possibly be contained in my forthcoming books about my experiences on this deployment to Iraq. Although a news agency might copyright their respective stories on my deployment, I reserve the right to reproduce those news stories in my forthcoming books. Darby Hillcrest, 7-12-2004.

Thank you very much. Our deadline is Tuesday afternoon, and our paper comes out on Wednesday. If you can't answer this right away, we could still use your information some other time. If you want to check out our paper, you can read parts of it on the web at yadayadayada.com.

I wish you the best of luck and, when you're done, a safe trip home. You are in a lot of people's thoughts and prayers over here.

Sincerely,

The Editorial Staff

12 July 04

20:08 I am beat. We returned to Scania at around 16:10, and I hit the ground running. Not only did we get hit at Kalsu last night, but Scania has also fallen into some bad luck today. Early this morning, a local, national female, age 38 and mother of 6 was accidentally shot in the head and killed by another unit passing by the camp. Also, a Lieutenant Colonel and a Command Sergeant Major were killed just south of here in an accident with a Hadjie Truck driver on MSR Tampa. It has been a horrible 24 hours, and I am absolutely exhausted. I pray that we don't get any retaliatory fire on us tonight. God bless.

13 July 04

When my wristwatch alarm clock woke me up this morning, my first thought was, "I am alive, thank you, God." One more day down, one more day closer to going home.

Good news: I received my first positive feedback from a golf company. Out of the dozen or more emails and letters that I sent out, only Callaway Golf responded positively. They said that their foundation would be sending clubs out to us soon.

Other good news this morning: CPT Morehead (S3 Air-Operations Officer) gave me copies of two FRAGOs (follow-on orders that add or make changes to preexisting larger base orders), one FRAGO dealt with regular "Joes" (soldiers) submitting stories into PAO for possible publication in the command newspapers and the other dealt with LEAVING THIS PLACE! It addressed the initial planning process for the transition of OIF II (us) and OIF III (our replacements). Boy, is that a positive thing!

19:41

I spent most of the day working on the investigation with SGT Corales. It looks pretty messy for the MP unit at KALSU. It appears that they might have shot a Local National's house on purpose. Heads could roll for this.

I wrote a friend of mine who is in the National Guard back in California:

> Hello,
>
> Thanks for emailing. It always picks me up to hear from you and your family. I have a recommendation, and **YOU BETTER TAKE THIS ADVICE!!!**
>
> DO NOT COME TO **IRAQ** OR THE **SINAI**!
>
> YOU DON'T NEED THIS SHIT!
>
> I SAY AGAIN, DON'T THINK ABOUT COMING HERE. DO THE KOSOVO OR BOSNIA THING. STAY AWAY FROM THE MIDDLE EAST!
>
> I won't get into detail; there are a multitude of reasons. You must trust me on this. The biggest challenge you would face here is being a SGT, SSG, or even a WO1; you won't have the clout that is needed to make a difference with anything more than your section, team, or squad. You have too much to offer to be put into this position and, frankly, are too valuable to be put on a ridiculous mission of guarding a front gate, tower, or patrol. (That was supposed to be a compliment; don't take it any other way.)
>
> Here is one of my many examples: we have a West Point graduate, a former Armor Captain with some six to eight years of active-duty

experience. Well, he is a Sergeant and in charge of a patrol team of two vehicles and six soldiers. What a waste of talent, but that is the way it is.

You would have difficulty accepting the mediocrity that you would see. I have acted in ways here that would have gotten me kicked out of the AGR system and NG. I have stood up to 06s and 05s when I thought they were dangerously incompetent and making wrong decisions. I have gotten away with it for now, but I am a Major (04) in combat with a combat mission and have a combat arms background. For all those reasons, I have eluded a court martial. But I know I am right and sleep at night. (You wouldn't believe how fucked up the logisticians from the AC and Army Reserve are. They are clueless about force protection and combat operations. I call them dangerous!)

I know you too well, and you would also speak up when you have seen some of the shit that I have seen, but you would probably end up in the brig with a criminal record and a BCD (Bad Conduct Discharge). You don't need to put yourself in those situations. (And you would probably be right in your convictions; any Marine would!)

As your best friend, do whatever you have to do to keep the momentum of your business going. Keep on track with that. Your wife and son need a provider, not a war hero (trust me - I want nothing to do with the hero business). Bosnia or Kosovo are nice and clean six-month deployments that anyone worth their salt could do standing on their head. I say try to avoid those deployments, too. Keep on track with your career. We aren't getting any younger. If the WO (Warrant Officer) thing doesn't materialize soon, I recommend IRR or getting out. Stay on track with your career; besides, I will need a golf partner when I get back.

I love you, Brother,

Darby Hillcrest

I guess that is how I felt today. Let me sum things up; as I previously mentioned, I was at KALSU when the night before last, we were attacked by enemy rockets, a Local National was shot in the head and killed right outside of our northern entrance, and the last time this happened our camp was mortared by the enemy, and we sustained injuries, and a Lieutenant Colonial and his Command Sergeant Major were just killed in a vehicle crash, just south of here, are you getting the picture here? Where is my Jack Daniels? I need a shot of something strong! There isn't much JD to be found here, but if you know the right people, you can get your hands on the local flavor; it is called "Hadjie Whiskey." This is pretty rough stuff. Even on the label, it says, "Industrial Strength." What is Industrial Strength Whiskey in the name of Pete? *(Alcohol, in this instance, was the desire, but not actually acted upon, just my imagination in overdrive.)*

Last night, I was very apprehensive about things, particularly the high probability of getting another enemy mortar attack. They just lob them in, and where she lands, nobody knows. And I have seen the damage that just an 80mm or 100mm mortar can do, and it isn't pretty.

14 July 04

Worked on the 15-6 investigation into the MP shooting incident at FOB Kalsu. This evening, a tremendous explosion took place at 02:50 on the morning of the 15th. We all jumped out of bed and onto the deck. It sounded like a 120mm firing very close to our tent. There was only one round shot, which indicated that it probably wasn't enemy fire. We found out later that it was a big truck's tire blowing up. We are jumpy, I suppose.

15 July 04

We received intelligence reports that Scania is going to get hit with a mortar attack between 2300 and 0100 tonight. We don't know if it is our CSC Scania or the Scania trucking company in Baghdad. (Talk about confusion; there is an Iraqi trucking company located out of Baghdad with the same name as our camp, Scania.)

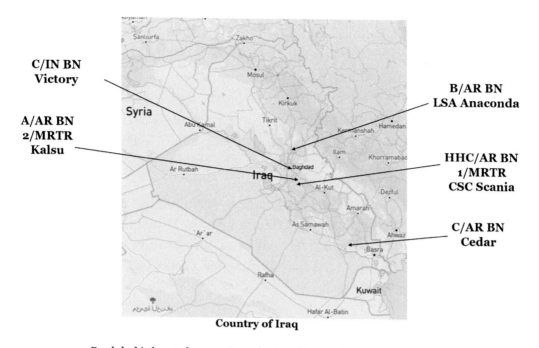

C/IN BN
Victory

A/AR BN
2/MRTR
Kalsu

B/AR BN
LSA Anaconda

HHC/AR BN
1/MRTR
CSC Scania

C/AR BN
Cedar

Country of Iraq

Baghdad is located approximately 60 miles north of CSC Scania, Iraq.
Map by John J. McBrearty.
Source: © OpenStreetMap (data is available under the Open Database License)

Nevertheless, we have beefed up our roving patrols with additional gun trucks and put the QRFs on alert. We have Stryker vehicles (4) on station at the ECP (entrance control point), as well as the MP units on post postured to defend the camp.

This afternoon, I lifted weights with CSM Hunts, and CPT Cantez tagged along. I like the idea of working out in the heat as it gets our bodies acclimatized to the extreme temperatures.

2300

I suited up my "battle rattle" (body armor with Kevlar & NODS) and made my way to the BDOC (can the army possibly come up with more acronyms?) Nothing was reported as out of the normalcy of routine. At 23:30, the Mortar Section fired off three rounds of IR Illumination. I captured some of that on my video camera through my NODS. I stayed at the HQ until around 00:30 or so and then returned to bed.

16 July 04

I could barely get out of bed on time. I threw on my uniform, grabbed my rifle, and quickly made it into my office. I scrambled to shave in my office and then brushed my teeth outside with a bottle of water and a toothbrush that a wonderfully nice family from Sacramento sent me in a care package. I fired up a pot of Starbucks coffee and read my emails. I had a really nice email from my wife. I must have said the right words in my last email to her; she was really cool in this email. I have a plan to surprise her and the rest of my family by taking 15 days of leave in early August 2004. It should line up perfectly with our move into the new home. Hopefully, I will be able to help out with the move. They will be surprised out of their minds. This is weird; Annette wrote me that Junior said yesterday, "Daddy's coming home." Very strange.

NOTE FROM AUTHOR: Folks, you will hear me say the following throughout this manuscript; "God works in mysterious ways." And he just did! JM

This afternoon, I wrote a story about one of our soldiers for our camp newspaper and brigade newspaper and a second story about one of our medics saving a life.

17 July 04

Today, I received a typical email from one of my staff officers, 2LT Tonic, our battalion communications officer. I noticed a quote that he added to the bottom of the email, and I thought it so accurately depicted the American soldier that I must share it with you all;

> "It is the soldier, not the reporter, who has given us the freedom of the press. It is the soldier, not the poet, who has given us freedom of speech. It is the soldier, not the campus organizer, who gives us the freedom to demonstrate. It is the soldier who salutes the flag, who serves beneath the flag, and whose coffin is draped by the flag, who allows the protester to burn the flag."
>
> -- Father Dennis Edward O'Brien, Sergeant, USMC

I have to admire Father O'Brien, as I think he had things figured out pretty accurately. I only hope that the rest of the American public has the same sentiment.

Today, I also had a moving email sent from Leanne, a childhood friend. Leanne was my next-door neighbor all through my younger years growing up in Pennsylvania. She was one year older than me, and she was an only child. I believe that she had some older stepbrothers or sisters from her father's previous marriage, but I don't think they were close. Leanne's mother and my mother were also the best of friends. Leanne and I had one big commonality: we were both children of alcoholics. Her father was a very heavy drinker and out-of-the-closet drunk, whereas my mother was more of a closet drunk that we hid from the world. In any event, Leanne and I both have some youthful scars that we have carried around all of our lives. Although I haven't been super close to her in our adult years, our lives have wandered into one another once again at the loosing of my parents last year. My parents were surrogate parents for Leanne. My sister and I were as close to Leanne as brother and sister. It is too bad that my sister has also shunned Leanne out of her life as well?

Dear Darby,

I am very proud to know you and to know that we have known each other for a very long time. I tell my children, and for that matter anyone else who will listen, how very much we appreciate that you and your men are risking your lives to preserve our freedom. I know that our parents are smiling down at us right now. You and I go way back, and I know the real Darby, the one who loved to play with Army men as a boy but who also cried when his friend's mom died, as he was in Marine Corps boot camp at the time, and he couldn't be there to console her. I am learning as I mature that our lives are interwoven by the initial friendships that we forge when we are young. I am very thankful that you lived next to us for so many years and that despite changes in our lives, we were able to find our way back into each other's lives.

I am sad that your sister has chosen to go her own way, but if God wills it, maybe we'll find our way back to each other again. However, I don't have time to deal with pettiness; at this point in my life, there are many other important issues and concerns.

The newspaper article was very well written and gave a glimpse of your everyday life.

Love, Leanne

18 July 04

Today, I awoke to the bright lights being turned on by a greeting, "Hello honey, I am home!" Major Rickets reported into the "Major's Pad" at around 08:30 this morning. I helped him move furniture around and get his stuff into the tent. For furniture, we are talking about cots and bed frames, nothing fancy. I have my quarter of the tent sectioned off with camouflaged poncho liners.

19 July 04

MAJ Rickets's first day on the job here at CSC Scania. This afternoon in our commodities meeting, I couldn't help but notice everyone's 1000-yard stare. Everyone looked "fried," burnt out. At the meeting's conclusion, I mentioned to everyone to try to get eight hours of sleep a night and get themselves on a physical training program, and oh yes, don't forget to get that one day off a week. It is almost like a joke. When the boss doesn't put into policy a day off, we don't take one, hence the burnout. When I last brought the subject up, Slacker nearly bit my head off? Later, when he heard rumors that "Slacker won't give his staff time off," he immediately tried to put that fire out by telling the Sergeant Major and me, "...of course, if they need time off, give it to them..." WTF?

20 July 04

Time is flying; the 20th of July and another month is down. Only a few short, SHORT weeks until I get to go on leave! Talking about excitement is an understatement.

Today, I got up a little early to work out with CSM Hunts. We lifted weights in our typical "old man" fashion, supersets. That allows your heart rate to be increased with little or no rest time between sets. I feel great! We followed our workout with a light breakfast and then into work. Fired up the Starbucks and put Linkin Park on the computer. My "Hadjie" speakers that I bought are the envy of the battalion, and I play it loud often. If you come into my trailer (that expression cracks me up as if we are now officially "trailer trash"), you better be ready to rock!

Yes, I am in pretty good spirits today; I am just thinking about leaving. I have been surfing the web trying to buy a few presents for my wife, Annette. I would like them to arrive just prior to my return home. I have had some trouble ordering online from Nordstrom, so I searched the web. I somehow ended up on a "gentleman's" website. Normally, we can't access any type of pornographic websites through the government system, but I think that the website folks are up to this. If a website has certain words in it, like "nude chicks," there are automatic blocks that search for these types of words. However, now the website types are not necessarily putting those types of words in their website titles, which opens up more markets, hence my stumbling onto this site. Well, this site had hundreds of photographs of women in either lingerie or swimsuits; they actually gave you a choice! The reason why I bring this up is to address the subject of sexuality. This is a subject that I haven't delved into much for a multitude of reasons. Primarily, I have found that on this type of deployment, you don't think of it often. It only becomes an issue when you have complacency or downtime. I have to admit, my curiosity got the best of me this time, and I did a bit of "surfing" on this website. My reasoning and justification, to myself anyway, was that I was going on leave soon. If I wasn't going home, I would have hit delete and moved on my merry way. As far as this website is concerned, I guess they bait you in with many beautiful women in sexy clothes in order to lure you into purchasing a membership. Membership on these types of sites enables you to access their model's posing nude and, most likely, some more advanced types of pornography. So, the moral of the story is that the good Major is staying away from that stuff and focusing on his return trip to his loving wife.

Today, I have the task of writing several letters of reprimand for CPT Crader. LTC Slacker is hot on him about not doing the leave paperwork for a soldier going on emergency leave, as well as his weapons accountability. Today, I also wrote another complaint to the mess hall for their suggestion box, asking for them to extend their hours of operation as they had during the "surge" from the transition from OIF I to OIF II.

Junior had some kind of incident with daycare. Nightmare.

21 July 04

Yesterday, a 1st Infantry Division soldier became the 900th U.S. military death in Iraq since the beginning of the war in March 2003. The soldier was killed by a roadside bomb while on patrol in a Bradley fighting vehicle in Duluiyah, 45 miles north of Baghdad. This week alone, there have been a total of five deaths, and the week is not even over yet!

More than 60 foreigners have been taken hostage in recent months, and there were fears that the action by the Philippine government would lead to more kidnappings. The Philippine government gave in to their demands to withdraw troops from Iraq to prevent the beheading of the 46-year-old father of eight who had been held captive for two weeks. Spain withdrew troops after a Socialist election victory following a terrorist attack in Madrid.

Meeting this morning, Col Nosey was in rare form. He says, "Why wasn't I informed about A Co. soldiers showing up here?" "Sir, if you want me to stop what I am doing and report to you every time a soldier shows up, I will do that then." *(My staff loves it when I stand up to this pompous prick!)*

22 July 04

Worked out with the CSM and CPT Cantez at 07:00; it was unusually cloudy and very humid. Today, much of the staff went to Hilla (Babylon). CPT Crader and his A Co. crew came down from Kalsu. A SGT sustained injuries at Kalsu this morning when he was trying to break open a .50 caliber round, and it exploded on him. He received some fifteen stitches from the accident. A Co. will pursue disciplinary actions for misconduct and being unsafe. We are still waiting to hear a word about where the rest of A Co. will go; we suspect it will be LSA Anaconda. That place is known as having received the most attacks of any other post in theater.

Cantez, Kanister, and Barnum, all located in the BXO/S4 trailer, are talking shit about the Marine Corps. Cantez; "I saw the CSM sitting with some RECON Marines in the chow hall, and man, they were filthy pigs!" Kanister; "That is because they go out to the field ten days at a time on RECON missions." Cantez; "What the hell is RECON doing here?"

Hillcrest: "Don't even waste your time SSG Kanister, guys that talk shit about the Corps, only wish they could be allowed into the Corps."

At 13:45, KALSU sustained another rocket attack, with five rockets impacting and exploding in the camp. No injuries or major damage were reported.

I wrote a letter to COL Nosey that complained about the mess hall staff not responding to my complaints that I put in their suggestion box. I cited them on several instances of inefficiency and laziness. At our morning meeting, the mess hall supervisor must have forgotten to read as he only read complimentary comments. Go figure?

23 July 04

Here are some of our recent statistics: our manning strength for the battalion is 186 presently here at Scania, our total patrols to date are 1,183 and are made up of primarily day and night motorized patrols with about a dozen foot patrols, joint IP (Iraqi Police) patrols are five, we have arrested or detained 152 individuals, we have conducted a total of seven ambushes/raids/cordon & search missions and have reacted to fourteen QRF (quick reaction force) missions. We have had one KIA (killed in action), nine injuries to hostile fire, and twelve non-battle injuries. C Co., located at Cedar II, was involved with relocating the ROM (refuel on the move) point called KENWORTH to inside the wire at Cedar II. A co. is still preparing to send the rest of its company? Where? That is the five-thousand-dollar question right now. We want them. The Marines (the 24th MEU) have now requested that they stay at KALSU, and our Brigade wants them to help out security up at LSA Anaconda. One platoon has already been cut down to a prison on the Kuwaiti border. Here in Scania, we continue our mission of force protection of the camp and have completed four civil affairs projects in the last two weeks or so. We had nice dedication signs made for the projects, which are printed in both English and Arabic.

On the bigger picture, the 10th Mountain Division Soldiers are now pretty much all here in theater, and our camp will have less traffic because of that. The 11th MEU (Marine Expeditionary Unit) is also currently deploying into theater.

On the way back from noon chow, CSM Hunts told me about a soldier from the Engineers who is assigned to us, received a "Dear John" letter from his wife and was reported to be suicidal. A "Dear John" letter is the most feared part of being away in combat for a soldier, as so much is out of your control. (A "Dear John" letter is a letter sent to a servicemember by their significant other, terminating the relationship. In other words, getting dumped!) This is also one of my greatest fears. We are going to get the soldier moved here to Scania from KALSU and let them see the post Chaplain and stress team OIC.

Today, I am reviewing several legal investigations: one about soldiers going to the Stars and Stripes newspaper with a story and not telling the chain of command, another about accountability of weapons, and another about falsifying submissions for purple hearts by two members assigned to A Company. Needless to say, our Legal NCO, SGT Corales, is a very busy guy.

Today, we received word that while on emergency leave, MSG Moocheff broke several of his toes by dropping something on his foot. This was quite a convenient move as he is allowed to stay at home on medical leave, vice vacation, or emergency leave until he heals. LTC Slacker had to say this about Moocheff; if it smells like shit, if it feels like shit, I wouldn't eat it because it probably is shit. I stated over lunch about Moocheff; if it looks like a rat, and it smells like a rat, and it feels like a rat, hell, it probably is a rat, and I think Moocheff is the rat!

This afternoon, I cleaned and organized my office. I had many care packages stacking up, and they needed organization. A lot of what hasn't been consumed by or used by our soldiers goes to the local nationals. I separated school supplies from the first aid and hygiene items and, of course, munchies. I also spent considerable time going through the boxes and locating anything with an address on it. We must destroy these items for security reasons. About once a month, I put on my pyro hat and burn all that stuff (burn pits).

The proverbial "burn pits" in our camp.

24 July 04

I would sum up today with one word: Diarrhea. I got hit hard with it today and didn't feel like doing anything all day. Today is my son's 3rd Birthday, and I certainly wish I was with him. Today is also a moving day for the family; we are moving into our new home. It will be a long and hard day for the family. I wish too that I could be there to help out.

25 July 04

It is Sunday. I was very depressed today. I couldn't put my finger on the reason why? I slept in very late (this is a first). I guess having hit the commodes yesterday close to a dozen times wiped me out. When I came into my office, I got online, but no emails from home. I suspected that as the family had been moving all day long, and you know what a monumental task that can be. They probably don't have phones yet, and the cable installation hasn't happened yet. I wrote a loving email to my wife.

25 July 04

Hi Annette,

I know that you will be without email for a few days, but I wanted to express myself to you in this forum anyway. I love you very much, and it gives me great pleasure to be able to provide you with the home of your dreams. We did it together and earned everything that we had together. Thanks for sticking by me over the years. This Iraq War situation is a phase in our lives and will pass. We will someday look back on these days with a significant sense of gratification. Thanks, too, for taking such good care of little Junior; I know that it is no easy task to do by yourself. I am also very happy that you have the flexibility to purchase the furniture that you deem appropriate for the home. You always got the most bang for the buck, and I know that you will be getting the best for the least. Tell Nina and Junior that I love them very much. Enjoy the new home!

Love,

Your husband

As I was trying to get online, which can often take half an hour or so, I put on Linkin Park's "Hybrid Theory" CD. There is one song that always moves me in a particular way, "In the End." The first time that I remember hearing this song and really listening to the lyrics was on a plane ride from Philadelphia, PA, to Southern California. I was seated next to my daughter, Nina, and she let me listen to her CD for a while, and she had this song playing. I had just left my parents, who were now residing in a Nursing Home. The lyrics to this song brought me to tears on that plane ride, as they still do today. The song reminds me of my father and our relationship over the years. As I have often said, my father truly was my very best friend in my life. His death, just a few short months prior to our mobilization, crushed me emotionally. The Linkin Park song goes like this;"..it doesn't matter how hard you try.....time is a valuable thing. Watch it fly by as the pendulum swings...the clock ticks life away....watch time go right out the window...wasted it all just to watch you go...I tried so hard and got so far, but in the end, it doesn't even matter...I had to fall and lose it all, but in the end, it doesn't even matter..."

The song brings up my memories of my father working so very hard his entire life, and, in the end, he went out as most of us will go out: an elderly man in failing health who is struggling from day to day just to live. Having to "fall and lose it all" reminds me of myself because I have been down this road with my life, quite literally almost losing everything due to scrupulous and dishonest business partners. "In the end, it doesn't really matter" reminds me of my father. Remembering that plane ride with my daughter, that line stuck in my head and always brings me to tears. On that plane, I remembered seeing my father in the Nursing Home, seated in a wheelchair, knocking on death's door. And in the end, it doesn't really matter how much you have when you go; what is important is how you spend your time when you are here. The song tells of "watching time fly right out the window," which reminds me of all the time as an adult that I didn't spend with my parents and now wish that I had. For me, the song is a reflection of life itself and a reminder that how we invest our time is what really matters and not so many materialistic trinkets that you can't take with you. It reminds me of how important it is to identify what is really important to you in your life, such as your family, and to take actions that won't adversely affect your relationship with them and, of course, spend time with them. That, to me, is what life is about. I believe that when an individual figures this out for themselves, they are one with God (or Allah, or Abraham, or whomever they might worship).

The more I philosophized over my inability to rationalize my emotions today, the more I later realized another deep-seated reason that I didn't want to face. That reason? Today is my big sister's birthday. Here I am in the middle of a combat zone in Iraq, a very foreign and uncomfortable place, and I haven't received so much as one letter, one email, a care package, or even a postcard from my sister and her family while I have been deployed. I have received dozens of correspondences from my wife's family, her parents, her brother, her sister, my in-laws, uncles, and aunts, as well as my numerous cousins. I am deeply saddened that my sister has turned herself and her entire family against me and my family.

Nothing on this physical earth is worth getting in the way of family and the love of family. I really feel sorry for my sister and her family, as I feel that they are not one with God.

So that is partially why I am very emotional today, the fact that it is my sister's birthday, and I can't wish her a happy birthday because she won't let me. I think that someday, she will truly regret not having been supportive of her brother in his greatest time of need. She has also lost out on her only nephew's first three years of his life; this is a travesty!

Unfortunately, when my parents died, so did our family, and so did my relationship with my one and only sister. I am not just saddened by my sister's actions this day but also ashamed of her for her lack of support, which smells of non-patriotism. If this non-patriotic atmosphere existed in our pre-colonial days, there might not have been a United States of America at all.

It is mysterious how the Lord works.

10 Jan 04

I just stumbled across an old letter to my sister that I wrote and re-read. I guess that fate is playing its hand in my life. I feel that I conveyed myself well to my sister in that letter, and frankly, I don't understand her actions, and I probably never will. Life is so short. I really feel sorry for my sister; she doesn't have God in her life. Life is so short.

26 July 04

Monday, BUB discussions included trailer disposition in the camp and KBR hiring more locals. Nosey still has problems with the interpreters on the post. He doesn't trust them, based on the intel he got from LTC Milling (consider the source). Nosey said that "we" need to start talking to each other. He was disturbed about the conflict of getting a reception area shaded at the Smythe Gate, and he wasn't aware of it. He was also mad that he didn't know about the three mortar rounds being fired over the weekend (unfortunately, no one knew about this except the mortar section and CPT Castellano is correcting this screw-up). Nosey wanted me to follow up with the PX regarding soon-to-be expired food being distributed to the locals.

27 July 04

09:00

I saw the BC (Battalion Commander-LTC Slacker) and CSM Hunts off as they left to go to Camp Victory in Baghdad.

09:45

Major Rickets came into my office with word from the G3 that a FRAGO will be forthcoming today regarding the A Co. movement piece. He said that they could be assigned to a "DELTA Force" in the Anaconda area. I summoned the staff members here and had a staff meeting. (There is a good definition of DELTA Force in the Glossary of Military Terms at the back of this book.)

NOTE FROM AUTHOR: Anything involving DELTA Force or SPECIAL OPS (Green Berets) is considered TOP SECRET, and I won't be able to discuss this in any kind of detail. Sorry about that.

14:00

This afternoon, I read some emails sent to me from military.com, a commercial company that focuses on the military. It is like an online magazine. They posted a story written by a Lieutenant here in Iraq, who was also a 2003 West Point graduate. The Lieutenant spoke of the horrors of combat duty, and frankly, it was quite humbling. We/I haven't seen nearly the extent of action that this guy spoke of. Yes, we have seen dead Iraqi bodies, but he describes brain matter and intestines all over the place. I can't make that claim. And honestly, I am not ashamed of that. I guess I am a bit older and wiser, and our combat situation suits me just fine. I don't need to be in the middle of Baghdad to do house-to-house, door-to-door street fighting like that young Lieutenant. He mentioned that this experience was different for each of us, and he wasn't kidding. I just don't want to come off sounding like some seasoned war veteran who has seen "everything," not for one minute! All of us are seeing different things and at different magnitudes. Hats off to that Lieutenant and his soldiers!

One thing that helps me keep my spirits up is the continued banter from CPT Cantez (a cynical little fat man) and MSG Myler (an old Vietnam Vet and our lead cook). They have known each other for some fifteen years and are a scream. Cantez starts it this time, "Hey, old man, don't you have to go count some napkins or something!!!" Myler responds, "Shut your mouth, 'Little Man,' and get off that computer so I can get some work done!" Cantez; "Work, you ain't done an ounce of work since you got here, HELL YEA!" Myler; "I'm going to have to hurt you. Don't let me over there because I'll have to hurt you!" Cantez; "Go on, old man, get back to the mess hall and make some flap jacks or something....." This goes on and on, and it is a crack-up! All in good fun.

We gave Cantez a ration of shit for taking a nap at 10:00. The CSM got him up at 05:00 for PT, and we are trying to get him to lose weight so he can get promoted, but it is a struggle. We kidded Cantez about his PT, and getting up early kicked his ass, and he needs naps. He said that this was his first nap here. Sure, sure.... I jumped on my computer to produce some pictures I got of him sleeping on the floor at his desk. It was a scream!

28 July 04

Last night, today, and every day, I think about what I am going to do while on leave. I can't get it off my mind. Holding and touching my wife again is like a dream. I still haven't told them and plan on just showing up. They will be quite surprised. I plan on renting a BMW from Budget or Avis Rent-a-Car. Why? Because I can, and because I never owned such a car, and it could be the last civilian car that I ever drive, you see life differently from this experience, this experience of mobilizing with your National Guard unit, venturing directly into combat duty in Iraq. You see death constantly and live on "the edge." It changes you, partly for the better and maybe partly for the worse? How have I changed? I don't know, but I do know that you look at life so differently now, or at least I do. Money and material possessions mean absolutely nothing to me right now. I could literally wipe my ass with money, as all I want to do is survive, to get home and raise my son, to get home and walk my daughter down the aisle and to get home and hold my dear wife at night in front of our new spacious home. I pray several times a day, at a minimum, before each meal. I pray for my wife, my son, my daughter, our three lost comrades, my two deceased parents, and my sister. Sometimes, I add in other family members or other soldiers whom I think need help, and often that is LTC Slacker. I pray for God to grant him the wisdom to make the right decisions and to do the right thing. I thank God for all that he has given me and for all that I must live for.

28 July 04

Slacker and CSM Hunts are still at Camp Victory in Baghdad. The morning BUB with Col Nosey was uneventful and surprisingly quick. The issue of drinking and drugs came up, and Nosey said that if he caught any being sold at the Hadjie market, he would shut them all down. Rickets and I spoke with him following the meeting. I brought to his attention part of the MCI Commander's Intent: support economic development & set conditions to establish and allow economic growth. Perhaps Nosey didn't get that memo?

We are still working on the issue of moving A Co. out of KALSU. I received a call from the Task Force Tacoma's Commander, LTC Messing. He informed me that one of B Co.'s Lieutenants lost his rifle and that he wants to relieve him, and BG Killman wants Article 15 charges brought up on the officer. I took note of it and will try to inform Slacker when he is available today.

29 July 04

I started the day at 07:00 doing PT with CSM Hunts and CPT Cantez. We did our routine of lifting weights super-sets at the MP's outdoor weight bench set up. This is followed with some chow, cheese omelet, ½ a biscuit, ½ a bowl of oatmeal, juice, and a banana for the road. Ten emails in my us.army.mil account; one email from a JAG (Judge Advocate General) who is stateside prosecuting MSG Chord (no longer a First Sergeant) at Ft. Lewis, WA, for alleged sexual misconduct with his female soldiers. They are requesting that a witness have their leave time extended in order to testify. The soldier has had two weeks' leave, and the trial is another two to three weeks, and Slacker says, "Hell No!" I don't blame him; they can get the soldier to do a videotaped deposition and return him to duty here in Iraq. Fucking JAG pukes!

30 July 04

This morning's BUB was somewhat uneventful; as a matter of fact, we ended both that meeting and the force protection meetings at an unprecedented 09:35. Slacker was in a mellow mood, which permeated amongst the staff. CPT Cantez went with some of the other staff; 1LT Tonic the S6 and CW2 Cliffs to KALSU. They are all working on the A Co. move up to LSA Anaconda and here at CSC Scania. Major Lukes is still visiting from the Brigade Headquarters. He is taking 1LT Youngham up to Anaconda this evening. She will inventory and organize our Class VIII (medical supplies). I received a disturbing call from the Brigade's CPT, Smythe, asking to speak to MAJ Lukes. I informed him that he had probably already left for Anaconda. Smythe told me that the Chief of Staff, LTC Café' didn't want LT Youngham coming up to Anaconda? I didn't understand that and let Smythe know that they were already gone.

Today, I spent part of the day writing the Internet Cafe's essay *(eventually featured in my book, **COMBAT ESSAYS**)*. It is difficult to finish because I keep getting interrupted from time to time. We are expecting a full moon this evening, and it is extremely hot, maybe pushing over 125 or so. At evening chow, I sat with CPT Randerson and MAJ Rickets. I couldn't help noticing the long-lost stares in their eyes. I guess I have it, too. I made light of the fact that it was Friday evening. Randerson said that he was going to hit the PX following chow, and I said jokingly, "So a big night on the town, this Friday night!"

This morning, I read an email from my wife, Annette. She spoke of marital problems between some of our close friends. I wish that I was back home to help them.

How do I feel today? Well, every time you go anywhere, and we are just talking on the post here, you sweat. For example, if you have to use the latrine (to take a pee), you have to grab your -weapon, hat, and sunglasses and make your way to a porta-potty. Inside the porta-potty, it is at least 20 degrees hotter than the outside temperature (note: The outside temperatures hit 120 regularly here). The other option is to take a long walk to a trailer with plastic toilets inside. At least there, they might be air-conditioned; however, they often smell awful. And by the way, to walk anywhere, like I mentioned before, you sweat. So, your choices are to sweat in the porta-potty or walk a great distance to a possibly air-conditioned facility, and of course, sweat. That kind of sums up life around here: darn if you do and darn if you don't! There aren't many great options for anything around here.

All of those factors that I just mentioned are compounded multiple times if you have to leave the wire (go outside of the camp). You are now talking about wearing 50 pounds of gear that includes body armor, Kevlar helmet, etc. You sweat just putting that stuff on, let alone walking around or chasing some Hadjie bad guys. Those boys doing the urban fighting have it rough. It encompasses many dismounted operations (walking or humping-soldiers slang) with all that gear on.

Today, MAJ Rickets wrote the OPORD (operations order) for the A Co. to move to LSA Anaconda and here. I proofread it and sent it to Slacker for signature. I also helped him draft a FRAGO regarding mandatory PAO training. We currently have three 15.6 formal investigations going on: one for weapons accountability, one for improper PAO procedures (soldiers granting interviews and not informing the chain of command), and another for possible improper awards submission (purple hearts for some soldiers at KALSU).

I am still scheduled for leave and should be leaving on the fifth of August. That is in only six days! To say that I am excited would be an understatement! I spend much time fantasizing about seeing my wife and family and all the fun things that we will be doing during my surprise visit home. I can't wait!

31 July 04

Up again at 06:30 and did PT with CSM Hunts. Cantez is still at KALSU and headed up to VICTORY (in Baghdad) later today and couldn't join us for a workout. Today, I slugged around all day; I guess that I am burnt out. Nine months and no days off can take their toll on you. Prior to that, in preparation for the mobilization, I worked my AGR job seven days a week for several months straight. I really need that two weeks of leave. Since I was going on leave, I decided to search for my wallet. I haven't needed it for over four months now that we have been in theater, and I put it away somewhere. I decided to unpack the large crate that I had behind my desk in my office. It contained a bunch of history books, as I was knee-deep into my master's degree when we got mobilized. I also have civilian clothes, spare socks, extra PT gear, batteries, and a few golf clubs (I snuck those onto the deployment). I found my wallet and repacked my box. I wrote a lengthy email to my wife, Annette. In it, I spoke of trying to get this **COMBAT JOURNAL** made into a movie someday? We will see, I guess.

Who wouldn't want to see this movie: A National Guard Battalion Executive Officer faces nearly impossible odds during his deployment to Iraq; an absolutely intolerable Commanding Officer, a sister from Hell, dysentery almost daily, train-equip-and mobilize 1,000 citizen soldiers who aren't normally full-time soldiers, away from his family for over 2-years, and oh yes, the enemy is trying to kill him!

I also wrote to friends back at home and purchased about forty postcards for my trip. I plan on writing to all my relatives while I am traveling.

I spoke with Slacker today about some issues with A Co.'s equipment and moving it to LSA Anaconda, as well as some legal issues regarding one of our officers. Slacker was in a pretty good mood today, and I think it is partly due to his working out this morning. It is a good stress reliever for us all. And quite frankly, today, there isn't much going on at the FOB.

I started my day with a telephone call from LTC Cafe,' the Brigade Chief of Staff. We discussed A Company's mission in Anaconda and their need for certain equipment. Apparently, their mission is more complicated than the leadership has led us to believe. A Co. will have some static guard duties and escort missions for VIPs, probably VIP detainees. They will be working with DELTA Force (DELTA Force is the most highly trained elite unit in the US Military. They are the Army's equivalent to the Navy's Seal Team 6) and the CIA (Central Intelligence Agency). All information and correspondence about the mission is highly classified and is disseminated on a need-to-know basis.

How do I feel today? Tired. I can't get my wife's beautiful curves out of my mind since I will be leaving for home in just five short days. I also think of all the stops and visits that I wish to make when I get home. I plan on visiting the Division Headquarters as well as my hometown Armory. I'll probably take my three-year-old son Junior there with me and get my favorite Mexican food. I also plan on purchasing a large roll of Astroturf and shipping it to myself in Iraq for our golf course project. Today, I thought about my son a lot. I guess that I really miss him and his sister,

Nina. I also thought about missing my connecting flight through Ireland so I could enjoy visiting the country of my ancestors for once in my life. I would love to do that, but I know deep down that I probably won't. I don't break the rules, ever, unless it is to benefit my soldiers (and I would consider that possibly bending the rules only). The longer we are away, the longer it is for the next guy to go on leave, and I don't want that on my conscience.

1 Aug 04

Today, the internet is down, as well as our outside camp telephoning capabilities. The signal folks apparently obtained the incorrect "FILL," which is the word for communications specifications that radios are set to and operate from.

At approximately 12:00, our soldiers were shot at on the MSR that runs through the camp. The roving patrol was chasing off some illegal traders on the road, and one of the Iraqi males returned fire at the soldiers. The traders evaded arrest by running into a tree line and various canals. Our soldiers returned fire but didn't hurt any Iraqi Nationals. The trader who fired on us was not recognized as a local and was more than likely an outsider to the area.

CPT Cantez returned last night, exhausted from his two-day trip to KALSU and BIAP (Baghdad International Air Port). CPT Randerson's investigation of our missing weapon and weapon serial number accountability had to be turned over to MAJ Rickets as we overlooked the fact that Randerson is a newly promoted Captain and was outranked by several other Captains who were being investigated. This is against Army Regulation, and Rickets now has the ball. Slacker confided with me this morning in my office, stating that BG Killman would be visiting Scania in mid-August and that he would have to break the news to him about another missing pistol. The real ugly part of this mess is that it has not been accounted for since NTC, Ft. Irwin, CA, in February/March of 2004. Holly cow, Batman!

14:00

I just returned from the DFAC (chow hall), and I am soaking wet in sweat. The distance can't be more than two or three football fields, and I am drenched! I wear an undervest identical to what the DEA Agents wear. Most of the senior staff members ordered these vests at their own expense when we were at Ft. Lewis, WA. At that time, we hadn't received our body armor with SAPI plates (small arms protective inserts) and weren't sure what we were going to receive in the way of body protection. The vest was expensive, around $800.00 or so, but what the heck, it is only money, and I can't spend it if I am dead. My daughter Nina has asked me several times to always wear my vest, so as a promise to her, I wear it everywhere, with the only exception of sleeping in bed. When I do sleep, it is right next to my bed, along with my body armor and helmet. Wearing the undervest does make you sweat. Unless there is an immediate threat or intelligence to that effect, we don't have to wear body armor while on this FOB.

Today's lack of connectivity is a reminder of how reliant we have become on the internet. Our ties to home are severed without this instrument of communication. If we had no internet, we would be sending and receiving letters that take three weeks to get to their destination. I really miss starting my day with the opening of an email from my wife. The day just won't be the same until I hear from her. I might venture down to the internet cafe to try my luck there. Today is Sunday, so I must be available for church services at 16:00. This will be my last Lay Leader service until I come back from vacation in about three or four weeks. I am looking forward to attending church at my regular church at home. When I am there, I will ask them to mail me several of their monthly missalettes for us to use in our services here.

19:36

SPC Gibson of the Mortar Section from KALSU joined me at evening chow as I was finishing my food. He seemed a bit upset as he asked, "What is it with that SGM Moans guy?" Apparently, Moans chewed out Gibson's ass for coming into the mess hall in a dirty PT uniform. I explained to Gibson that SGM Moans and the mayor's staff have never left the wire and don't have a clue that there is a war going on outside of the safe and secure gates of this camp. They have no clue what you guys went through at KALSU and that you don't even have a laundry facility. We went on and on about how

156

f__d up they are. Then SGM Moans came up to me, and Polity told me that the soldier was way too dirty to be in the mess hall. I told him that it was over 120 degrees outside and that the soldier had been working in that heat all day and was from KALSU, where they don't have laundry facilities. SGM Moans went on and on, and I stopped him and said, SGM Moans, you need to get over this; there is a war going on outside of this post, and soldiers get dirty. Moans didn't like hearing that and said that "we" always use the excuse that there is a war going on...

The SGM left, and SGT Moody came to the table, whipped out his notebook, and took down Gibson's name and unit info. I tore the paper out of Moody's book and said that I authorized his uniform and to have SGM Moans direct his inquiries to me.

Talk about lame; SGM Moans of the Mayor's cell hassled one of our Mortar-men from KALSU. These guys are Infantrymen, and they are tough customers. This guy's first day at Scania and Moans jumped his shit twice. This time, it was for having a dirty uniform; hell, KALSU doesn't have a laundry service! Moans and I went at it. I defended the soldier in front of a bunch of our guys and stood by my actions. The soldiers loved it.

2 Aug 04

One word to sum up my day: exhausting! I lifted weights with Sergeant Major Hunts at 07:00. Today, we were both putting up a lot of weight; I guess the training is paying off, and we are getting stronger. Cantez slipped in on us around 07:30; he has his challenges waking up. We hit chow by 08:00; I had two cheese omelets, oatmeal, and juice. At 08:30, I reported to the BDOC to go with the HHC Soldiers on a raid. *(I wrote a decent essay about this event entitled "On Patrol" and put it in my book, **COMBAT ESSAYS**).* I went with SSG Rolley's vehicle, and little did I know, this team was going dismounted! What that means to a forty-four-year-old Major, who is primarily an Armor Officer, is humping. Humping is what we call hoofing or walking very long distances on patrol. Luckily, the weather was on our side, and it didn't break 110. However, the body armor, Kevlar, ammunition, weapons, etc., trust me, are very heavy, probably over 60 pounds or so. I also brought my DV camera along for the adventure. I figured that this would be a prime video opportunity. So, there I am, humping through the farmlands of Central Southern Iraq, with all my gear, trying to keep up with the likes of twenty-three-year-old Specialist and SSG Rolley, a former schoolhouse Infantry Instructor.

The purpose of the mission was to capture illegal traders in close proximity to the camp. Yesterday, there was an incident where one of these traders brandished a weapon at our soldiers and fired. We won't accept that, and this is our response.

After what seemed to be a never-ending movement to contact, we heard on our radio that one of the fire teams adjacent to us had apprehended two suspects. Captain Castellano was with a team that linked up with our team, and we hoofed it back to the rally point. Unfortunately for us, Castellano and his mounted soldiers (riding in up-armored HMMVWs) got their signals crossed and missed the link-up point. This meant that we had to hump back to the MSR, fuck it was far, and we were hot, tired, and sweating from head to toe. I did get some great videos despite my challenges to keep up with the young citizen soldiers. We had to plow our way through several canals that were almost waist-deep. When you step foot in these canals, you stir up the debris from the bottom, much like you would when stepping in the ocean or the bay or river. However, when you do that here, you smell centuries and centuries of smells, anything from sewage to dead animals to decaying crops; it is absolutely dreadful! I kidded with the other soldiers on the drive back that at lunchtime; I was going to find LTC Milling and SGM Moans' table in the mess hall and sit with them so my smelly, sweaty uniform and body would gross them out to not end. The troops got a big kick out of that. SSG Sauley stated, "Wow, sir, you are really cool; we hate those Mayor's cell assholes too!" When we returned to the base camp, I spotted CPT Castellano screaming at the top of his lungs at the detainees; he would have made Tony Soprano quite proud; "I have told you, traders, to take your illegal shit out of my camp area! Where are you from? Ash Shumali (a local town)? Yes, you are, you aren't from around here, and you better not come back and trade your crap in my area again! And I know that you understand English, so quit faking that you don't understand!" (Note: All of this dialogue was also translated into Arabic by our interpreters.) It was quite a scene as there were numerous soldiers dismounting themselves and their equipment off their HMMVWs. After a brief AAR (after action review), the leaders discussed the good and bad points of the operation. Overall, it was a success as no Americans were injured, and we detained two criminals. After an interrogation session through our interpreters, we handed over the suspects to the local Iraqi Police for processing.

Detainees taken during patrol.

3 Aug 04

I thought that I would include information similar to our BDOC (Base Defense Operation Center) daily reports to shed light on our day-to-day operations. The next several pages contain reports that are not much different from what we used in Iraq.

2LT Ronsen

0001-0800 03 August 2004

Report period 02 August 2004 0000-2400

Page 1/1

Summary:

Item No. Time Event

0000 Duty Officer 2Lt O'Shannon

0200 Duty officer 1LT Watchmanez

22,23,24 0535 SGT Gilmore fell from Tower 1. He sustained a laceration to the head and an ankle injury. Medical was informed.

35, 37, 38, 40, 0902 Operation Trader Joe's began to get traders. Two traders were caught and sent to Ash Shumali Police Station.

49, 50 1100 Duty Officer MSG Rasper

1600 Duty Officer 1LT Watchmanez

72, 21, 49 Hunter 34/35/22/27 established TCP vehicles were searched, and nothing was found.

Shift Significant events 03 AUG 04

NONE

Viewed by

CPT Castellano 03 AUG 04

Last night, MAJ Rickets got a call from CPT Crader at KALSU stating that the Marine Corps Colonel wouldn't release the A Co., Armor Battalion AR Mortar team from the base and that he had an MNCI order stating such. Rickets followed up with a returned call to Crader.

This morning, the medics from KALSU arrived with 1LT Atkins (PA). The Armor Battalion cooks also arrived. The Brigade cooks who were attached to ours are preparing to move out at 08:00 for Anaconda. Today, I plan on catching up on paperwork that I want closure on before my departure for leave.

Today, CPT Cantez went to Talill with SSG Colan, and SSG Kanister is still on leave. The office is quiet. SPC Ison stopped in and waited to meet with SFC Barnum. However, Barnum was two hours late. Ison is a unique duck, a college-educated man who works in the technical field of topography and geology. He is very opinionated and often outspoken. He previously worked in the TOC (tactical operation center) and now is a machine gunner on a gun platform (machine gun mounted HMMWV).

*Callaway Golf donated golf equipment
for the troops in Iraq.*

4 Aug 04

The 0900 BUB was uneventful. The big event today was receiving a record number of packages, 52. Callaway Golf really came through for us and sent me some 24 or so golf bags with clubs. Big Bertha drivers, irons with graphite shafts, you name it, it is here! WOW, that is all that I can say. OPERATION IRAQI PUTTING GREEN is on its way! Tomorrow, I will get the price quote and samples of AstroTurf from one of the Interpreters who went to Baghdad today. CPT Cantez tipped me off yesterday about the large mail delivery for today, and I coordinated with the HHC Supply Sergeant to have a 5-ton truck standing by for when the mail truck arrives. The mail truck is a very large 10-ton truck with a PLS (pallet load system, which has a very big crane that lifts a large connex container.) I helped the Sergeant load and unload the 52 Callaway boxes in a supply connex so we could keep them under lock and key and hide them from LTC Slacker and the Mayor's Cell so they wouldn't rush to judgment about my golf course plans.

NOTE FROM AUTHOR: "This was a hush-hush covert operation because if the brass had known about the golf course project prematurely, they could have very well nixed the entire project. It was my thought process that said, once I get all the equipment and land in place, how can they say no?"

CBS Los Angeles Sports Central telecast.

My leave got delayed another week since A Co. left KALSU, and their HHC soldiers came down here to Scania; we also inherited three of their soldiers who are currently on leave (R & R). That fact, along with an unexpected emergency leave, has caused all of our leave dates to be bumped up another week. I actually don't mind this, as I can spend the week putting together the golf course plan and finish up the stories that I have committed to writing for the camp and brigade papers. I am also very behind with writing OERs (officer evaluation reports). I still haven't told my family about the leave and want to keep it that way. This is the second delay for my leave, and I will believe it when I actually see it.

5 Aug 04

I can't believe that the entire day has slipped by, and I haven't written one word until now! I spent part of the day going through the backup disks from my previous computers. Initially, I was looking for a personal file that had all my relatives listed on mailing labels. I wanted to use this when I mail them all postcards while flying home. I didn't see the BC all day and only saw the CSM late in the afternoon. Hunts went to KALSU in the morning to check on our remaining Mortar Section, which is still there supporting the Marines. I don't know what Slacker was up to, and frankly, I don't really care.

6 Aug 04

Things are really heating up in the surrounding areas. Here are highlights similar to last night's BDOC log entries:

04 on 06 Aug

A SPOT report from the MPs: Imminent attack possible on Camp Delta, at Najaf and in Al Kut, the Governor of Wassif Province has decided to turn control of the city of Al Kut to the Mahdi Army, and the IPs have decided to go over to the Mahdi Army. 100 to 150 Sadr Party members have been massing on the other side of the river from the front gate of Camp Delta.

Heavy enemy activity in the surrounding cities means trouble for us. We are plusing up our Roving Patrols outside of the camp and initiating mortar illumination firing missions. Last night, the Marines were involved in heavy fighting, which rendered two KIAs and many injured. Each of these cities, Al Kut, Najaf, and Diwania, is less than one hour's drive from here. Diwania is only about ½ an hour south of here.

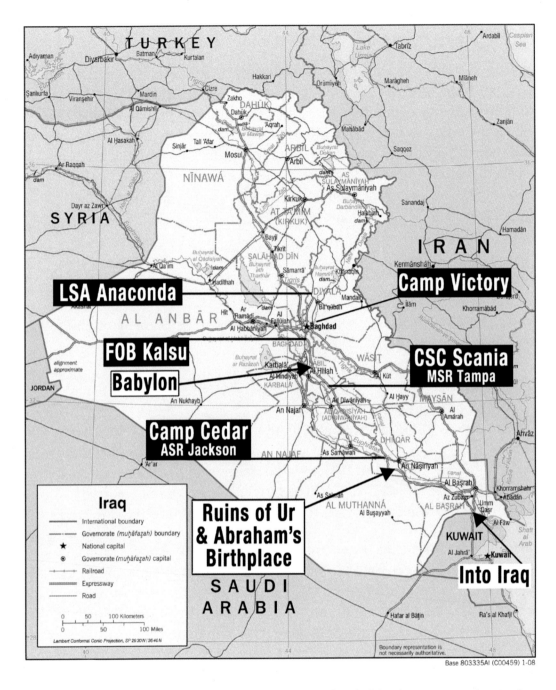

The cities of Al Kut, Najaf and Diwania are less than one hour's drive from CSC Scania. Map by John J. McBrearty. Source: The World Factbook, CIA Maps.

Also, yesterday, in the village of Al Zabar, over 15 MM (Mahdi Army militia) posters were observed, and the inhabitants were very tense in communication. Hunter 22 and 27, SSG Tucker, and SSG Rassler Roving Teams stopped in the town of AL Zabar to give water to the local children. As the children approached, men (about military age) started hitting and shouting the children away. The general attitude was hostile. He observed an increased number of military-aged men in the area. At that time, they noticed fifteen or more posters with mixed versions of pictures of Sader and versions of Humvees' burning posted. Regarding the posters, one of the men said it was a democracy. They could post whatever they want. This town is approximately four kilometers northwest of the .5A Bridge. This type of behavior is atypical for our area of operations. As a result, we will send our S5 representatives out there and attempt some communication with the local populace.

Coalition forces battled militiamen loyal to radical Shiite cleric Muqtada al-Sadr in several Iraqi cities Friday, saying they killed about 300 militants in Najaf over two days of fighting.

Two U.S. Marines and an American soldier were killed in Najaf on Thursday, and 12 troops were wounded, the military said. Fifteen U.S. soldiers were wounded in Baghdad.

In Najaf, 100 miles south of Baghdad, U.S. helicopters on Friday attacked militants hiding in a cemetery near the Imam Ali Shrine in the old city at Najaf's center,

In April, the Mahdi Army militia launched sustained attacks on U.S. and coalition troops in several cities, the first major Shiite violence against the Americans. The confrontation dragged on for two months until Iraqi politicians and religious leaders negotiated a series of truces.

Al-Sadr blamed the United States for the violence in Iraq (news - websites) in a sermon read on his behalf Friday in the Kufa Mosque close to Najaf.

The clashes between coalition forces and militant Shiite cleric Muqtada al-Sadr's Mahdi Army flared in Shiite communities across the country, killing dozens of other Iraqis.

7 Aug 04

The threat level was increased. Body armor is required within arm's reach in place of rest and work. The IBA with helmet carried is required in the market. The weapon's status remains amber (the weapon is considered substantially safe, loaded magazine in the weapon, bolt forward, and the chamber is not loaded, which allows the shooter to rapidly transition to red or black status).

16:40

Death, again. I opened an email from the Brigade's PAO that had the following attachment:

DoD Identifies Army Casualty

The Department of Defense announced today the death of a soldier who was supporting Operation Iraqi Freedom.

Spc. D.M. of Ypsilanti, Mich., died on August 5, in Landstuhl, Germany, of injuries sustained when an improvised explosive device detonated near his patrol on August 4 in Balad, Iraq. Spc D.M. was assigned to the Army National Guard's Infantry Regiment, Washington National Guard.

The incident is under investigation.

I have a massive lump in my throat and feel like crying. It just kills me to have another 20-year-old soldier die in combat. What a loss. This price of freedom just keeps on rising.

Today, CPT Castellano and MAJ Rickets went out to Ali's house for lunch. They addressed an issue of a hashish dealer in the area. The dealer was actually there, along with a city council member, to plead his case.

At approximately 0010, the North CP reported a KBR truck hit an IED at 4A. There were no casualties.

8 Aug 04

Sunday was a quiet day, almost routine; I slept in for a few hours, missed breakfast but made it to work, lunch, church, work, dinner, the hooch, watched a horror flick on my personal DVD player, and crashed. Pretty uneventful, which we like around here. *(Like police officers describing a shift at work- "a slow night at work is a good night for us cops")*. I did speak with my wife this evening, which I think cheered us both up a bit.

At 0010 hours, Scorpion MSR patrol reports that MPs were escorting a convoy in the vicinity of bridge 4A and encountered an IED, which detonated disabling a commercial truck.

Patrols reported observing a smoking box in the vicinity of 4A, in the same location and at the same time as the barricade placed the previous night. The convoy started changing lanes when the box, an IED, exploded. A commercial KBR truck lost five tires and damaged the trailer. No injuries or death were reported. MP Security teams secured the vehicle and took it back to CSC, Scania.

9 Aug 04

Today, I had a startling revelation: Several of our soldiers had their own personal websites on the internet. The sites contained information and journals about their deployment. I spent several hours going through a SSG's website and found it to be quite harmless as far as operational security goes. Other than his atrocious spelling, his journal was pretty harmless. It was brought to LTC Slacker's attention that SGT Freedom also has a website and posted photos of Slacker with some jokes stating that he, the CSM, and the local Sheikh sat around all night bad-mouthing women. Needless to say, Slacker caught a case of the ass and lit up Freedom. *(The funny thing is that Freedom was probably correct with his findings? Just a hunch.)*

10 Aug 04

Time is flying by, but I had time to get this entry made. I spent some of the day polishing my ninth essay about the Bridge dedication ceremony that was conducted on the twenty-ninth of July 2004. *(Most of these essays can be found in my book, **COMBAT ESSAYS**).* I also took SGT Freedom on a walk around my proposed golf course site. We measured off the T-Boxes, fairways, and greens. I came up with a total of four par three holes that we could build inside of our compound. I also added two practice putting greens and an optional driving range that would be just outside of our rear gate.

Word is out that LTC Milling is really pissed that someone has been putting anonymous complaints in her mailbox and threatened to file an IG complaint against her. It is a joke in the camp that we finally found a means to get "under her skin," and we are enjoying that! Hmmmm....

0033 Tower 5 reported 20 rounds and were fired approximately 600-700m from their position.

8,9 Hunter 25 and 33 check the area. They talked to LNs in Al Bakhan, who said a white Toyota pickup with 3-4 individuals carrying 3 AK 47s shot into the air. The truck traveled toward Ash Shumali. Hunter 33 talked with the Ash Shumali Ips, who said nobody passed through town fitting that description.

11 Aug 04

0535

An IP (Iraqi Police) CP (Command Post) was attacked at .5B. The IPs saw the rovers passing and waved them down. They requested assistance from an interpreter and brought an IP to BDOC. The IP reported that a lieutenant was killed, and the attacker was wounded and carried to jail. Other attackers were wounded but fled. CPTs Castellano and Ridges were informed.

As you can see, it has been volatile in the last 24 hours. I joined the CA team this morning at 08:30 for the bridge dedication with local dignitaries.

Bridge repair near CSC Scania, Iraq.

IPs' Attacked, Counterattack

ROV (Roving Patrols) Assisted

0400 hrs.

5B Road Vic AD Deghghara Iraqi Police Checkpoint attacked,

2 IP KIA, 1 AIF KIA, 1 AIF WIA, ROV team in area. IP requested assistance.

ROV Hunter 20 team patrolling .5B was flagged down by IP. IP requested their assistance. Their checkpoint was just attacked, killing IP personnel. IP requested to speak with the translator. Brought IP officer to CSC, Scania. S-2 informed; he spoke with IP with translator. The IP reported that a lieutenant was killed, the attacker was killed, and one was wounded but died. Other attackers appeared wounded but fled. The second IP also died. Reports MM activity increased in the area. IP suspect MM safe house in the area.

0700 ROV Hunter 33/36 team escorted IP to his station at Ad Deghgharah. At the station, Chief of Ad Diwaniya requested an ROV escort to Ash Shumali PD (Police Department); he was concerned with MM attacking. 2 IP trucks and ROV team escorted IP chief. As they traveled, LNs ran up from side of road, flagged down IP, and reported Mahdi Militia in a house nearby, the ones who attacked the IP last night. IPs pursued, request ROV assistance. Attacked the house, and a firefight ensued. 2 MM ran out of house, and shooting continued. 2 MM captured; 2 MM evaded. IP searched the area, unable to locate IP retained MM members for questioning. No injuries or fatalities to Attacking IP or ROV team.

18:30

We had to mandate that the camp go to increase the threat condition of the camp and have everyone wear body armor and Kevlar helmets. The threat is all around us and has hit the local IPs (Iraqi Police) practically right outside of our gate.

21:00

I made my way from my office, in full battle rattle, to my tent. The scene was quite ominous as you hardly saw a soul out and about. The setting was serene, quiet, and downright spooky. Whenever there is a significant threat like there is now, people don't come out to play. They stay "hull defilade," as we refer to a tank taking cover.

2345 August 11, 2004

Hunter 34 brought in a death threat note from the Ash Shumali IPs. The note was given to the Ash Shumali IPs from the Mahdi Army. The rovers brought it in and had it translated.

17 0204 Hunter 38 reports Deghghara Iraqi Police were attacked again at approximately 22:00 hours on 11 August 2004. They requested assistance from Hunter 38 and 39 by showing a force in the area.

1118 Roving patrol reports they have detained an LN dressed all in black and green who was hunched down in bushes observing convoys entering and exiting Scania. The individual was handcuffed and brought to BDOC, then taken to the Ash Shumali IPs. The IPs had the individual make a sworn statement that he was not militia. He will be released to his father and, if caught again, will go before the judge.

12 Aug 04

Full battle rattle again today; the threat is close. SFC Barnum told me today after noon chow that the Iraqi Policeman who was killed yesterday by the Madi Army was the Lieutenant that I had my picture taken with several weeks ago. The pain of death continues. Today, I literally felt sick to my stomach.

I have second thoughts about leaving my men behind to take leave, but the thought of seeing my little son, college-age daughter, and loving/sexy wife outweighs my guilt. I know the little three-year-old particularly needs me in a major way, and Annette says that he is a bit of a discipline problem. *(Hell, what little boys aren't?)*

Today, I wrote OERs (officer evaluation reports) and took some time to clean up my assault pack that I will be taking home with me. We had a satellite installed in our office today. It started getting cramped, so I told LT Tonic to get the numerous batteries that were temporarily stored in our office out of here! He complied, and I am happy.

We have increased our platforms (gun trucks-up armored HMMWVs with a machine gun on top) from teams of two to teams of three and four.

2147

One loud explosion was heard between Towers twelve and nine. Estimated 300 meters west of MSR. Possible mortar attack. All towers/stations reported noise of blast. Steel rain QRF was sent to investigate checkpoints and MSR. No trucks were parked on MSR at that time. Hunter 20 was sent to search for an area west of Scania and set LP/OP. Mortars stood up. Hunter Six informed. No injuries reported. 2255 hours, nothing further was observed. Completed stand-down of units involved.

2355

Small arms fire at .5A Bridge upon convoy entering Scania. Reported by North Check Point and convoy crews. Hunter 35 sent, patrolled the area, set up OP, and monitored another convoy passing area; Hunter six notified. No injuries reported. Nothing further was observed. Continued patrol.

North Check Point, CSC Scania, Iraq.

0147

Hunter 37 reports a loud explosion heard for about 2-4 seconds coming from outside of the wire, but no flash was seen.

0313 Hunter 33 reported IPs from Al Hamza said it was a small bomb in a house. No injuries were reported. They were limited in information because they did not have an interpreter. It was given to them in broken English.

XO's assessment:

The attacks that have been taking place throughout CSC Scania's sector have been the result of MM movement around CSC Scania's

AO (area of operations). Given the level of communication and the unwillingness of the local population to collaborate with the MM, the MM path of least resistance is around, not through. The fact is there is limited presence of the Multi-National Forces out of key areas of concern. This has allowed the MM to maximize the utilization of ancillary roads. Patrol routes and TCP locations that have been successful in inhibiting the mobility of the MM have been bypassed. Through reports, it appears that the roads and small towns that are just out of CSC Scania's AO are being used regularly to move troops and supplies. Moving the focus of manpower to the enemy while maintaining optimal force protection is a balance that can show significant results and hinder operations in distant key locations.

INCIDENT REPORT: Small Arms Attack on IP Checkpoint

LOCATION OF INCIDENT: IVO Ad Daghgharah,

DATE OF INCIDENT: 11 AUG 04

DATE OF REPORT: 12 AUG O4

REPORTING OFFICER: SGM WESTMINSTER, OPERATIONS SGM, Armor Battalion, CSC SCANIA,

OVERVIEW: IP checkpoint was attacked by 10-15 MM members armed with AK-47s and RPGs. The initial attack resulted in 1 IP KIA, 1 IP WIA (later DOW), 1 AIF KIA, 2 AIF WIA. AIF were believed to have fled to a safe house in the area.

Roving patrol from Armor Battalion AR was flagged down by an IP officer, who was brought to CSC SCANIA to provide update to SCANIA S-2. Upon returning to the IP Station at Ad Daghgharah, they met with the Chief of Police of Ad Diwaniyah, who requested escort to the IP Station in Ash Shumali.

While en route to Ash Shumali, locals flagged down the patrol and identified the safe house. Approx. 20 IPs and AR BN Patrols responded. A brief firefight ensued, and the AIF fled from the house, resulting in 2 detainees. 2 AIF evaded on foot. The detainees were transported to Ad Diwaniyah for questioning. There was no damage to U.S. personnel or equipment.

IP Checkpoint was attacked again, resulting in 1 IP WIA. Overnight, IPs in Ash Shumali received written death threats at station.

CURRENT STATUS: CSC SCANIA increased FPCON to CHARLIE and instituted a uniform change to SIERRA. Additional patrols were sent to reinforce IP checkpoints in Ad Daghgharah and Ash Shumali. AR BN mortar section on stand-by to launch illum (illumination) O/O (on order). IPs currently have 6 in custody from the original incident.

FUTURE OPERATIONS: Continue FPCON CHARLIE / SIERRA through at least 13 AUG 04. Maintain close communication with IPs as the situation develops.

13 Aug 04

Today, I am down with a nasty sinus cold and slept in until about 09:30. It was a very long day for me, laboring along with this illness. At 10:00, I attended a PAO briefing put on by CPT Morehead. It was for the S5 section, and I asked a few staff officers to attend. The class was based on a FRAGO that I published this week. I supplied them with PowerPoint slides and reference materials for the training.

19:24

The BDOC is jumping! 50 Madi Army militants just overran an IP station just to our NW. The IPs have asked for assistance, and we have called up our QRFs (quick reaction forces). We have six platforms (vehicles) in and around 4A and stood up MP teams for support. We moved one mortar gun tube within range to the north end of camp. Over 100 Madi Militia took over the IP station to our south. We put out through the camp to go to full battle rattle and cut the phone and internet. The mood was tense. The camp was very quiet.

Here is another typical day at Scania (*War is Hell!*)

Item No. – Time -- Event

05 – 0040   H37 OP set up, observed area, no significant activity detected.

10 – 0145   H37 hears blast estimated range 2 K, NW, nothing further detected. No flash seen.

0313   H37 contacted IPs from AL Hamza, who reported a house was bombed earlier, no IPs injured, IPs did not elaborate further.

18 – 0349   H35, Set OP at .5B, also developing mechanical steering difficulty, no significant activity detected.

14 – 0300   H37 discovers two boxes near footbridge, suspect IED, shot 2, M16 rounds, no detonation, cleared boxes from area.

23 – 0542   H37, Set TCP on MSR, 32 vehicles searched. No weapons found.

29 – 0655   H34, Set OP at 2A, no significant activity detected.

43 – 0942   H33, medical aid follow-up conducted, crewmember sent into camp to have stitches removed.

44 – 0944   NCP, medical aid, follow up for child seen the prior day.

46 – 1000   Tower 12 reports two TCNs involved in knife fight, broken up by passing unit. T12 reports one wanted to buy alcohol, and the other disagreed about it.

73 – 1815   H45, contact LN in area, reported convoy attacked with IED, earlier at, vic. of .5A road north. Crater 1 foot deep, 2 feet in diameter. Team on site.

74 – 1835   Situation develops. H45 on scene, location item 73, an LN drove up and reported MM from Hamza, three

kilometer west, is headed to site, other Hunter 4 elements alerted and en route. Defensive position set one Kilometer SE. At 1840 hours, 258 MP QRF activated.

1908 hours Mortars alerted, moved to fuel point for range.

1920 258 MP set OP at .5A, prepared to assist Hunter 45.

2007 H45 relays over 200-Armed MM in Hamza, holding mayor H42 relays information, that Al Daghgharah IP subject to attack at 2200-0600., Also, stops search vehicle similar to the one used in Al Daghgharah attackH45 relays information that Hamza IP station was taken by MM.

The 2022 base was placed on heightened alert with full battle gear.

2041 Hunter 3 platoon RED CON One H43 contacts IP in Ash Shumali, IP contacts Hamza unsure if situation is clear.

2051 Stand down 258 MP,

2104 Mortars stand down, internet café phones reopened.

105 – 2107 Steel Rain MP Vehicle crashed into carrier RTO, and Driver hurt. Medics alerted and responded.

109 – 2121 Hunter 42 Set up a TCP searched three vehicles from Daghgharah; LN reports no unusual activity there. No weapons found.

126 – 0010 Hunter 31, reports Mayor and IP Colonel from Ash Shumali just came from Hamaza, Reference item #74; Mayor of Hamza has control of city. They report several MM earlier entered Mosques preaching

propaganda. IP left to arrest them, but MM evaded them.

130 – 0119   Hunter 32 crew, WIAs, hit by IED on 5A road approximately 400M southeast of IED site Reference item # 73. Patrol escorted to Scania, 1 MEDEVAC out, 1 RTD (returned to duty), vehicle disabled H31 team returned to site to investigate found crater 1'deep 3' wide, cleared brush eight feet around. H-6, K-6 informed. Patrols alerted & continued.H31 team continues patrol with rest of platoon.

0555   Nothing further significant reports.

Serious Incident (example) (these are always done whenever a soldier is WIA or KIA).

14 August 2004

IED Strike on ROV patrol, Two WIA

0119 hours, H31 reported IED detonation on H32 ROV Vehicle, sustaining two WIA: 1 WIA, MEDEVAC, 1 WIA RTD (Returned to Duty).

H31 was traveling westbound on .5A road vicinity 1A bridge with H32 in lead H36 second. The element was patrolling in white light, traveling east at 55 MPH. No traffic on the road at that time. Detonation occurred on the left side of vehicle. The explosion spewed shrapnel, punctured the gunner's left leg, and caused minor laceration on the driver's neck.

H32 Driver increased speed, and gunners fired into the area around blast site, and team continued up to MSR route with H36 as wingman. H31 in trail stopped before entering site. H31 instructed the team to rendezvous near MSR.

Injuries assessed, and first aid was applied. The team departed to hospital. H32 vehicle started to slow down due to damage sustained. The injured gunner was transferred to H36, which departed rapidly to hospital. Injury to H32 driver was discovered at that time.

H31 escorted limping H32 Vehicle. All four tires were perforated, the windshield cracked, as well as possible motor damage. Vehicle left in motor pool.

Detonation occurred estimated 400 Meters from IED site 13 Aug 2004. Prior event occurred on 29 April 2004; six daisy chain explosives were disarmed by IPs.

Just another day in paradise!

Second Act: R&R; Visiting Home

15 Aug 04

R & R trip home. An absolute traveling nightmare! 0700, the convoy left from Scania to Cedar. Three other members of the Armor Battalion and I jumped on a convoy with the MP boys from our camp. The trip south down MSR Tampa is a treacherous one, to say the least. There are times when you have to drive down the opposite side of the road to avoid the dust from the trucks in front of you; Lord help us if an oncoming vehicle approaches. The road is scarier than the Madi Militia. *(But not as bad as Southern California freeways!)*

MSR Tampa, Central Southern Iraq.

We arrive at C Co. at around 11:30 or so, not bad timing. C Co. had their rovers take us over to the PAX (passenger) Terminal at Tallil at around 12:30. The Airman who waited on us was pretty cool. He said that there was no record of us flying out of Tallil, but would get us on something. Our flight left at around 22:00. It was a C130 military air transport plane, and it took us to an airport in southern Kuwait. From there, we bussed to the large post, Doha. The infamous Doha, where civilian attire is authorized, and there is a Starbucks in the PX, along with many other fast-food restaurants. It is amazing to us that this is also considered a warzone? It is so far removed from combat operations. We didn't even have our weapons; we turned them into C Co. for safekeeping.

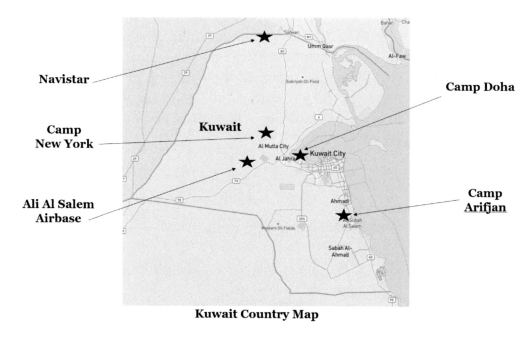

Kuwait Country Map

Map by John J. McBrearty. Source: © OpenStreetMap
(data is available under the Open Database License)

We go to a big hangar-type building around 02:30 or so and get a few hours of sleep. We attended a safety briefing at 07:00 as well as a customs briefing, followed by an intense customs search of all our bags. This took hours. From here, we go into "lockdown," literally. We are held in a building that is declared customs inspected and can't leave. We waited all day for a night flight out of Kuwaiti International Airport. We were bussed there in the middle of the night and boarded the aircraft, which is a civilian charter that typifies the government's selection process by rendering contracts to the "lowest bidders." I have never sat in such a cramped aircraft in all my life. It was absolutely deplorable conditions to travel ½ way around the world. After about twenty minutes of flight, we were informed that we were returning to Kuwait. They didn't say why initially, but by the looks of this crappy aircraft, it could have been anything. Later, we found out that the landing gear wouldn't go up. Are you kidding? We returned to Doha for three hours of sleep to get up the next morning and do the same routine all over again. The second time, we did make it out of the Middle East. BTW, how long have I been traveling for? And I haven't even left the Middle East yet. *War is hell!*

Our first refueling stop was in Budapest, Hungary. This was a good 2-3 hour stop, during which we could not exit the aircraft. *Good grief!*

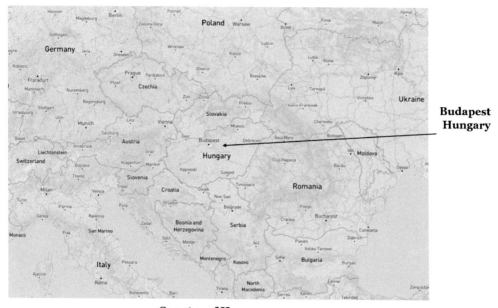

Country of Hungary

Map by John J. McBrearty. Source: © OpenStreetMap
(data is available under the Open Database License)

From there, we flew to Bangor, Maine, where we were warmly greeted by VFW members and their spouses, much like they were on our way to Iraq. I took plenty of pictures of the event as well as some videos.

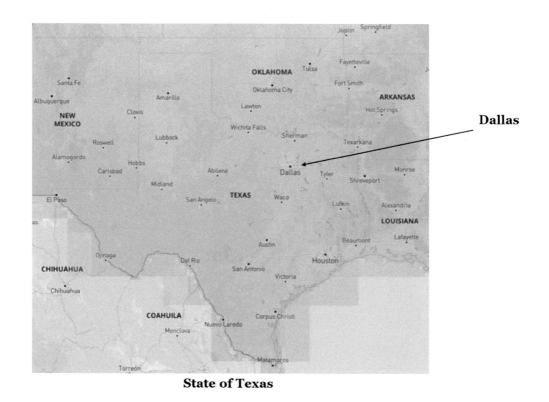

Dallas

State of Texas

Map by John J. McBrearty. Source: © OpenStreetMap
(data is available under the Open Database License)

After about an hour's stop, we mounted up with a new crew and headed for Dallas, Texas. In Texas, we were also greeted by some well-wishing family members of traveling soldiers. From Texas, we barely made our connecting flight to Ontario, California. We were the last to board the aircraft, but we made it. We got into Ontario around 18:00 or so.

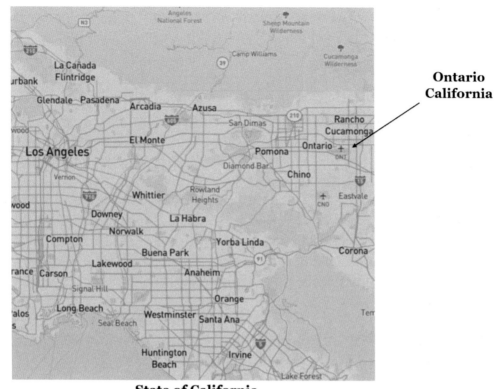

Ontario
California

State of California

Map by John J. McBrearty. Source: © OpenStreetMap
(data is available under the Open Database License)

It was nice to see the Armor Battalion members greet their families at the airport. I made my way to the rent-a-car complex at the airport and bartered for the nicest car that money could buy. I ended up with a Chrysler 300, which looks a lot like a Cadillac. It was a beauty!

I drove immediately to our new home. I parked and walked up to the front door, ringing the bell. Little Junior was the first to run up to the door, and he yelled, "It's Daddy!" I heard Annette make her way from the computer room to the hallway, and she said, "No, it can't be Daddy." She saw the uniform first before recognizing me. I think she was scared of having a uniformed person at her front door, as that usually means that someone is there to give her some bad news-like your husband is DEAD! She identified me, and we gave each other a big hug and kiss as Junior held onto my leg for dear life. Junior said, "I want to work in the Army, Daddy." *(Good heavens, no!)*

NOTE FROM AUTHOR: For a career military officer, you would probably be surprised to learn how I raised my two children. Not once did I ever mention anything about them affiliating with the military. Our home was a home of education and encouragement. I directed both kids in the direction of the sciences, which has resulted in both of them working in the medical profession. My daughter is an Internal Medicine doctor, and my son is completing his pre-med degree in biochemistry. My wife and I raised our children with the philosophy of them having better lives than their parents. So far, so good.

The visit home has been a strange one for me. I had second thoughts about leaving my comrades behind in Iraq, but on the other hand, I did want to see my family and new home. I particularly wanted to see my son as I know he is growing quickly, and he misses me terribly.

Nina wasn't home, but Annette informed her about my visit when she came home that night from a day at Disneyland. I saw her for the first time the next morning, and I gave her a big hug.

Several days have passed now, and I am finally over the jet lag. That tired feeling lasted a good three days. We went to a restaurant or two and did some shopping. Annette took Friday off work, and we had our window blinds installed.

30 Aug 04

The trip home was delightful. I spent just about every available moment with my family. Junior has grown much and now talks in sentences and is potty trained. I bought Nina a new laptop for her college studies and myself one for my video editing ventures and writing projects.

I got some golf in but played horribly; I was very much out of practice. Annette's computer crashed, but my Marine Corps buddy Luke is trying to fix it. I finally got online with the new computer and sent an email to Cantez, Slacker, and Hunts with our new home telephone number.

Nothing else new. Initial feelings of guilt, being here and not there. My wife says that I am distant and don't look her in the eye much, as if guilty of something? Eating well, but my stomach is in knots, and I am defecating heavily? Maybe it is nerves. *War is Hell, folks!*

I would have to sum up the whole R & R experience as the Army's truly best idea of the war. Taking care of its soldiers is what this leave meant to me. Getting a chance to visit with loved ones, you can't put a price tag on the experience. My son Junior is almost another year older, and I was able to experience that. When I left, my daughter had just graduated from High School and started college. Now, she has an entire year of university behind her; oh, what a difference! She is so much more her own woman than the fledgling youngster that I left last November. She is truly finding her way in her life. I got a chance to see my new home. That in itself was amazing to me. Annette has done an extraordinary job of decorating and processing the whole nightmare of selling a house and buying a new home.

I hit Starbucks every day that I was on leave. On the second day of leave, I stopped at our local Armory. My parking spot was still there, and although all the other dedicated spots were taken, mine was empty (just like old times). I brought my son with me, and he immediately got acquainted with a basketball and the one hoop that was mounted on the drill room floor. A Specialist dressed in Desert Camouflaged Utilities said that seeing me was like seeing a ghost. He immediately (ran) up the stairs to inform the other staff members that I was there. I followed him up the stairs as his actions were so blatantly awkward that I had to find out for myself if anything funky was going on. There wasn't, however, as I greeted SSG Malton and an SFC whose name escapes me, but I do remember that he was bipolar and not allowed to deploy or carry weapons. The NCOs sure seemed defensive and immediately stated what they were doing that minute, "Oh hello, Sir, I am trying to fix this PFC's pay situation...." I stopped them all in their tracks, saying that I wasn't here to check on them but just to check in from my leave and say hello. I also wanted to visit my office. Malton got a key and took me down to my office. I found it as I had left it in November, and I was ecstatic! I heard rumors that all my stuff had been shuffled around, but this wasn't the case. I was happy and after checking in with the TSD fellows (Active-Duty Army trainers) and two recruiters, and then I left. I took my son to my favorite Mexican Restaurant where "they know your name." I had my usual chicken burrito, wet with sour cream and red salsa, lots of salsa. Junior had his usual chips and salsa with a white milkshake type of Mexican drink. The next day, I regretted having eaten this meal but enjoyed it as I ate it. I made it a point to eat out at least once a day while home, and of course, there was Starbucks at the beginning of each day.

I golfed twice with one of my buddies. The first excursion was at Indian Hills Golf Club. This was a beautiful course that was inexpensively priced. Rather than playing 18 holes, we played 9 and hit the bars afterward. This is what "guys" do, so I am not apologizing for it! We took back roads to a dive bar in Corona where the battalion had busted some of its members of A Co. attending the bar in uniform on drill weekends. The chicks in the watering hole were pigs *(sorry, this is how young soldiers talk)*, but the bartender was HOT. We each had a beer and a shot, along with a snack. From there, we returned to my home (I wasn't driving). At home, we had Subway sandwiches with our wives and kids.

I also saw my best friend, Luke. I called him upon my return to civilization, and I mentioned that Annette and Nina were having a horrible time with their new computers. Luke came to the rescue as he visited and analyzed the situation. He had to take the computer with him to wipe the hard drive and reload the software. Luke is a bro! That was it for my visitors. Other than a visit to Los Alamitos to see the Division Chief of Staff, I pretty much stayed at home with my family. I played a second game of golf at the Navy Golf Course in Seal Beach, CA. I was so out of practice I really sucked. But I had fun.

2 Sep 04

The night before my flight out, I awoke at 0200 and couldn't return to sleep. I keep thinking of all the things that I had to do before leaving the house: take out the trash, hide that empty bottle of JD (Jack Daniels), kiss my wife, etc. At 0400, that alarm went off, and I was up. I packed my computer and loaded my stuff into the car. I showered and kissed my wife goodbye.

3 Sep 04

06:30 Flight out of Ontario, CA to Dallas, TX, and of course, only two of the four traveling soldiers from my unit, SPC Ellius and me, arrived. Ellius is a fifty-year-old something Specialist (this is quite unusual in itself; usually, someone of his age would at least be a Staff Sergeant or higher), of Hispanic descent, and a chain smoker with a raspy smoker voice. When I checked in for the flight, the airline attendant immediately put me in a first-class seat. I asked why, and she said that that is just what they do for us. I was quite honored. SPC Ellius also got a first-class seat and was situated in front of me. When the flight attendant came around, I asked for a vodka and orange juice (it was 07:00). The attendant said, "Orange juice, right?" and I corrected him by stating, "That was vodka and orange juice." He replied, "Superb choice, my favorite!" He kept them coming, and by the time we landed, I was buzzing.' We flew to Dallas without any problems. After waiting for what seemed to be an eternity, we made our way onto an ATA chartered aircraft terminal. Ellius is a chain smoker, so whenever an aircraft touches down, he be-lines it for the nearest smoking area. I agreed to watch his bags as he sucked away on his cancer sticks. After almost an hour and telephoning my daughter, I finally met up with Ellius. I asked the big question, "Ellius, do you like a cold beer?" His eyes lit up like a kid at Christmas; he replied, "Hell yes, sir!" I suggested that we take a cab to another terminal so we could indulge a bit without the worry of other soldiers seeing us. It didn't take much to convince him, and before you knew it, we were on the next shuttle bus to Terminal A. When we entered the terminal, we were met with different looks than we got in Terminal B. We soon realized that Terminal B in Dallas handles all the charter air, and the military always flies the cheapest aircraft, and that is charter air. So, the military guys in uniform aren't seen in the other parts of the airport. We were quite an attraction for the civilians. Immediately, we were assisted by the airport security staff, who guided us to an American Airlines supervisor who gave us a bogus pass to enter the terminal. We told them that we wanted to get something to eat and drink and that terminal B was too crowded with GIs. They bought my story, and we were in. After the routine shakedown past security, we hit the first stop, the nearest watering hole, TGI Fridays. Utilizing some discretion, we chose a table farthest from the entrance and away from the view of the terminal. We ordered two beers and two shots each and told the waiter that we were in a hurry. Ellius wanted to eat something with the booze, so he ordered soup. I ordered up a plate of French fries, and we were in business. A gentleman at a nearby table couldn't help but notice our rushed drinking. He came over and stated that he had a close friend who was called up by his reserve unit for duty in Iraq. He bought us a round of drinks. Later, another younger fellow also bought us a round of shots. Everyone that we met in that terminal thanked us for our duty and sacrifice. We were both overwhelmed with gratitude. It drove me to tears (but God forbid that I show it to anyone) as I knew that this was the last American experience that we would be having for another six months, or for an eternity for that matter? That last memory for Ellius and I was quite a good one, and we often talked about it during the whole trip to the Middle East.

Ellius and I ate and drank it up in another terminal of the Dallas airport prior to our departure. We were pretty toasted for the flight. I stumbled across a Chilies Restaurant and treated Ellius to dinner. We gorged ourselves!

We hustled out of the terminal and made it back to Terminal B. I was among the last on the plane. Some soldiers in line said, "Major, they asked for all Majors and above to go in first class." SPC Ellius answered, "This is my Major, and he is the best. He is with us and doesn't need to go in first class. He is one of us troops."

NOTE FROM AUTHOR: I can't tell you how good that experience felt. It is one of those memories that you take with you to the grave. Those words from that Specialist still ring in my ear. I love my soldiers till this day!

Ellius and I got on the aircraft and got lucky on the seating. We sat on the left side of the airplane about midway to the back. We left the middle seat open and put our gear in it. When an NCO later asked if the seat was taken? Ellius replied, "Yes, he is in the head (lavatory), not feeling well..." Well, the NCO bought it, and we had some extra room for the fifty-hour flight.

Hot flight attendants. It seems to be a trend with international flights. What a great way for the GIs to last remember American women! Really hot and friendly, too!

After several delays at zero dark-thirty (a slang term referring to evening hours), we took off. Our first stop was Shannon, Ireland. It was quite beautiful. This was my first time stepping foot on Irish soil, and I was very excited. I bought a bunch of souvenirs from the gift shop. One couldn't help but notice the robust selection of spirits in this small part of the airport. Unfortunately, we are not permitted to partake while traveling in uniform.

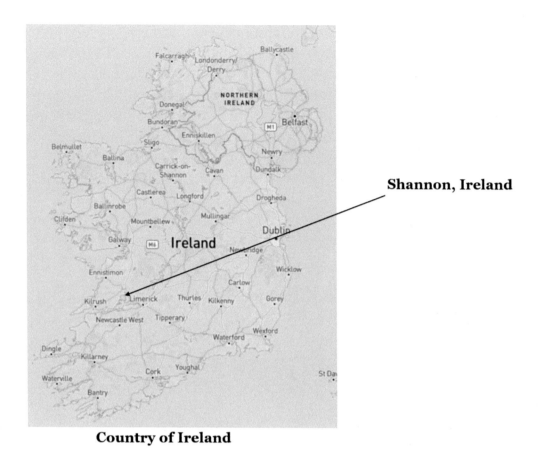

Shannon, Ireland

Ireland

Country of Ireland

Map by John J. McBrearty. Source: © OpenStreetMap
(data is available under the Open Database License)

From Ireland, we flew over the Irish Channel, England, the English Channel, and parts of Europe, Hungary, Turkey, Iraq, and eventually into Kuwait.

From the airport, we bussed to Camp Doha, Kuwait. The buses were what we call "Hadjie Buses" and were manufactured by either Hyundai or KIA. The only noticeable difference between these buses and those used in America is that they are considerably smaller, and they use a stick shift versus an automatic transmission. I slept on the entire second leg of the flight and the bus ride. After some briefings, we bunked up in the same building 6 (but a different squad bay), from which we departed. On the first leg of the journey, I really had panic attacks about the flight. The captain of the airplane said something about delaying the trip for maintenance, just like our previous experience with this airline (remember the landing gear mishap?) All I could think about was my little boy and how he needed a father figure so much. While home, I played ball in our big 1/2 acre backyard with him every day. He and I had so much fun together; the thought of not returning from Iraq in one piece to continue that relationship would be just too much to bear. I could not stop thinking about that. I never, never in my whole life felt so horrible! The thought of not seeing that little guy again really was breaking me up. Of course, I missed my wife and daughter, but that little guy had me hook, line and sinker!

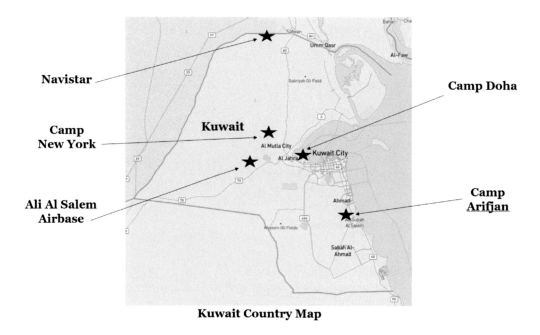

Kuwait Country Map

Map by John J. McBrearty. Source: © OpenStreetMap
(data is available under the Open Database License)

Third Act: Returning to the Belly of the Beast: Iraq.

4 Sep 04

We arrived at Camp Doha, Kuwait. After the briefings, SPC Ellius and I took showers and then hit the rack. At 05:30, I awoke to go and pick up my body armor and helmet that I had left behind on the trip home. At 06:00, SPC Ellius and I ate chow at the post mess hall. The food was plentiful but far from the restaurant dining I had been accustomed to during my R & R. After chow, we hit the rack again. I slept until 11:30 and forced myself up. Sometime later, Ellius and I went to report to the Brigade's LNO and called into our Battalion in Iraq. From there, we hit Starbucks at the PX and did some shopping.

Later that afternoon and evening, I wrote some forty-three postcards to relatives and friends. I toted all these around during my trip, anticipating several long waits for aircraft. The postcard breakdown goes like this: Annette & the family, in-laws, Cousin #2-Cousin #3-Cousin #1, Leanne, sister & brother-in-law and family, brother-in-law's mother (married to an Iraqi immigrant), cousin (on mother's side of the family), college buddies, Annette's aunt & uncle, cousin (father's side), my old acting coach from college, several other cousins (on father's side), best man from my wedding and former college roommate, USMC buddies, my daughter's babysitter when she was a kid, other cousins, wife's uncle, (mom's brother and family), my father's caregivers, childhood friends, Annette's doctor brother), aunt's & uncles on my mother's side, more cousins on my mother's side, Annette's teaching close friends), several of Annette's cousins, Annette's grandmother, and our former neighbor.

I know I will only hear back from less than half of these folks, but that doesn't prevent me from writing them. My basic message to most of them was that we were now completing the first six months of our deployment, that I had visited my family on R & R, and that I stopped off in Ireland on my way home. Most of my friends and relatives know that I am Irish and hold my Irish heritage close to my heart, and this stopover really was important to me.

5 Sep 04

We waited all day for a flight, but it didn't happen. The powers to be here told us that late in the day, there would be a 14:30 meeting tomorrow to discuss our flight. That is over 24 hours here in Doha. Between writing my postcards, sleeping, and hitting Starbucks at the PX, I didn't really have much time to do anything else. I wanted to hit the gym, but that, too, didn't happen.

Fourth Act: Operation "Wild Turkey"

5 Sep 04

While at the PX, SPC Ellius and I picked up some tactical drinking accouterments for the field, sometimes referred to as a flask. When we bought these items, he mentioned that he bought some Wild Turkey on R & R and brought it with him. I didn't give it much thought, but at around 11 p.m., I heard the words, "Major, get your flask. We're filling up!" He didn't have to say another word; "Operation Wild Turkey" was in full swing, and I was a major player. Like two High School kids sneaking booze into the prom, SPC Ellius and I worked together as close as a Neurosurgical team. Objective: To download the contents of a Wild Turkey bottle into our flasks with the following conditions: 1) No spillage. 2) No observation of any 3rd parties. The stress rose, and the heat was on, as was a testament to our sweaty brows. The seriousness of the situation couldn't be greater. Together, we picked up the slack of one another's weaknesses in tandem as if we were tag-team wrestlers. Once we hit the fifty-percent solution, Ellius broke a smile and laughed, stating, "Sir, we make a great team!" The good Major nodded as he had the lookout and didn't want to waver from those ever-important duties. The squad bay that we were in had racks (bunk beds) all around. Luckily, not every bunk was filled. A bunch of Marines headed out earlier for Mousel. *(I love the Corps, but hey, Marines, get the fuck out!)* LOL

The setting reminded me of "The Three Stooges" television show where they said, "Step by step, inch by inch....." *(Younger folks need to google that one. It is quite a crack-up!)* The moment was tense. Eventually, the mission was completed. All flasks were filled, and as Ellius pointed out, "There is only a couple of GIGGERS left in the bottle, sir, let's kill that now ourselves." We killed those giggers and continued with the night. Later, we washed our previous day's underwear in the latrine sinks with some body wash. That was Ellius's idea (maybe I can put this good soldier in for a medal someday)? What a cool way to pass the time, as a rapid journey back to our destination wasn't happening any time soon. This is another example of how sometimes officers need to shut up and listen to their NCOs; they usually have the answers.

Later that evening, Ellius spent a good half an hour cleaning up his bunk area. There had been some Wild Turkey spillage, and he used what was left of that body wash that we used to wash our clothes in the latrine. He then spent an inordinate amount of time repacking his duffle bag, the bag that he smuggled the WT in. Again, the dedication and thoroughness of this troop amazes me. If you could see my rack area, it looks like the frat boys have arrived with "shit" spread out everywhere. Again, officers need to respect their NCOs and other enlisted soldiers.

To conclude, Operation Wild Turkey was a complete success! Apart from a large number of Marines that joined us in our squad bay later that evening, the events went off without a hitch.

Tomorrow will bring us another adventure, I am sure. Luckily, here in Kuwait, we are so far removed from any combat action it is highly unlikely that any combat will be involved.

6 Sep 04

Today, we visited the Marble Palace at Camp Doha, Kuwait (an MWR facility for coalition forces that included a swimming pool, television, games, and decent air conditioning). You must see the photos to get the real significance of this location. It is an R&R setup for combat troops. Man, it was nice! Starbucks poolside on the beaches of Kuwait, and did I mention golf? Yes, golf! They had a driving range, two putting greens, and a putter-golf course. Batting cages, volleyball, and horseshoes. Inside the palace, there was a snack shop, a sweet shop with a variety of candies, a large music room with all the equipment to do a rock concert, and a TV room. It was beautiful.

7 Sep 04

14:20

We had an accountability formation and jumped on a bus around 15:30 or so. We joined a convoy and headed up the MSR Jackson. Boy, was it hairy! Two breakdowns, and we ventured through several large towns. I took over 100 photos on the trip. Man, was it dangerous.

I eventually bedded down at 18:30 (or was it 20:30), skipping chow. I have no clue what day it is or what time it is. I was completely exhausted.

Fifth Act: Combat Action

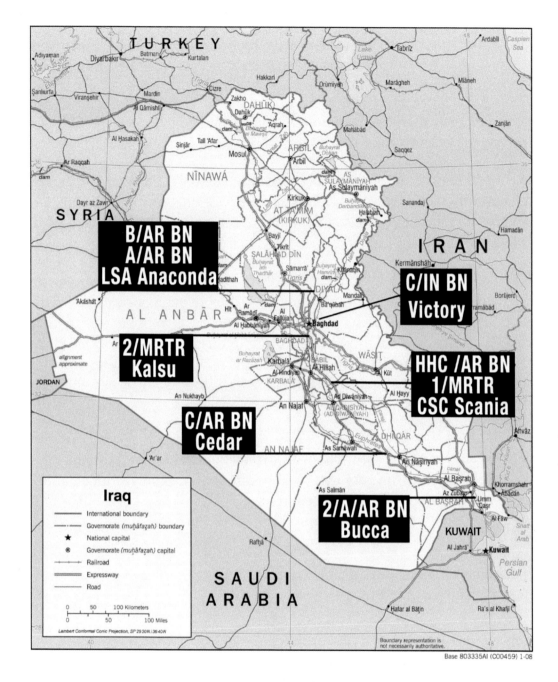

Map by John J. McBrearty. Source: The World Factbook, CIA Maps.

8 Sep 04

I am back at CSC Scania.

Up at 04:00, yes, 4 a.m. My clock is still on California time. I hit chow at around 05:00. I had breakfast with 2LT Long, who works the night shift.

He said that the snipers reported an extremely large increase in vehicular activity on Kieve (not sure of the spelling-sorry). This could be a precursor to things to come.

Today, the American death toll in Iraq surpassed the 1,000-person mark, an unfortunate milestone in history.

This horrifying milestone didn't hit me until I sat at breakfast in the DFAC on the morning of the 9th. It hit me like a wave of uncontrollable emotions. I just wanted to cry. I held on as I sat next to SPC Bonilla, one of my R & R travel buddies.

Work-wise, I am really up to my ears: OERs (officer evaluation reports) for myself and other officers, awards to write, sitting in on an awards board of which I am the president, my promotion packet needs to be created, taking an APFT (Army physical fitness test) for my promotion paperwork. And yes, Slacker strikes again, as he dumped an investigation on my ass about a shooting at our southern checkpoint. Help!

1149

South CP shot at a blue suburban with two passengers for not stopping after several attempts to get them to stop. The vehicle finally stopped and turned around. No injuries were reported.

2344

Knight 6 and Knight 7 board a helicopter to Anaconda. The expected return is Saturday, 11 SEP 04

9 Sep 04

I am still not over the jet lag, and I awoke around 04:30. I got up and off to chow at 05:30 and in the office by 06:00. I spoke with LT Long and CPT Bordham in front of the S5 office about some awards that they had submitted, then got into my email and brewed up a pot of Starbucks. I again tried to call home, only to be greeted by an answering machine. Since I don't think that my wife is back online, I am making efforts to call her. I got lucky on the home phone line, and we spoke for about twenty minutes.

The big event: wireless internet! We got hooked up online at 15:00 at the MP's HQs for a $200 fee (each person). No problem; for unlimited wireless and unsupervised internet access, we would have paid any price.

14:00 Meeting with the staff to discuss their issues and suspense.

Today, I spent time writing my OER support form because I have to submit a promotion packet for our state's Officer Manning Roster's yearly update. You must be on this list to even be considered for promotion as a field grade officer. I hope to have my OER updated and submitted for this board.

Taha came into my office with a few problems with the units on post, not wanting to switch interpreters. We spoke for about ½ an hour (he likes to talk in several languages). Eventually we developed several courses of action to follow.

A Korean Major also came into my office requesting one of our soldiers to continue working as his interpreter for the next two weeks. I told him that it would be no problem and that he would work it out with his company commander.

Another very fast-paced day with much paperwork to do. Thank goodness there are no attacks or enemy activity to deal with; I am just too far behind in my work.

There is a noticeable difference between those soldiers who have taken leave and gone home for their two weeks and those who haven't. The R & R soldiers seem so much more relaxed and not as stressed. The rest all really look run down, tired, and stressed. This has been a long deployment, almost a year, and we are just burnt out! No days off will do that to a person.

Good news, we anticipate the mayor's cell leaving in the December timeframe, hallelujah! There is also talk that COL Nosey will be transferring to Arifjan, Kuwait, soon to be the OIC of the redeployment out of theater. That would leave Slacker in charge, and that is fine with all of us. He is better off in charge when there is no one around to answer to.

10 Sep 04

I finally slept in, so I guess that I am over most of my jetlag. Rickets and Cantez got up at 06:00 to do PT, and I didn't get up. Maybe later in the day, I'll get some weightlifting in.

Chow has improved as the DFAC now has eggs cooked to order. I am so proud that my recommendation (complaint) was recognized and implemented. Unfortunately, it took several anonymous letters to COL Nosey and LTC Milling to make it happen. I threatened to complain to higher authorities if some things weren't changed for soldier care.

NOTE FROM AUTHOR: I didn't elaborate much about it here, but I actually consider this one of my finest contributions to our unit on this deployment. One thing about the military, and probably in the corporate world as well, is that often your boss won't go along with your good ideas because they weren't their ideas, and they won't get credit for the ideas. I have learned over the years to work around the system to get what I want for myself and or my soldiers. Sometimes, you have to create an environment in which your boss thinks that it was their original idea; that way, they know that they will get credit for it if it succeeds. In this case, I saw that the mess hall had the personnel and resources necessary to make cook-to-order eggs, omelets, etc. I thought what a morale booster this could be for the troops, getting restaurant-level cooking here in this fucked up country. So, I submitted the request anonymously through the mayor's suggestion box. It actually took many attempts to come to fruition, but I did succeed in this, yet again, another covert mission for the troops.

Additionally, I just got to thinking of what my dearest friend and former college roommate would think of this story. He had an active-duty career in the Army Special Forces (Green Berets). He is also one of the most decorated war veterans of our generation. My buddy saw the shit! I mean, the shit! He did a tour in Afghanistan, where he and his A-team saw an inordinate amount of combat. He had the life-changing experience of losing two of his fellow comrades to enemy fire, both of whom died in his arms. What would this war hero think about my "omelet story"? The point that I want to make here is that each and every soldier, airman, sailor, or Marine has a different combat experience than the next guy/gal. I believe that each and every one of us did our part and contributed equally in our own way to the success of our respective missions.

I can't help but notice attitude. I see some bad attitude amongst our ranks. I have the most visibility with the officers of the battalion, and I see attitude. It could be several things; we are all just plain old burnt out, as in me sitting as the president of the awards board, not all awards have been approved, and some have been downgraded, and this really has a tendency to piss off people. I know because I had an award downgraded once, and I thought that the Colonel who did that was way off base. Or it could be a combination of things. We will have to do what we can to get everyone's spirits up. Maybe putting on some skits or a funny video or something like that.

15:00

Our second awards board meeting with me, 1LT Olouski, 1LT Obannon, MSG Moocheff, and a SGT from the mortar section (I forget his name). We have made much progress with the process of reviewing award submissions. In our previous meeting, we kicked back a bunch of awards for rewriting. They came back and were pretty much outstanding. It is great seeing progress. I believe that the awards that we are approving and moving forward with will get approved.

I am told that CPT Morehead was really pissed off this afternoon and wanted to speak with me. I bet it is because one of his submissions was recommended for downgrading, and one was put on hold because of a legal action pending on the soldier. He needs to get over it without personalizing the issues.

I am very happy today as I visited Chrys at the MWR tent, and she showed me the AstroTurf that she obtained from her supply warehouse. I couldn't believe it, four big rolls and a bunch of putters and golf balls. We are on our way. I told her that she just saved me about $500 in costs, as I was just about to purchase the turf from the Iraqis. I also met with CPT Phillips, the company commander for the Engineer unit assigned here. I informed him of the plan for the golf course and asked for his help dropping some dirt down for our greens. He was most helpful and said to just let him know when and where to make the drops. Now, I just have to get the final decision from COL Nosey on the location. I propose a small triangle behind the MWR tent. The second location is near my office. I will talk to him tomorrow.

Astroturf obtained in preparation for building a golf practice facility for American soldiers at CSC Scania, Iraq.

Earlier, I met with CPT Chang of the Korean Air Force. He was having trouble getting tents for his transient Korean soldiers coming through Scania in a few days. The mayor's cell would only give him four tents for 400 soldiers and wouldn't budge on getting him anymore accommodations. CPT Cantez tried to work something out with LTC Milling but got nowhere. I telephoned COL Nosey and asked him to intervene, and he said that he would. We have a vacant postal tent and a vacant LNO tent presently, which could be used, and I am sure there are more opportunities out there.

The internet and external telephone system were down all day due to some problems in Doha. I directed the BDOC to contact Anaconda by SAT (satellite) phone with a sit rep and to check on LTC Slacker.

11 Sep 04

Anniversary of the bombings in 2001. I wanted to write something profound considering the day, but I just couldn't find it in me. But I did come across an old letter written in May that I never sent off. It was written for my High School class. Here's a look:

From the Desk of

Major Darby Hillcrest

TO: High School Class of 1978

SUBJECT: LIFE

DATE: May 19, 2004

Dear Fellow Alumni,

The responses to Meggy's email have been overwhelming. I am not in a position to email everyone, so I came up with the idea of a concentrated effort. This is a response to the many alumni that did email or write me. Many expressed their support and concern for our well-being overseas. Thank you all very much, and please say a prayer for my men and women.

A FRIEND

It is funny; the last letter that I wrote was to my "very best friend in my whole world" hopefully, we all have someone that we can trust and enjoy the benefits of such a relationship with as I have with my Marine Corps buddy, Luke. Luke and I went together through NROTC U. S. Marine Corps OCS at Quantico, VA, many years ago and have always remained close friends. Friendship, have you experienced true friendship? Friendship, to me, is trust. Trusting someone with what is important to you; your home, your life, the life of your spouse, or the ultimate, the life of your child:

THAT IS A FRIEND! A TRUE FRIEND! If you have had the pleasure in life to experience this phenomenon, embrace it as you are truly blessed. If you have not, pursue it because that is WHAT LIFE IS ALL ABOUT. The reason why I bring up the point of my friend Luke is that the letter that I wrote him gave him guidance on how to handle my business and personal affairs if I don't make it back home. No one here wants that to happen to any of us, and we do everything in our power to prevent it, but war is war, and things happen. You never know. This is my reality.

EGO

To some degree or another, we all have one. Some EGOs are bigger than others. Folks, there isn't time for EGO where I am right now. I have seen people get killed because of EGOs, and that is tragic. My motive for writing you after all these years, or for writing a book for that matter, is not EGO based. I could care less what people think of me; again, there is no time for that. I guess at the age of 44, what I find important to me now is what my three-year-old boy might think of his father in the event that he doesn't make it home from his combat mission. I also think of how I would be remembered by my nineteen-year-old college student daughter, Nina. (Is a proud father tooting his horn? You bet your ass he is! I love my daughter so much; she means more to me than life itself!) I am so proud of Nina. She is going to make a superb Physician. I often wonder, "Did I spend enough time with her as she grew up?" Little Junior could just be the next TIGER WOODS. Look for his name in "Golf Digest" magazine someday because I bought his first set of golf clubs when he was 8 months old! At age 2 he could swing and hit the ball. Moreover, at age 3, he is dangerous, yes, dangerously good at hitting a golf ball with a golf club.

MY LIFE

When we graduated High School, I spent "Senior Week" like many of you in Ocean City and Margate, New Jersey *(yes, I know that I just "grabbed my audience" because if you don't have a memory from that experience, well, you must have been living under a rock back then!)* When we left high school, and when senior week was over, I went to Ft. Knox, KY, for Reserve Officer Training

Corps (Army ROTC) Basic Camp in preparation for my Plebe year at Valley Forge Military Academy and College (VFMA & C). I enlisted into the United States Marine Corps Reserve (USMCR) the following summer. Although I was already in college and in good standing to become a Commissioned Officer in the military, I felt that it was important to start my military career from the very bottom; a Private in the USMC. I have absolutely no regrets about that decision. In later years as an officer, I sensed that the enlisted troops that you led actually showed you greater respect than the other officers because I was once one of them, formerly enlisted. I digress; after another year at VFMA & C and my USMCR affiliation, I transferred to Temple University and pursued a degree in Communications. I participated in Villanova University's NROTC program and received a commission as Officer of Marines upon my graduation from Temple in August of 1982. Following college, I served on active duty with the Marine Corps. While at Temple, I met my lovely wife, Annette. We had our firstborn one year after our marriage (a novel concept these days, marriage before childbirth?) (Excuse my cynical commentary, hell, I am 44 like many of you and have earned the right to bitch about things from time to time!)

After my hitch with the Marine Corps, I threw myself into theater study with world-renowned thespians Sanford Meissner, Bob Carnegie, and Jeff Goldblum. I eventually got my Screen Actors Guild card, but I never really landed any big parts in Hollywood. The first role that I auditioned for was that of a Marine Corps 1st Lieutenant. No joke. My previous work history was that of an active-duty Marine Corps 1st Lieutenant! Needless to say, the Hollywood dimwits of that particular project didn't think that I was the right guy for that role????? WTF! That, my friends, is how Hollywood works. Good luck with that life! Not for me. I wanted to be a rock-steady provider for my family and raise my kids in a good neighborhood. Hollywood was not that answer and was certainly not a neighborhood to raise a family that I was comfortable with.

Eventually, my calling for the military life drew me back in, and I was once again reacquainted with the military via the National

Guard. I found one of the best-kept secrets in the military; the Active Guard Reserve (AGR) program. As an AGR, you serve on active duty with all of the appropriate benefits of active-duty military, all the while working within your home state. Through a series of assignments, I landed the position as Executive Officer of an Armor Battalion. This battalion is an enhanced Armor Battalion and is assigned to one of only fifteen enhanced brigades in the U.S. Army. The enhanced brigades are better equipped and better trained than the regular Nation Guard and Reserves. If the Active Component Army is in need of additional forces, such as in a wartime situation, they first utilize the enhanced brigades. What are the consequences of being a member of an enhanced brigade? Deployment to Iraq in support of Operation Iraqi Freedom. A philosophy that Sanford Meisner stressed in his teachings to his younger students was to *experience life*. He said go out and live your life for 20 years and then come back to me, and you will be ready to become an actor or filmmaker. He said that you have to draw on human experiences to be a real actor or filmmaker. I hope that my life experiences and combat action will make for an interesting book or movie someday.

WRITING

I am not an OXFORD-trained literate by any means. My book, **COMBAT JOURNAL**, will be about how and what I feel going through this life experience. I am still developing my nonfiction writing techniques as we speak. My writing background has been mainly writing dialogue for the screen or school newspapers. The ***American History, A Veteran's Perspective*** book series is my first efforts into the literary publishing world. Commerciality is the furthest thing from my mind. If I do not land a book deal, I will then publish my memoirs by myself. Eventually, I hope to produce my story into a motion picture. These aren't grandiose dreams, it is just my world, and I see them as quite attainable. I will base the motion picture on my real-life experiences in real-world combat operations in Iraq through 2004 and into 2005. I guess that I feel that I have a story to tell. Anyway, folks, these are my dreams. You have to have dreams in your life.

At the time of our deployment, I was decisively engaged in a master's degree program in American History. Unfortunately, I had to put those academic pursuits on hold until after we returned home.

In addition to my duties as Battalion Executive Officer and writing the book about my adventures in Iraq, I am putting together a DVD scrapbook for the battalion.

FAMILY

I married the most beautiful girl on the Temple University campus, Annette. Annette was a professional ballet-jazz-tap dancer while attending Temple. We had several classes together, started dating, and the rest is history. Annette has since entered the teaching profession and has earned her Master's Degree in Education.

MY BEST FRIEND

My best friend was my Father. Unfortunately, my father passed away on May 25, 2003, just one year ago. Yes, this has been quite a year for my family, as we also lost my Mother just two months before Dad died. If you haven't lived through the experience of losing a parent, my dear friends, you owe it to yourself to start preparing now, as it can be a rough ride. My Father was truly my best friend. To lose your Father and your best friend all in one day was quite life-altering. Man, was that a difficult experience! I miss that old dude!

SISTER

I only have one sister, and she has chosen not to support me in the war efforts of our country. Too bad, all I know is that if our founding fathers did not support one another at the time of our Revolution, our country would have never happened. Enough said on this subject. I think that her actions are tragic, and I would not wish this situation upon my worst enemies. (Did I tell you that somebody shot at me this week, I guess *they* would be considered a real adversary?) Put that into perspective when you get into your next argument, particularly with your own blood relative, like a sister. It saddens me not to be supported in the war effort by a family member, but I deal with it. Despite her convictions, I still love her. To have the freedom to disagree without fear of persecution, what a wonderful country we live in. Enough with my problems.

MUSIC

Linkin Park does it for me; I love their music. I guess it is the rocker in me at heart; I have always loved to rock and always will. You may or may not remember me playing the trumpet and bass guitar during High School in several rock bands? Here in Iraq, there are only Arabic-speaking radio stations, so we have to listen to CDs, MP3s, and of course, iPods for our music. I spend quite a bit of time listening to *Linkin Park*, *Alice in Chains*, *Led Zeppelin*, and the *Rolling Stones* (old-school rocker or what?)

9-11

Folks, 9-11 is our Pearl Harbor. What I am doing is a direct result of 9-11. Trust me, my life changed dramatically from that date. I worked 7 days a week for a year following that tragic day. The culmination for our family, obviously, is this deployment. The deployment is in excess of eighteen months in length, with a high likelihood of an extension. When I left home, my son, Junior, was in diapers, and my daughter Nina was leaving High School and starting her first year of college as a pre-med student. When I get back, Nina will be a junior in college, and Junior will be ready for preschool. I guess that is my commitment and sacrifice to our country and all of you; I missed out on those precious years (not to mention one heck of a 25th High School Reunion this year!) Luckily, my wife Annette, who is made of bedrock, is holding things together quite well. I am one of the lucky ones over here. (*If all goes as planned, I will be home by late May '05 and will be visiting family in Pennsylvania in July '05.*)

HOBBIES

Golf, weights, and more golf. Writing my **COMBAT JOURNAL**.

LIFE IN IRAQ

This is the way it is for a soldier in combat. You have to prepare for the worst. We buried a fellow Soldier from our Camp this week, as well as another Soldier from our brigade. I have attended TOO many memorial services! The price of freedom has come with the color of blood, as it has since the conception of our beloved country. I hope the American people will not forget about our sacrifices for the cause of democracy and freedom.

IN SUMMARY

Combat duty is tough, but we do not have it that bad. No matter how bad things get, I know that there are Soldiers and Marines over here that have it far worse than us. The frequency of enemy attacks is lessening, and the Iraqi people as a whole are taking a liking to us. The Iraqis appreciate our humanitarian efforts that we have accomplished. Unfortunately, those efforts don't often make the front-page news.

MORAL OF THE STORY

The moral of the story is to live each and every moment of your life like it could be your last. Tell your loved ones that you, in fact, love them. Spend more time with your family. Look at yourself in the mirror and ask yourself the hard questions. None of us is invincible, and we will all die at some point. How do you want to be remembered by family and friends? What I do know is that when you go out of this world, all you have is your family and maybe a few good FRIENDS. Make the most of that and cherish your loved ones.

God bless,

And remember, I wish peace, love, and happiness to everyone.

(from Greystones Yearbook, 1978)

I hope to see some of you in July 2005!

Your friend,

Major Darby Hillcrest
Executive Officer
Armor Battalion
Central-South Region, Iraq

*This letter was also included in **COMBAT ESSAYS**, American History, A Veteran's Perspective, Volume II.*

I had a long talk with CPT Morehead about the awards. He was shocked to hear that his Lieutenant was not being considered because of his still pending legal action against him (this was Slacker's call, and, in all fairness, it isn't uncommon for a commander to make this choice). Morehead assumed that the issue was dropped. Morehead was also very upset that SGT Freedom's award was being downgraded from a Bronze Star Medal to an Army Accommodation Medal. I explained that the board had done a pretty good job with standardizing its evaluation, and Freedom would have another chance for a BSM before the end of the tour, which would give him two medals versus one medal. Regardless, Morehead wasn't happy. It is a funny thing about awards; people take the issue so personally. (Much more to follow on this subject later.)

12 Sep 04

Sunday, the day of rest? Hardly. I filled sandbags from 08:30 to about 11:00, cleaned the tent, and avoided the mayor's cell folks. Koreans everywhere! I am glad that I helped out MAJ Chung (ROK); he is also glad now because things are running smoothly for him.

Iraqi Nationals and soldiers of the Armor Battalion filling sandbags at CSC Scania, Iraq.

Slacker is still gone, and all the battalion-level problems keep coming into me. I have never been busier since he and CSM Hunts went up to see the Brigade Commander in LSA Anaconda.

We just got a FRAGO from MNC-I stating that there is an extreme increase in enemy activity and that the threat condition was heightened to expect attacks imminently. We have beefed up our patrols and put everyone on alert. We are also at the camp's maximum capacity, with the Koreans passing through along with their many MP escorts. The Marines are also stopping here as they travel through from Najaf.

The weather is cooling down for us, only getting up to 110 or so. Thank goodness, I say!

The chow hall is absolutely swamped with people. I blew off lunch as I had my normal breakfast of an omelet, one French toast, and fruit and was pretty full all day. I also drank quite a bit of water from working hard out in the sun. At evening chow, I waited in line for ½ an hour. This was quite typical when we first got here when OIF I was leaving and OIF II was arriving.

Today, I cruised the web with the wireless internet that we bought into from the MP guys (they are actually Field Artillery FA turned into provisional Military Police MPs). I learned today that there is an abundance of FREE pornography out there. Call me naive, but my wife does not allow me to venture into such things. I guess that I learned that when it comes to my boy Junior, we are going to have to control his internet access from the get-go! I think that you could find any kind of strange fetish to your heart's desires out there, and it is pretty scary.

Today, I lead the Catholic service as the Lay Leader, as I have done so every Sunday while here at CSC Scania. The two Protestant Chaplains were very glad to have me back from leave to help. I don't know why; it is no big thing for me. I think it is just a calling for me.

Exterior of Chapel at CSC Scania, Iraq.

13 Sep 04

Monday. Today, I spent too much time in meetings: 09:00 BUB, 09:45 Force Protection Brief, 13:00 Battalion Staff meeting, and 15:00 Awards Board meeting. In today's meeting, COL Nosey announced that we are going to have a golf course added to the camp. I was putting green around the MWR tent. I later took 1ST Villa to the proposed area, and we measured off the perimeter. We then went to speak with KBR about getting lumber for the project. We were met with nothing but resistance. They said to put the request through the mayor's cell, or they couldn't help us. I told them that it was bound to get fucked up if they had anything to do with any of it. They agreed but wouldn't budge on anything unless directed by them. Get this: the lumber we want to use was obtained by the Army for soldiers to use and is only stored with KBR. More red tape! Watch things get fucked up, my friends; just watch! Lord, give me strength!

The only big issue that came up from the awards board was SGT Freedom. Initially, we thought the award justified an ARCOM. CPT Morehead was livid with those results and confronted all members of the board. He ended up with me, and I told him that, as written, it didn't warrant a BSM. He asked me to rewrite it for him. I agreed to help him out and stated that we would reconsider the award. Later, we did, and I found some credible achievements in the award. I changed my mind, and so did one other member of the five. The other three still weren't convinced that this E5 deserved a BSM at this stage of the mobilization. I decided to send it forward, stating that the board had a split decision and would discuss it with LTC Slacker. Later, I discussed it with Slacker, and he agreed with me and felt that the award was warranted, even at this early date.

I heard that Slacker was looking for me to discuss why I was involved with the Koreans and their living arrangements. I figured that instead of talking with him when he was pissed, that I would avoid him until he cooled down. I did, and he never brought it up. LTC Milling probably said something to him because I ratted her and her staff out to COL Nosey for not being cooperative with the ROKs (Republic of Korea). The ROKs, on the other hand, got what they wanted: housing for their troops during a hot summer day in Iraq. They got this because I raised the red flag to Nosey when they weren't getting cooperation from the mayor's cell Idiots! The ROK's have expressed their gratitude to me several times.

*NOTE FROM AUTHOR: This is an example of why I wrote the book **MILITARY LEADERSHIP LESSONS LEARNED**. MAJ Hillcrest went out of his way to help fellow coalition forces. He didn't ask permission from his psychotic commander or incompetent mayor's staff* *but went directly to the approving authority. He knew how to work the system to his advantage, and he prevailed. This is one of dozens of examples of good leadership lessons learned. Those ROK soldiers were quite grateful and will not forget MAJ Hillcrest any time soon.*

14 Sep 04

06:00 Got up for PT. I lifted weights in the MWR tent, but I didn't see Cantez and Hunts. They got up at 05:00, went walking, and did the stationary bikes.

07:00 I showedered and hit chow at around 07:30. I ate with LTC Z, CPT Cantez, CPT Randerson, SGM Westminster, a Lieutenant, and MSG Rasper.

08:00 As I approached my office, I noticed CPT Morehead speaking with LTC Slacker in front of Slacker's office. At 08:20, Slacker came into my office to spread his joy. He has hit an all-time low. He said that he didn't want me in any more pictures for the press? I almost couldn't believe what I was hearing. "Come again?" I asked. He said that it is the Brigade's perception that I have been in too many pictures that have been forwarded to the PAO. They want pictures of other people from the battalion and not me.

Well, this has taken the wind out of my sails. Just as I was literally preparing my video camera for another Civil Affairs dedication ceremony today, I got this from Slacker.

Slacker went on to say that he wanted to do some mentoring with me and mentioned that he hadn't done enough of that with me or anyone else for that fact. He said that there was a perception that I had a case of the ass for 1LT Fernandez and that I needed to drop it and move on. He said that he investigated his flight issues with the Brigade's air liaison people and found that Fernandez only missed one flight of his own accord and that the other missed flights were legitimate. I told him that the second go around with the board, I chose not to process because I wanted to speak with him first since I was going to council LT Fernandez. He understood. I also went on to tell him that on the last Bridge dedication, I asked to have additional HHC troopers come out for pictures, and we had no one show up. I also had Morehead, Fernandez, and Freedom have pictures taken at the dedication, and I submitted those pictures to PAO. Slacker said that everyone's name was printed but Fernandez. I told him that it wasn't my doing; look at the California magazine. It has Slacker pinning an award on a Battalion soldier, and I specifically had MSG Rasper's name with the photo and news story?

It is my opinion that Slacker is jealous of me getting some recognition. If he wants his picture in the paper, he needs to get off this comfortable post and off of his ass and go out with his soldiers once and a while and do that. I would be glad to do pictures and stories on him, but he doesn't play that game. I also told Slacker that I asked many times to get other soldiers to get their pictures taken with the various mayors and whatnot, but they won't.

Another reason why I think Slacker is concerned about me outshining him is my wish list. I informed him that I met briefly with the Chief of Staff back in the States while on R&R. I also spoke to COL Raskins, the 2nd Brigade Commander, about my desire for promotion and my possible next assignments. I made sure that Slacker knew that I spoke to them and that they both requested my biographies and my wish list of follow-on assignments. Yesterday, Slacker told me to send my list through him so he could endorse it. It seems to me that he is getting in the middle, maybe as a control mechanism, I don't know. Fuck him, I am sending the information out to all three of them as directed. Let the cards fall as they may. I ain't going to put my future in the hands of Slacker. No sir!

NOTE FROM AUTHOR: Looking back at this obtuse behavior from Slacker, his motives are quite apparent. As a senior Major with a successful combat tour under my belt and Slacker as a junior Lieutenant Colonel, it is inevitable that our paths will cross again in the future for the same assignments. No way did he want to compete with the likes of me. So, he did all that he could to keep me down. He did this fairly successfully, I might add, all the way through deployment and even in post-deployment with evaluations and awards. This is a true violation of Army Values that I feel compelled to live by. JM

CSM Hunts came into the office around 09:30, and I mentioned to him that Slacker was in earlier, spreading his joy. I told him that I wasn't accustomed to getting backstabbed by my staff. I also told him that the

OER rating chain was recently worked between CPT Randerson (S1) and Slacker, and I wasn't included. This made no sense at all because I wrote up the original rating chain, and as the full-time officer in charge, that was my job prior to mobilization. Also, I have the most experience with this subject than any other officer in the Battalion and possibly the Brigade. In any event, I mentioned to Hunts that the rating chain would fix this situation for me because, originally, all the battalion staff had me in their rating chain as either rater, intermediary rater, or senior rater. He agreed that that would fix these types of problems.

I also mentioned to Hunts that I was really flustered because as we started the CA (civil affairs) program, it was me who wrote the stories and took the pictures and video of the events, all of which was done before CPT Morehead came into the S5 shop. Now, Morehead wants to take over those duties, and I resent that. I bought all this video and editing equipment to make a DVD for the battalion and feel like a chump. Hunts said to not stop with what I am doing with the DVD stuff and not to let things bother me.

To conclude, Slacker has quite a knack for de-motivating his subordinates. I don't usually allow things to bother me, but this whole episode does. For him to tell me not to have any more pictures taken for the newspapers is beyond me.

Six more months of this shit? Fuck me.

11:30

I was picked up by the S5 section and went out to the Ibdaa-Gryaat River Basin for a dedication ceremony with the local Iraqi community leaders. It is a site where we had an important bridge/culvert repaired. It was a joyous occasion as we took some pictures and videos with the local village leaders. A great sense of accomplishment was the common emotion for this occasion. Again, part of our strategy is to work harmoniously with the local Iraqis, which can result in a safer environment for our soldiers to conduct business.

Before	Current

An important bridge/culvert repaired near CSC Scania, Iraq.

13:30

I ate chow after returning with the S5 section, spaghetti with meatballs. I eat it without the meatballs because of my gout condition. Unfortunately, today, I am having a reaction to the malaria medicine that I took last night and have had diarrhea several times.

I got the word from MSG Moocheff, who returned from the States and is acting as the HHC First Sergeant until SFC Randerson returns from leave, that we have one more stack of awards from C Co. to push through the board this afternoon and that Slacker said that these would be the last push for this time. I realized that I had to get cracking on my awards that I was writing for Cantez and Randerson. I wrote them up this afternoon and later sat in on the awards board. All went well with the board except for 2LT O'Shannon. He got really immature when I instructed him to rewrite an award for SFC Barnum. The wording wasn't powerful enough, and he resented having to rewrite it. He really acted like a little hostile kid. I say, fuck you and do it, you little piece of shit, Second Lieutenant! That is how it is.

NOTE FROM AUTHOR: You would never find this kind of insubordination in the Marine Corps! OoRah! Unfortunately for this officer, his cocky, holier-than-now attitude followed him throughout his military career. Like they say, "You can't fix stupid!" And you can't fix this poor excuse of an Army Officer. JM

17:30

I am beat and making my way to my office. Slacker sees me and calls my name. He yells, "Corales is doing far too much on this investigation; it is your job...." (Now Slacker is dictating how I should conduct my independent investigation? Perhaps it is not so independent after all?) I replied, stating that I had been devoting a lot of time to awards.

Later, Hunts, Cantez, and I were hanging out in my office, and we talked about Slacker and how difficult he has been lately. We talked about our hooch being dirty; we bad-mouthed the mayor's cell (what else) and bagged on Slacker. Maybe it is the diarrhea, or maybe it is him, but I have had it with this poor excuse of a commander!

15 Sep 04

Good old diarrhea again. I am pretty sure this is from the chloroquine phosphate malaria medicine that we are required to take. I didn't take it while on leave and took it Monday night with only some crackers and cheese. I usually take it with a full meal. In any event, the effects are quite debilitating. I would say that I hit the latrine yesterday around a dozen times. Today was a bit better, but this morning, I really felt like staying in bed.

In this morning's BUB, there wasn't anything significant covered. The ROKs will be traveling through on the 17th, which will cause less congestion on the post and in the mess hall. We scheduled mortar missions for tomorrow night at 21:50. It appears that the postal unit will be visiting two days a week now versus once a week. This is quite good for our soldiers. Originally, we had no postal visits. The mayor's cell is also in the process of hiring some Local Nationals permanently to do various odds and ends on the post. I couldn't help but notice that SGM Moans' tent and bunker were being sandbagged by a team of around eight or nine LN's. The rest of the units on this post had to stack their own bags, and many of us even filled our own bags. I guess that the mayor's cell beats to a different drum again. There was also discussion of redeployment. We have staff members who will go to a weeklong planning conference for redeployment in Kuwait in about a week from now.

The force protection meeting following the BUB didn't amount to much. Following that meeting, I read up on the investigation that I am conducting that has to do with the shooting of a Local National at our South Check Point on the sixth of September. The base planning meeting at 13:30 also seemed very routine, with nothing significant covered.

This afternoon I had the CSM do my height and weight and tape for my paperwork for my OML Board. (In order to stay in the Army and be considered for promotions, you must meet their height and weight standards-no fat asses!) LOL The OML is the officer manning list board where the decision makers in your respective state prioritize field grade assignments of their officers. To be considered for promotional positions, you must be evaluated and listed on the state's OML. I also emailed my updated officer's biography to our S1, along with my wish list for follow-on assignments.

I received a cool email from my childhood friend:

> Hey Darby, this is for your book on what your counterparts are doing in Afghanistan. Do you remember my cousin Tim at all?
>
> I hope you are well. I think of your well-being daily, and we pray as a united nation for your safety while carrying out your mission. We are very proud of our armed forces, and I cry every time I hear the national anthem at an event. The solemn services for 9/11
>
> We're a testament to the lasting pain and significant, senseless loss here. Abroad? Well, it depends on the party you're in. I think the Democrats see our war effort as senseless. We see it as necessary. How do you see it these days, and what is your general impression of the sentiments of those who serve?
>
> Our old crew and my family all send their best regards.
>
> B.

Hello B.,

It is always a pleasure to hear from you.

I have two points of view about the bipartisanship that currently exists in our beloved country. First, as a soldier, I am bound by duty and honor to follow the orders of my superiors, hence my deep loyalties to our president, commander, and chief. So, in my capacity as a soldier fighting in a war on foreign lands, I refrain from commenting about politics. I do, however, think that it is sad that some Americans are making the war a political issue because it compromises our security and the well-being of our troops. It is downright unpatriotic! Well, there you have my two cents.

I was able to get out for a two-week R&R trip home. I got the opportunity to see our new house for the first time, which was quite exciting. Little Junior is speaking in sentences (kind of like sentences). Nina looks more like an adult every day. Annette is holding up well despite our adversity.

It is interesting to note that while traveling across the globe in uniform DCUs (desert combat uniform), I received nothing short of a VIP reception. I was upgraded to first class at the insistence of airline employees and passengers and never paid for a drink or meal. Even my rental car was a luxury vehicle at compact car prices. I truly believe that our country is behind us. I will never forget those experiences, and I brought those stories back to the troopers in the field.

The sentiments of our soldiers are in keeping with our nations to defend our rights of freedom and dignity to our fellow men/women. We see the immediate results of our occupation and efforts here, so we feel pretty good about being here. Unfortunately, the vast humanitarian efforts being accomplished every day here by soldiers/sailors/ Marines/airmen, etc., don't make the front pages. Such is life. We are past the ½-way point of being in Iraq and can't wait to get home.

Keep in touch.

Your friend,

Darby Hillcrest

16 Sep 04

May the soap opera never end! Just call this camp "Peyton Place"! (Note: Peyton Place was a novel that was later turned into a drama series. It was noted for being a small town that harbored terrible secrets and scandal among its residents.)

Is this an appropriate comparison to CSC Scania, or what?

It is 03:00, and I got up to take a pee, and I feel like absolute crap. I feel so bad from the diarrhea that I decided not to go to work on time and sleep in. At approximately 08:05, I hear at our tent's door, "knock, knock." I know what that means; there is someone out there who might not normally come in who wants to come in. It was CSM Hunts, and he informed me and Rickets, who was still sound asleep in the bed, that LTC Slacker was stomping mad like you have never seen before and that we needed to check in with him pronto. He said to prepare to take a beating. Hunts mentioned something about a driving incident with the S5 section and an altercation with the BDOC, and Slacker was furious.

I told Hunts and Rickets that my stomach was still f'd up and didn't feel so hot but that I would be there shortly. Rickets got there first and walked out of Slacker's office with a stack of sworn statements.

Castellano was seated with Slacker and, got up and left when I came in. I sat down and told Slacker that my stomach was still in turmoil, and I was sleeping in because of that. He said that the others should have said something, and then he wouldn't have yelled for you. (Yeah, right!) You need to get to the TMC and get some meds. I pulled out two bags of pills and said that I had already been there. Slacker said to go back for some stronger medicine (you see, he is always right!)

Slacker went on to inform me that there was a drunken party last night in the S5 shop and that the BDOC staff attempted to break up the party and got into an altercation with the S5 staff. Apparently, LT Fernandez pushed LT Mates of the BDOC out of the S5 trailer and that there was a fight going on in the trailer. Slacker was really pissed. He said that all officers involved in the drinking incident would have General level Article 15's. He said that Morehead and Fernandez are going down. He said that he would cancel Fernandez's promotion.

Later, I had a conversation with Rickets, and he told me that he had spoken with Morehead about the incident. I told Rickets that he couldn't speak to anyone involved with the incident without reading them their rights. Rickets plays things off like a know-it-all, but he could not fool me. He does not have a lot of experience with investigations and must be careful with this one. I told him to contact a JAG to get some ground rules and guidance and to meet with SGT Corales ASAP.

The rest of the morning, I conducted interviews for the South Check Point shooting incident from the sixth of Sep 04. A Full-Colonel from NGB (National Guard Bureau) was here visiting, and LTC Slacker had his head far up this Colonel's ass! I couldn't get a word in edgewise with him.

I had to inform 1LT Youngham that she wasn't going on a trip up to Anaconda with the S4 section this weekend. It was a convenient trip with MAJ Lukes from the Brigade S4 shop. They are an item, and the Chief of Staff, LTC Coffey, said that he does not want Youngham to visit Anaconda ever again. She was pissed! I guess I ruined her weekend plans. Frankly, I don't care if Lukes and her are an item. She is separated from her husband, and I don't know his status. As far as I am concerned, they are two grown adults and can make their own decisions.

In an Associated Press release today, an intelligence committee report to the President reported that there lies a strong possibility of civil war in Iraq before 2005 and that the situation is tenuous at best.

This evening, I received an email from a reporter from the L.A. Newspaper with a link to a National Guard story that he wrote. It is a Q&A with two of our NCO's. I was disturbed by the story because I didn't know about it ahead of time. Leave it to this reporter; he is a slippery devil.

At evening chow, I sat with LTC Slacker, who was hob-knobbing with the COL from the National Guard Bureau. CSM Hunts was also with them, and they were done eating when I sat down. They talked and talked about jerks that they had worked with in the past. It seems like this COL is recruiting officers for NGB. Slacker doesn't have a full-time job or career to speak of and has been wanting to get into the full-time Guard workforce for quite some time now. But starting out as a Lieutenant Colonel is not ordinary. However, Slacker is the ultimate kiss-ass, and he could possibly find something with NGB (located in Washington, D.C.)

This evening, Cantez returned from his trip to BIAP (Baghdad International Airport). I told him about the activities last night, and he couldn't believe it. We both can't believe how stupid the S5 guys were to have so much commotion and disruption last night. Apparently, CPT Morehead got in a fight with an English soldier. The whole situation sounds like it really is going to explode in their faces. With Article 15's, the officers' careers could be toast (finished).

As LTC Slacker stayed up late in his office brown-nosing with the NGB COL, CSM Hunts visited us in our trailer. Cantez popped in the Rob Zombie movie, "1000 Corpses." It was funny watching Hunts and SSG Kanister react to some of the violence.

I left the office late, around 21:30 or so, and hit my tent. Surprisingly enough, MAJ Rickets wasn't there playing his typical video games. This evening, he joined the KBR folks at Ali's for dinner and must have been late. I got out of my uniform and watched an episode of The Sopranos. I had the lights off and was easing into sleep mode. Rickets eventually came in, turned on the overhead light, and started up his video games on his new 30" stereo television. I have my section of the tent quartered off by several camouflaged poncho liners held up by a green cord. Needless to say, there isn't much privacy and absolutely no hearing privacy at all. After the Sopranos, I read one of my Time magazines from cover to cover. I am several weeks behind in reading Time because of my trip home. After almost an hour of reading, I turned off my light, and by then, I had the overhead light turned off, but Rickets continued with his earsplitting video game. I asked him to turn the noise off, and he responded, "I'll turn it down." Well, that wasn't the answer that I was looking for, and the time was now past midnight. After fifteen excruciating minutes of sci-fi sound effects, explosions, and guns firing, I couldn't take it anymore and asked him again to turn off the sound. He resisted, and I responded, "This isn't KALSU, and we have schedules here after 11 P. M. we need to go to headphones." Rickets replied laughingly, "I think not!" I got up and ventured out of the tent to use the restroom (which is a porta-Potti located behind the MWR tent near our tent), and as I walked out, I said, "It's frigging after midnight!" I walked around a bit as I was frustrated and getting worked up over Ricket's insensitivity. I don't like pulling rank about things like this, or anything for that matter, but Rickets is a crude man who thinks pretty much only about himself and his own needs. Just a week ago, when we were cleaning the tent, he stated, "We are going to have to move our living area into some of your area," which meant moving my space in and giving me less space. I told him emphatically no, even if the thought was disrespectful, but not to Rickets. Cantez doesn't even come into the tent any more because Rickets is so difficult to be around.

When I returned, the television and lights were out; I guess he got my drift. But I lost an hour's sleep from this bull shit as it got me worked up. I put my headphones on, listened to some heavy metal, and eventually drifted off to sleep. Thanks, Rickets, for nothing!

18 Sep 04

Payton Place, once again, as my office was graced with a visit from COL Nosey with two bottles of whiskey.

After Nosey left somehow, we got on to the topic of this place being a movie and discussed who would play us in the movie. CSM Hunts picked Tony Soprano for me, and Cantez picked Tim Robbins for me. This is a fine example of how varied points of view can be. Those two individuals are as similar as salt to pepper?

I visited the tent twice this afternoon as I was doing errands like getting a bag of ice from the Class I yard (Class I is what we refer to as food and water in the Army) and getting my laundry done. On both visits, MAJ Rickets was sound asleep in his rack. I guess if I stayed up until 01:00 playing video games, I'd need a nap too!

Class I (food, rations, and water) storage yard, CSC Scania, Iraq.

I scored big time at the Hadjie Market today by buying all five episodes of the Soprano's series on DVDs. These were in-box sets that were produced in America and top quality. All five seasons sell for $110.00, while in America, one season sells for around $90.00. I also feel better buying a DVD in a plastic DVD case that you would find in a store because you know that it isn't a bootleg copy. The bootleg copies are in flimsy plastic bags with a color poster of the DVD versus a plastic box.

15:35

I went into Slacker/Hunt's office to speak with Slacker about the soldiers involved in the drunken fighting incident in the S5 section trailer. I brought up the fact that all the soldiers and officers involved were just submitted for awards. Slacker became pissed and immediately answered, "They get their awards! I am not punishing their whole careers for one isolated incident!" I replied, "But sir, the regulation says that all promotions, awards, formal schools, etc., get put on hold pending legal actions..." Slacker interrupted, "I say push the awards forward!" I left the office. CSM was in the office at a distance, and as I walked out, I could tell what he was thinking, that I was there trying to again save Slacker's ass, and again, he rejected my advice. Slacker has no regard for Army regulations.

18:00

I just returned from chow, where it was quite crowded because the Koreans are still here on post. Today, it was quite warm, around 120 degrees. When I went to the Class, I saw the thermometer in the sun read 140.

Temperatures often reach 120 degrees in the summer months at CSC Scania, Iraq.

This afternoon we saw SGM Moans from the mayor's cell stopping the MPs that are here to escort the ROKs into their staging area. Instead of parking the four-wheeled armored personnel carriers in an area in front of the office trailers and mayor's cell where there is plenty of room, he had them crammed into a very small out-of-the-way area that required quite a bit of maneuvering. The mayor's cell strikes again.

ROK four wheeled armored personnel carriers at CSC Scania, Iraq.

Depression. Days like today really do take their toll and make you depressed. Here, we are away from anything that resembles our normal lives in America, and our so-called "leader" does everything in his power to make us miserable. I just don't get it? Slacker and I have such different leadership styles it is insane. I believe in mentoring and developing subordinates rather than harboring all the control and making all the decisions, Slacker is the opposite. He is driving us nuts! He is upset about the S5 drunken fiasco, but I say don't take it out on all of us. He knows that he will have to answer for their improper behavior because it is a bad reflection on his leadership (or lack thereof).

In the evening, after hours, I took a long-needed shower. I usually brush my teeth and often shave at night before showering. I use the Force Provider facilities on the southern portion of the LSA (Life Support Area), near the KBR living area. I find those facilities are less used and a bit nicer than the other lavatories and showers on the eastern side of the LSA. Sometimes I shower every other day, and sometimes I shower every day. It is just such a big hassle to take a shower; here is the sequence of events: I lock up my pistol and my wallet in my tent. Change out of DCU's into PT uniform with sneakers. Pack my small green laundry type of bag with shower and shaving kit, flip flops (shower shoes), clean underwear, and a small bottle of water (I don't brush my teeth with the tap water as it had its origins from the Euphrates River). Now, I strap on my rifle onto one shoulder, put the laundry bag over the other shoulder, and walk to the latrine, which is about 1/16th of a mile away from the tent and a few tents away from the shower point. I will do my business and then walk to the shower tent. From there, I do all the usual things that one does when showering; only I do it with my rifle. Not everyone takes their rifle to the shower, but I always do! I do this for two reasons: first and foremost, we are the protectors of this camp, and I feel that we must be prepared to protect this camp 24/7, at any time, day or night, and secondly, it is a Marine Corps thing. Each Marine is a rifleman, and you just don't go anywhere without it in combat. Period. I don't see how others don't follow this, but I do. So, I reversed the steps of dressing in clean underwear, putting my PT clothes back on, loading up my bag, grabbing my weapon, and returning to my tent. The time frame is thirty minutes. That is a lot of time and a big hassle, and that is why I don't take a shower every day. I do if it is in the 120-degree range and I am getting nasty, but not if I don't have to. That is what we use baby wipes for.

19 Sep 04

I slept in since it was Sunday. I saw Slacker in the mess hall at lunch, and he was in PT clothes. I heard he didn't even get into his office today, so I guess that I am safe with sleeping in until 10:30 or so. I got to the office by 11:00 and had a list of telephone messages. Some pertained to the shooting investigation that I am doing from September 6 at the South Check Point.

I conducted the Catholic service at 16:00 as the Lay Leader. I always enjoy doing that; it gives me a chance to go to church and say a few prayers for my soldiers, my family, and my parents.

Rickets confronted me today, confining in me that he was worried about his investigation and that if he starts asking where the party guys got their booze, it might lead back to our Chief Warrant Officer, that it is rumored he has gotten booze for all the staff, to include LTC Slacker. I told him to voice his concerns with Slacker and do what he thought was best.

I am really buried in paperwork. I think that I have figured out why Slacker is in such a bad mood; maybe he is afraid of something coming back to him regarding the S5 party blowout. In addition, maybe that is why he does not want SGT Corales to help us with our investigations? Corales is very experienced at this stuff and knows what to ask and look for when it comes to finding dirt.

Today was an extremely quiet day on the camp, and I believe that I was the only one working; Cantez even pointed that out?

20 Sep 04

At 08:00, COL Nosey popped his head into my office and asked me to confirm a rumor he had heard about some LNs attempting to rob truck-driving LNs on the MSR inside the wire. I quickly checked my secret computer, but nothing significant had been reported from the previous night. I made a call or two and did get confirmation of the incident for him. However, the LN's got away.

I stayed busy with my investigation. Between interruptions and meetings, I didn't make a lot of headway or as much as I would have liked. I had breakfast, the morning BUB, a light salad lunch with CSM Hunts, a 13:00 staff meeting, and an afternoon dealing with A Co.

The issue with A Co., this time, deals with the logisticians that we sent up there to help them. They were to assist with A Co's command supply discipline program and facilitate an accurate property book (logistical records - see glossary) accounting and logistical reporting and accountability. Well, they were turned away by A Co. stating that their mission and location were top secret and off limits to Brigade personnel? Well, that bullshit answer wasn't going to cut it, so I got involved, as well as Major Lukes, the Brigade S4. Then CPT Crader (the Company Commander) played dumb, stating that he didn't know about SSG Kanister and 1LT Youngham's visit (Youngham is now assisting our S4 at the request of the Brigade COS-I didn't see that one coming?) Well, we dug up several emails to the First Sergeant that stated that he was aware of the visit and expecting them. The BC told me to inform Crader that he is close to getting canned and to play ball. When I spoke to Crader, he seemed defensive and almost accusatory, asking me, "Why does Kanister even have to come up here? We didn't ask for his help." When Slacker heard that, it was the straw that broke the camel's back. Crader is getting fired as the A Co. Commander, and the 1SG is also being relieved. I like Crader a lot, but he plays too many head games and is now working in Anaconda, where he is way too close to the flagpole and can't get away with the shit that he did while at Kalsu.

The weather today was pretty hot, but nothing like the unbearable heat of July and August. The mayor's cell has been busy cleaning as their Commanding General is visiting tomorrow.

I finally sent my High School class the letter that I wrote in May and later found on 9/11. I got the idea to finally send it on the 11th of September.

NOTE FROM AUTHOR: As I am doing the final edit of this manuscript, ironically, the date in this journal entry is 9/11/2004, and today is September 11, 2023. This is a solemn day for me as it is a day of reflection. My first thought of today was that of sadness for the families of the soldiers with whom we lost in combat. My next thought was to put several American flags out on my front lawn as a show of reverence for this sacred day. My next thought was how my family was so dramatically affected by the result of 9/11: Daddy's 2-year deployment away from home. Our family, for all intense purposes, looks pretty normal on the exterior, but inside, we all have varying degrees of some sort of manifestation of PTSD (Post Traumatic Stress Disorder) (my opinion, of course.) Our family would never return to what it was prior to 9/11. God bless you all on this most somber of occasions. JM

21 Sep 04

Yesterday, I finished the south checkpoint shooting incident investigation, and today, I turned it over to SGT Corales. I am so glad to be done with that one. I rewarded myself in the afternoon by surfing the net. All kinds of stuff out there, just there for the taking.

Today, BG Cambridge visited the post. He is the COSCOM (Corps Support Command) Commanding General. Colonel Nosey, LTC Milling, and her crew all work for him, so they have been in a rare form of late. I had never seen so much fuss for one individual before. Not us; when a general visits us, it is business as usual.

Today, I ate lunch with Slacker and LTC Z, the female college professor and stress management consultant. It was a boring lunch for me because, frankly, Slacker is a bore. Unless you like hearing Slacker talk about Slacker, then you are in luck.

Cantez and I have been making light of our third roommate, MAJ Rickets. He went to bed pretty early last night, around 22:00. He got up at 08:00 and was back in the rack by 09:00 and slept half the day? He gets more sleep than anyone else on the post! We make light of the fact that when the guys were up at KALSU, they didn't have any other adult supervision, and most staffers slept all the time. They remind me of my cat at home; he sleeps all day!

27 Sep 04

I will address my trip to Doha, Kuwait, shortly, but foremost on my mind is the MAYOR'S CELL. Upon my return to work this morning, I immediately checked in with 1SG Villa to check on the status of our lumber request for our putting green. Lo and behold, Villa said that my request was "shot down." The reasoning was that the golf course and putting green needed to go through a base planning committee for approval. More red tape! I am about to lose my mind and am staying away from the mayor's top idiots as I just might hit one of them!

Exhausted from the trip, having a total of six or seven hours of sleep in the past two nights and, traveling from Kuwait up to Anaconda (Balad, Iraq), and driving down to Scania last night.

Another mayor's cell issue, the September 2004 issue of the Scania Gazette, came out, and did one of my three submitted articles make the cut? No! I guess they weren't good enough for this sophomoric publication? I sent a nice email to MAJ Wanda Freakins.

> Hello Wanda,
>
> How are things?
> I returned from leave and was immediately sent on a

redeployment IPR down in Kuwait. I just got back from that. The IPR was fairly productive.

We haven't had a chance to talk much with our conflicting schedules. How is your Scania Gazette coming along? Could you use any of the stories that I sent you?

I'd like to get together with you when it is convenient to discuss future possible stories.

Let me know when that would be convenient.

I hope you had a nice time with your family during your leave; I certainly did. My three-year-old is now potty trained and talking in sentences. He is all grown up. When we deployed, he was in diapers and only saying a few words here and there.

Well, take care and keep in touch.

Darby Hillcrest

Before I went on leave, I sent her these stories and asked her if she used them not to edit them. The letter was very cordial and polite. I don't get these people? Are we at war with the Iraqis or with ourselves?

This afternoon, I spent two hours moving our furniture into our small, cramped tent. CSM Hunts was able to get us dressers made along with a coffee table. Even the KBR nitwits (American civilian contractors) said that Hunts must have had a lot of pull to get this request completed, as they aren't supposed to do these types of projects. I really had a tough time listening to this KBR dude that goes by the name of "Hillbilly." He spoke like a typical union dude. Fuck these assholes! Do they forget that we soldiers are the ones protecting his sweet ass? Dumb fucks, all of them.

Here is my Hell.

I just peeked in on the S1, CPT Randerson, and I asked to see what Slacker wrote for my OER (Officer Evaluation Report). It wasn't very well written at all. There was basically nothing of an outstanding nature to this OER. I don't think it has to do so much with his attitude for me thinking that I didn't perform well. I think it is due to his lack of experience in writing

OERs. This isn't the first time I have seen this with M-Day Officers (part-time soldiers-weekend warriors). To add insult to injury, CPT Randerson had the Senior Rater (SR) blocks selected, and they were not selected as the top rating! First of all, those blocks are for the SR to mark and should ALWAYS be left blank. Slacker had me checked off as average and not above average in his rater's section. For the rater, it is quite customary to give the officer an above-average rating, as there is no limit to how many above-average ratings he can give out. However, this is not so with senior raters (SR). The SRs are strictly regulated on the number of top blocks that they can give out; only 1/3 (or 24%) can receive this top rating. So, for the rater, it is understood that if you want the guy promoted, choose above average. Again, he doesn't have a lot of experience in these administrative matters. I should have written this one myself and let him approve it. Fuck me. It was the hardest military tour in my life, and I got the worst written OER in my life? Is this fair, God? Just get me home in one piece, please, God.

Slacker is absolutely the worst officer that I have ever worked for!

I will have to go about this one in a diplomatic manner. I gave so much information about my achievements in my OER support form, and he didn't use much of it at all? I put down quantifiable statistics, and he didn't use them? I don't get it? I am so fucking frustrated I could scream.

Another possibility is that he is jealous of me. Sometimes, these insecure types like to keep you down to make themselves shine? The jealousy perspective reminds me of an officer that I had the displeasure of working with over the years, Ike Weanie. He was a flaming fucking red-headed prick that was the quintessential backstabbing officer who tried everything in his power to make his peers (me) look bad. If he spent half of that energy forging cooperative relationships, Ike could have been a real leader. But he did not and is not a leader. Don't get me wrong, Ike is intelligent and a hard worker, but watch out, he will fuck you every time if you are any kind of competition for him. Hell, he will probably make GO someday (General Officer). *Good guys in the National Guard don't always finish first!*

I digress; back to Slacker...we are both Armor Officers in the same organization and only two to three years apart in date of rank. When it comes time for higher promotions and assignments, we will be in competition with one another someday. They only have so many Colonel and General slots in the state. I can only hope that I am wrong on this account and blame the lousy OER on Slacker's inexperience. However, Slacker is a smart man, and it is quite possible that this is his long-range plan for me. I am at the end of my rope! *(Much more to follow on this subject in* **COMBAT JOURNAL** *Part 4 of 4.)*

AUTHOR'S NOTE: About Slacker's jealousy of me runs deep. Very deep. I think it has to do with my job and his lack of a job or career. He has desperately attempted to apply for full-time National Guard permanent positions (AGR, State Active Duty, etc.) to no avail. The organization just isn't equipped financially to hire Lieutenant Colonels for entry-level positions. You could literally hire three Sergeants or two Lieutenants for the price of one Lieutenant Colonel. The fact that I have a secure and permanent AGR position really gets under Slacker's skin. This is my assessment. It is difficult to fathom why someone hates you so much, but this makes some sense to me. Very similar to my sister and all her psychodrama. My wife and daughter informed me of how my mother told them how jealous Sherry was of me and for her entire life, ever since I was a baby. I guess I was blind to this as I always respected and loved my sister dearly.

ADDITIONAL NOTE FROM AUTHOR: It is interesting to note that the issues I just raised have actually given me a plethora of storylines for the motion picture concept behind this **COMBAT JOURNAL**. *My sister has inadvertently helped me develop quite a prolific storyline to put on the big screen. This week, I wrote the synopsis for the screenplay, and the subplot wrote itself, the jealous sister. It is almost amusing how ironic life can come full circle.*

I just checked my OER support form, and I was right. It is full of good contributions that weren't alluded to in the Slacker's version. I have concluded that I need to speak with CSM Hunts and ask for his advice. I think that the ticket might be to write up my own version and give it to him to read. I am so fucking upset!

Annette reminded me that it was my mother-in-law's birthday, so I gave her a quick call. She was pretty happy to have gotten my call. I told her to tell the family that I was asking for them, and she said that she loved me. That meant a lot to me tonight.

28 Sep 04

Just in, hot off the presses! Word has it that LTC Emma Milling (aka: bitch from hell Mayor of Scania) is pregnant! OMG! There is some confirmation to the rumors as she has been in hiding for the last almost two months now. HOLLY COW BATMAN!!! I guess when I was gone, things really heated up around here regarding her pregnancy.

About the OER, I am rewriting my version and will present it to Slacker.

Slacker went to Baghdad with SGM Westminster to meet with LTG Gloom, the Chief of the National Guard Bureau. CSM Hunts and I had a long talk about the OER Slacker situation. I rewrote my OER and will have a talk with Slacker when he gets back.

Up at 0700, SOS (shit on the shingles-slang for creamed chip beef on toast-a standard in Army cuisine), omelet & fruit, work at 0800. Wrote my letter to the OML Board and my version of my OER. I reviewed some staff work and checked emails. I received my two large (50 lbs.) care packages from home and will open them tomorrow. Later in the day, I spoke with LTC Z for a while about my OER problem. She is a good listener.

Last night, I read a book about a guy who claims to have produced a film shot on DV (digital video) for $99.00. The book was pretty good, but I could have written it myself. Tonight, I am reading; "Rebel Without a Crew," another filmmaking book.

29 Sep 04

Another very hectic day! Up early couldn't sleep. Ate chow, but no eggs cooked to order were available, so I ate a bunch of fruit. Maybe not the best choice since I have been literally shitting my brains out for the last 24 hours. I finished tweaking my recommended OER comments for Slacker and got a quick salad lunch in before the military media showed up. I met them near my office and introduced myself. We all immediately clicked; heck, we have so much in common. I took them up on the roof of the BDOC and pointed out the camp to them. They were an NGB PAO Major, a TechSGT USAF Reporter, a PAO NCO, another Senior Airman USAF Combat Camera - DVD CAM, and a SGT USMC Reporter and Still Photographer. I escorted them to my office and let them use our phone and eventually took them to chow. We spoke a bit about my college film and television background and my writing interests. Following chow, we joined up with the S5 Section and walked out of the Smythe Gate for a bridge dedication at the village just behind our camp.

Bridge dedication ceremony near CSC Scania, Iraq.

It was a wonderful photo opportunity, and the PAO folks ate it up. The S5 guys put up a dedication sign; we took pictures with their staff and Allie, the local businessman whose life would remind you of an episode of the Sopranos. Later, the Mayor of Ashamali arrived, and we took more pictures. The PAO staff were absolutely astounded by how wonderful the atmosphere was in our area and camp. He had never experienced the Iraqi people who liked the American soldiers before now.

That night, we went to Shiekh Hatim's for a grand Iraqi dinner. What a wonderful experience.

Shiekh's castle. (NOTE: MAJ Hillcrest's brother-in-law's father was originally from Iraq, and his family actually knew this Shiekh.)

30 Sep 04

Another day off to a fast-paced start. I linked up with the PAO staff at breakfast. Apparently, SGT Freedom last evening invited them to come out with the S5 guys on a mission. The PAO staff agreed; however, I didn't even know about it. This kills me that guys like Freedom have such big fucking balls to make side deals without involving the chain of command and going through channels. The PAO staff didn't even mention it to me? Well, fuck, everyone! I try and I try to do things right and by the book, but a lot of soldiers cut side deals, particularly with the media. Most of them like being in the news, and that is cool, I just like to do things in accordance with Army policy.

I got an email from my wife today informing me that my best buddy Saul is getting orders for the Kosovo mission. Poor bastard is going as a Sergeant. He was a First Lieutenant in the USMC back in the 1980s. It is too bad that he couldn't go as an officer; I think he has a lot to offer the National Guard, and they are limiting his potential.

We are expecting the Governor of the Babil Provence, Waleed Amraan, to visit us today along with Ashamali Mayor Amir Malik Lehaymus. We will have a meeting with the BC and S5 staff when they arrive, and the PAO folks will cover it.

I asked the PAO reps to go out with our roving patrols this morning in addition to going with the CA guys. I was only able to convince the Marine Sergeant to go with them. It figures since it is the HUA type of infantry stuff. The Marine went with our SSG's crew, the same crew that I did the dismounted patrol with, so I know that he is in good hands. I later hooked the Marine reporter up with an interview with CPT Castellano to discuss the force protection mission here at Scania.

Temperatures are dropping, usually hovering around 80 at 07:00 in the morning. Today, it was around 77 degrees, and I almost needed a light jacket or sweater.

Today, I wrote my 11th essay and did my normal XO duties: OERs, 15-6 (investigation) about troops talking to the LA Paper without command authorization or knowledge.

14:20

I wrote a small note to CSM Hunts. The note asked him what kind of mood LTC Slacker was in because I needed to speak to him about my OER revision. Hunts knew that this was very important to me and that it is generally a touchy issue with officers. He told me that it was a good time and that he was in an okay mood. I later returned to his office, asking if he was busy. He looked like he was goofing around on the internet as he waved me in. I sat down, and he generated some small talk.

I then brought up the subject of loyalty and how important I thought that was and that I didn't want to piss him off. He said that I could talk to him about anything (really?) I mentioned that I had certain strengths and certain weaknesses. Slacker was very receptive as the PAO Officer had just been in his office and bestowed upon him praises of our CA program, our PAO program, and, in particular, me as the PAO POC. Anyway, I went on, and we talked about how much experience I had in writing OERs from my various OIC (Officer in Charge) positions and as the Deputy G1 (Division Personnel Officer). He agreed and said that I really was good at that and good at almost everything. *(Shit, if that is the case, then put it in my evaluation, you idiot!)*

I then told him that I had a problem that was really bothering me and that I wanted to speak to him about it. He said go ahead. I told him that the OER that he wrote could almost end my career and most certainly stop an early promotion. He immediately took offense to my comment and disagreed. (Now it is getting personal and veering away from professional.) We went on to discuss his point of view about OERs. I said to myself that I was doomed, as he just didn't have the experience that he thought he had. I told him about raters, and he told me about his theories of raters and how to rate, Outstanding Performance-Must promote, or Satisfactory Performance-Promote. I told him that as the full-time Deputy G1, I sat in on promotion boards with Colonels and Generals as the scribe (secretary taking notes) and saw firsthand how they made decisions. They look at OERS for senior officers (field grades) with time in grade in mind. First, a rater can have any number of Must Promote OERs that they rate, unlike the Senior Rater, who is restricted to only one-third (24%) of their officers and can have a "top block" (the highest rating). As an unwritten rule of thumb, they reserve that for field grade officers who have more time in grade than their peers and are closer to promotion. I told Slacker that the promotion board officers look at field grade officers getting a "promote" versus a "must promote" as the rater telling the board not to promote this guy. It is an inflated system, as it is in the Marine Corps (even more so), but nevertheless, it is the way it is. Slacker sighted some of his OERS as an example, and he says, "Presto here I am, a Battalion Commander, and made it to Lieutenant Colonel." I mentioned that I was an AGR (Active Guard Reserve Officer) and that this was my full-time job. I also mentioned that this is a combat tour OER, and that has much more significance, especially how well you performed under this kind of pressure. I don't think he was seeing the light. I also mentioned that the most important lines in the OER were the first line of the Rater comments and the last line. You must hit them hard; "MAJ ____ is an outstanding officer (or not so outstanding officer), etc. End the comments with similar strong language; "Promote this officer now!" He at least listened to that one without further confrontation.

Here is what is killing me. He said that he was planning on top blocking me on my last OER? Why then and not now? He believes that we are now doing "great stuff," and it will be recognized. I told him that I don't like to put the cart before the horse and that anything could happen between now and next March; an IED could get me, a drunk fuck could start a fight, a Hadjie could run me over with their truck, etc. I really have concerns about this guy and his methods. Here we are in the middle of a fucking warzone, a million miles away from our families, and this guy is fucking with his number two man? I don't get it. Not a smart move. He has lost any loyalty that I might have had for him, which was only out of respect for his rank and position, not from him.

Slacker said that he would look at what my recommendations were but wasn't promising anything. I emailed him my revised OER about an hour later.

Upon my departure, I returned to my office. CSM Hunts could see from my expression that things didn't go well. I asked to speak with him alone outside. I vented to him, mentioning that Slacker just doesn't have the experience with OERs, and he is truly making a horrific mistake with my career in the balance! I mentioned that I have never had a bad OER in my 18 years of military service and only had one OER with a "promote" vice "must promote" and that that was from a guy just like Slacker, a part-timer who didn't know much at all about OERs. I mentioned that I have written hundreds and hundreds of OERs and know what is required. I also mentioned that I insist on having the words "COMBAT OPERATIONS" and "OPERATION IRAQI FREEDOM" mentioned in my OER, and that just must be there. How in the fuck could he not know to do this?

In summation, here I am in the combat zone, apparently doing a pretty darn good job, and there is no mention in my OER from Slacker that this is a wartime combat zone Operation Iraqi Freedom Officer Evaluation. My friends, you be the judge?

I spoke with CPT Morehead about the situation without going into specifics, and he 100% concurs with me. (CPT Morehead has previous experience as a former AGR Officer, which implies that he probably has a good handle on Officer Evaluation Records and other administrative matters.)

I am officially at the end of my rope!

1 Oct 04

I was up early today, around 05:00. Today was daylight savings time, and no one remembered, and I didn't even know about it. I am experiencing a sinus infection, so I took an allergy pill that wakes you up. So, unfortunately, I couldn't go back to sleep. After laying there for an hour thinking about how I hate Slacker's fucking guts because of my OER situation, I got up at six. I did the normal shaving and brushing my teeth thing and made my way to the chow hall. Thank goodness they have eggs cooked to order again (the supply trucks must have arrived since yesterday). I saw Slacker, and of course, as a loyal XO, I am obligated to sit with him (just shoot me, please). My worst meals in theater have been while seated with this egomaniac. He never shuts up about himself and has no clue as to people's perception of him!) Even the reporters said to keep him away from the other press because he was rude and obnoxious. That is the absolute truth, too. It took every ounce of energy for me to sit next to him this morning. Other than a hello, not a word was spoken. He didn't stay very long; you could tell that he was not comfortable. He said something about the eggs and left. My sinuses are full and killing me. I don't think that I will join the CA guys on a mission this afternoon; I just don't feel good.

I have never been this depressed in my life. Perhaps when my dad died and my mother too maybe. Here is the way I see things: I have more responsibility than anyone else in this battalion, with the exception of the Battalion Commander. I have worked the longest hours and have done a pretty stellar job, so I have been told (by Slacker-CSM, etc). Why, then, is my OER an issue? Why wouldn't Slacker automatically put me as MUST PROMOTE (top raters block-highest rating) rather than PROMOTE (middle block-which is between MUST PROMOTE and UNSATISFACTORY PERFORMANCE, DO NOT PROMOTE)? He knows that I will be eligible to be promoted to Lieutenant Colonel at the conclusion of this deployment, and that is my desire. He just doesn't get it. I have concluded that if he doesn't change the OER to suit my opinions, I will call COL Raskins and consult with him. He writes the best OERs that I have read in the Division. He is a career AGR Infantry Officer who is a War College graduate. He commands a Brigade in our state and is a very, very intelligent man. He also is a voice of reason, objective and a superb mentor for guys like Slacker and me. He will tell Slacker that he is wrong and that I am right, but I hope that it doesn't have to come to that. Slackers will hold a grudge. Believe me, I will forever hold a grudge, no matter what the outcome. I am furious.

*NOTE FROM AUTHOR: Unfortunately for MAJ Hillcrest, this won't be the last OER incident with LTC Slacker. More to follow on this subject in further volumes of **AMERICAN HISTORY, A VETERAN'S PERSPECTIVE**.*

12:12

I just read the headlines on the internet regarding a coalition offensive that took place yesterday about 90 miles north of Baghdad in the city of Samarra. Some eighty Iraqis were killed, and another 100 were injured as the military fought to take back the town from anti-coalition forces. Also in the news was the first presidential debate, and it is said that Senator Kerri did well. However, I liked President Bush's comment concerning Mr. Kerri's line about how he described the Iraq war as a terrible mess. The President asked how troops could follow a commander and chief who would have a point of view like that.

Today, we will promote 1LT Artera. At 12:30, I am joining the S5 (civil affairs) for lunch with the Ashamali Mayor and will do another sign dedication.

From the first question Thursday night, Kerry went on the offensive, accusing Bush of leaving U.S. alliances around the world "in shatters" and ordering a war in Iraq that was a "colossal error in judgment."

Bush noted that Kerry voted to authorize the same war he now criticizes. "That's not how a commander in chief acts," Bush charged.

12:30 I went with the CA team to Mayor Amir Atim's house for a wonderful lunch. I dropped off three large boxes of goods: school supplies, first aid and toiletries, and pogy bate.

15:45

We returned from a bridge dedication.

16:00

LT Artera was promoted in LTC Slacker's office. I took pictures and videos.

16:15 - 20:00

I helped CPT Randerson write a response for LTC Slacker regarding a Congressional complaint that a PFC filed. He wants to go home and is saying that he needs to care for his mother.

My head is splitting, and I feel sick as a dog.

I got a great email from MAJ Corrigan:

Slacker instructs me to share this with the guys...

Sent: Friday, October 01, 2004 5:48 PM
To: CO, Armor Batallion
Cc: XO, Armor Battalion
Subject: Thank you for the invite to visit your troops!

Sir,

Thank you for the invite to visit your troops, dine with the sheik, and get a firsthand impression of your highly successful CMO operations. The trip far exceeded my expectations!

It is clear that you have the right people, working the right mission and giving them the top cover needed to be successful. I was particularly impressed with MAJ Darby Hillcrest (his media savvy, professionalism, and enthusiasm) and LT Fernandez & SGT Freedom (their CMO insight, vision, and genuine care for the Iraqi people.) Also, your enlisted drivers and security guys were great - professional and on the ball.

The strong bridges your team has built with the Iraqi people is a great news story that needs to be told around the world! I will do all I can to tell that story and get the media to visit - short of tying them up and throwing them on a Blackhawk.

VR

MAJ Corrigan
"It's Baghdad - Brother!"
Major Corrigan
Chief, Media Operations
MNC-I Public Affairs

I sent this out to our guys:

ALCON (all concerned),

I would like to personally thank all members of the AR BN for their efforts in making this happen. Below is an email sent from the NG's media representative here in theater. The success of our Civil Affairs and Public Affairs programs here at CSC Scania is a direct result of all the battalion's force protection and support efforts. Each and every soldier within the AR BN here at Scania is to be congratulated for their support of our mission. Keep up the good work.

Regards,

Major Hillcrest
Executive Officer
Armor Battalion
CSC Scania, Iraq

LTC Slacker received the following email from Major Corrigan:

I included the above-sited email. Could things be looking up? *We will see my friends, we will see.*

2 Oct 04

06:50

At South CP (Check Point), a vehicle started to enter the barrier, and they fired three shots into the barrier. Nine LN's coming from Diwaniyah to Karbala. The vehicle was stopped, searched, and released.

I woke up with a bad sinus cold. After taking some sinus pills, I shaved, brushed my teeth, and showered. The Army calls the shower units Force Provider Units, and they are enclosed in a metal container that could be placed on the back of an eighteen-wheeler truck. The Army then attaches a large tent to the front of it for the soldiers to use as a changing area. There are about twenty showers and twenty sinks in this unit, so forget about any kind of privacy. Heck, privacy went out the window that minute that we reported for duty at our home station Armories.

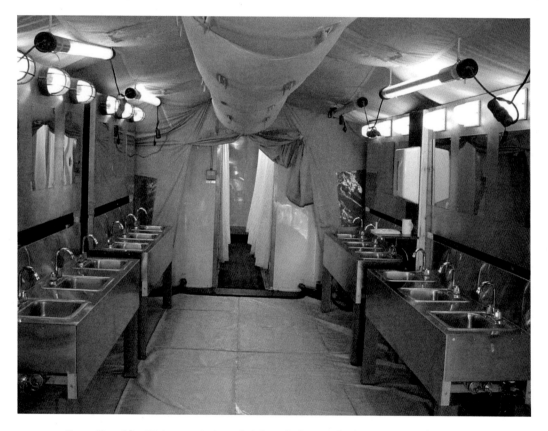

Force Provider Units consisting of sink and shower facilities at CSC Scania, Iraq.

Slacker dropped into my office today, and he acted in a conspicuous manner. He was too jovial. He said that he was in contact with COL Raskins about my OER. He said that Raskins said that the verbiage was good and warranted a top block by the Rater. He was making that change and attempted to explain himself for not doing so originally? I told him that it was imperative that all OERs state the words "Combat Operations or Combat Duty." He said that this OER only had one month of twelve in combat. I told him it didn't matter if it was one day of the OER; it was still combat action, away from home, etc., and that we need to recognize that for all the Officers and NCOs on their evaluations, he and I included. We left that conversation open-ended. I will fight to at least have those words added to the OER. I told him that that would be one of the only factors that would distinguish us from our peers. He went on about who California picked for War College, and he wasn't happy because he wasn't on the list. This conversation isn't over.

16:00

We had a promotion ceremony for LT Mates. I took pictures of the event which we held in the conference room. I later caught up on emails to the Stars and Stripes reporter as well as On Guard Magazine.

1510

Our MPs report two dump trucks rolled up and are burning on the MSR Vic 2B. No injuries, LN drivers. KBR Recovery 1 was sent out. H33 administered aid for slight injuries.

1738

H33/34 reports the trucks have been cleared off the road, but 6-7" of gravel remains. Notified MCT and South CP that southbound traffic must use caution.

3 Oct 04

Still sick with a sinus infection and feel miserable. It occurred to me last night that when Slacker spoke with me about my OER, he only talked about the OER that he wrote. He didn't mention my version. I bet that he didn't share that version with COL Raskins? WTF??? I think that I will send it to him anyway; I'll call it ODP (Officer Development Program).

I stuck my head into Slacker's office trailer, and he suckered me into a conversation. He said, "Sit down," I thought, shit, I'll be here for hours! Whenever CSM Hunts goes away, Slacker is by himself, and I guess he boars himself to death? I am stuck listening to his stories now, "Gees, thanks, Sergeant Major Hunts!" Slacker went on to discuss his disappointment with the California Army National Guard for not recommending him for one of their two War College slots. *(I believe that Slacker wants to attend the resident War College because it would give him almost an entire year of employment, more so than just creating upward mobility for his military career - the dude doesn't have a job!)* He later mentioned that, unlike him, I actually had other careers to fall back on if I didn't have the military. I told him that I had some offers but that I liked my AGR job and wanted to see it through to retirement. I said that I might write a book or make a film someday in my free time. I also told him that the Mayor of Ashamali and his people asked if I could come into their schools and give a lecture on Hollywood and show business. I thought that it would be good PR.

I arranged for Juliana, of the Stars & Stripes magazine, to visit our camp and do several stories. I emailed our state PAO in reference to the S & S coverage. CPT Laylock is also bringing the LA Paper here in a week or so.

0150

LZ was secured for medevac of TCN with chest pains.

0201

SEC 1 reports that 3 TCNs (Third Country National) were stopped at the MCT (Movement Control Team) shack for being intoxicated. Hunters 6 and 7 wrote banishment papers on them.

0402

Unannounced Chinooks landed on the MSR with 7 PAX. We were not able to make radio contact with them.

As you can tell from these reports, it was a very noisy night. Several Marine Corps choppers (helicopters) landed in our compound. Apparently, the 11 MEU will be passing through in the next two days.

4 Oct 04

The weather is still hot but cooler at night and in the early morning. I am just now starting to wear a PT windbreaker in the early morning. This morning, I wrote up a letter of input for 1LT Manalo, the medical services officer who failed to report for duty when we mobilized through Ft. Lewis, WA. He is up for promotion, and the State of California wanted our input. He eventually, like three months after us, reported to the Forward Support Battalion for duty, but we haven't seen him here in theater.

1034   Green 1 reports SP for Operation Trojan Horse. South CP detained one Blue Bongo truck/ supplier with contraband (Bongo trucks have the cabs on top of the engine compartment in the front of the vehicle and are quite common in this region). Three LNs were taken to IP. No other traders or TCNs picked up due to a lack of traders on wire.

Bongo truck in Central South Iraq, 2004.

1103

Blue Bongo truck unloaded traders on the west access road and was detained at the south checkpoint with contraband (alcohol, Viagra, and hashish). Traders turned the contraband over to the IPs.

13:00

Staff calls with the Battalion staff. I made the mistake of informing Slacker at lunch that I had to go to my staff meeting because, twenty minutes later, he walked into the meeting. This is supposed to be a staff meeting, where the staff flushes out issues with me, the XO. It is not a command and staff, which includes commanders. Slacker doesn't understand that by doing these things, he undermines my authority. This is a way of business with Slacker. You could see in the staff members' eyes their displeasure at having him there asking mundane, pointless questions of them. You can see the lack of respect these officers have for Slacker. He is the commander by default but hasn't earned anyone's respect. Slacker strikes again. You see, when CSM Hunts isn't around to keep him amused and occupied, stuff like this happens.

1900-2200 Roving patrols conducted vehicle checkpoints throughout our area of operations with nothing significant to report.

1732

H31 informed that the IP Colonel in Shumali has intel on the Mahdi Army operating in the Hilla AO (Area of Operations - the area around the military compound) with the intent to place IEDs. This coincides with intel the S2 gathered from a source at South CP this morning. The IP Col also said that the brick factory workers in Kiev are making explosives and that he needs more evidence to convict. IP Colonel will come to Smythe Gate tomorrow to speak to H6.

0005

MPs informed us that there was a drunk TCN detained at the MCT shack.

He was placed in the detention cell. We took his wallet and keys. His passport was not found. He's presumably a PWC subcontractor (logistical services).

Following evening chow, which I ate at around 19:00 or so, I surfed the internet and watched part of a B-Movie that I bought while home on leave. I picked up several movie sets from Best Buy that had ten movies in one set for a nominal cost of fifteen dollars. I like seeing these types of movies since they are not too far from what I worked on in college. Later that night, I went to the tent where, much to my surprise, I found MAJ Rickets reading in bed? He has his ritual of playing X-Box at a nauseating decibel level at all hours of the night. He said that he wanted to get rested up for his trip to the City of Hilla tomorrow. I read a book called "How to Write a Movie in 21 Days" and watched an episode of The Sopranos. All is quiet in the camp these days, and it is nice to have these types of relaxing evenings.

5 Oct 04

I got up at my normal 06:45, did the shaving thing, sorted some laundry, dressed, and went to chow. They must have been out of fresh eggs, as there were no eggs cooked to order this morning. Or they are expecting a surge of people and didn't set it up. So, I bypassed the eggs and had oatmeal and fruit with the BDOC NCOIC, MSG Rasper. The dude smelled like it had been a few days since he showered? I guess he has been busy? Most of the staff are gone today to Hilla or Bucca or on leave. I told SSG Kanister, "With all the staff gone today, it should be quiet, except that the Colonel has no one else to fuck with but us." Holly cow, as I said that, Slacker walked in. I just started laughing. I don't think he heard me, and honestly, I could care less if he did. He made small talk with Kanister and then left. I am still furious about my OER and won't let it go. I want to call COL Raskins to discuss it. I am certain that Slacker only showed him his version of my OER and not my proposed version. I want him to see it. I insist that OER have the words "combat operations" and "Operation Iraqi Freedom" in it when the OER rating period covered the time when we were here in theater. To omit this is an injustice, and I won't allow it for any of the officers. I am furious. *(Folks, you have seen nothing yet! Just wait for* **COMBAT JOURNAL** *4 of 4 and see how things get even worse for MAJ Hillcrest by the actions of LTC Slacker.)*

11:00

Slacker just busted into my office in a confrontational manner, announcing to me that only he would sign off on any board packets going out of the battalion for promotions for officers. I said, "Is there a problem? He said that there were blank PT cards and body fat worksheets floating around, and he didn't want any "pencil whipping" of any documents for promotions. I replied, "Sir, the only packets that I am aware of are yours, mine, and Cantez's? Is there a specific problem that you have heard of regarding this?" Slacker, "No, I don't know all who is up for boards (bullshit), but I don't want any pencil whipping of documents." I said it sounds like Randerson has something to do with this. Slacker, "No, he didn't say anything to me about this." (Bullshit) I said that if I was aware of anything, I would let him know. I also said that I would let the staff know. Slacker went on to say, "Some of the people around here's integrity isn't what I thought it was." This is a direct insinuation that I have some integrity issues. It is no coincidence that yesterday I asked CPT Randerson for a PT card and a body fat worksheet? Randerson has some loyalty issues and will be counseled by me for his trend of incompetence. This is the final straw for me and Randerson. He has blown my trust and confidence. (Keep in mind that Sergeant First Class Dwellers works in Randerson's office, and later, we discovered that he was a "snitch" for LTC Slacker.) As for Slacker, he ceases to amaze me. Forget that we have mobilized for 18 months, pulled away from our loved ones and family, and thrown into a combat zone, where we have not only taken on many casualties but have encountered four combat fatalities! And Slacker is making an issue about a PT test score's accuracy for a future promotion from here in the combat zone? Is it me, or is there something wrong here? I think that he doesn't want to see me promoted so quickly behind him as I will be his future competition. He knows that he can't compare with me because everyone he works with thinks he is a FUCKING ASSHOLE! Granted, I haven't won any popularity contests or anything, but I do tend to get along with the people that I work with. There are always exceptions, but I think that I do okay in this respect. I think Slacker is jealous. Well, enjoy the power and control now because once we are out of here, let the truth be told! The truth of his lack of leadership ability and that he is a chicken shit will spread like wildfire, and it won't have to come from me. The troops know, as do all the officers. Just let nature take its course. As is the current demise of LTC Milling (getting pregnant in the combat zone-good one, Norma!), just yesterday, CPT Artera (he was promoted this week) mentioned at dinner, "People like Milling and Slacker, and the way they act and treat people, they always get theirs in the end. They end up fucking themselves by their own accord." Boy, I couldn't agree more.

NOTE FROM AUTHOR: CPT Artera is wise beyond his years. Who knows what is in store for the future of LTC Slacker? Will karma play into the situation? We will see my friends, we will see.

It is funny; in some ways, I have to thank Slacker for being such a buffoon, as he is filling my pages with a plethora of entertainment for my readers. Let's see, who could play him in the Hollywood movie version of this book? Hmmmmm.

16:00

I got a fucked-up email from the Brigade PAO OIC and then later another from CPT Laylock that actually went to LTC Slacker first. This email was in reference to a Stars & Stripes reporter who was trying to get to Scania to cover our Civil Affairs program.

From: PAO OIC
Sent: Tuesday, October 05, 2004 2:10 PM
To: Kloster F. Killman
Cc: LTC Slacker
Subject: AR BN

BG Killman,

Sir, MNCI HQs asked me today about this Stars & Stripes activity. I was a bit embarrassed because, as the PAO, I was unable to acknowledge this important aspect of our mission.

R/

PAO OIC

Fucken dick, the PAO OIC. I sent them an email about a recent PAO visit and that the S & S visit hadn't been confirmed. Then Laylock sends this infuriating email:

Sir,

I sent an email to Major Hillcrest and haven't heard back from him regarding the LA Paper embed. Is he around? If not, is there someone else you'd like me to coordinate with? I have many questions and need to coordinate on your behalf ASAP. I apologize for having to go straight to you, but I don't have any other contacts besides you and the XO.

The embeds are arriving on 9 Oct, and I am trying to get there on 8 Oct. I need to finalize a plan in case I don't make it there on time.

Thank you,

CPT Laylock

Fucken bitch! She did this same shit before. If she doesn't have things exactly her way all the time, she always goes over my head to Slacker. Of course, she was wrong again, and I forwarded the email that I sent her to Slacker. Dumb bitch! I guess they haven't figured out that we get along just fine without the brigade's "so-called" assistance. We call that meddling!

Today, we received quite alarming intelligence that we are going to be heavily mortared this Friday evening. A credible local came up to the south checkpoint with this information. Our interpreters said that he was very frightened. He had gotten the info through a relative that the Madi Army was going to pay Iraqis that lived around FOB KALSU to come down here and mortar the hell out of us and get paid some $10,000.00 for it! Castellano drove up to KALSU to coordinate with the Marine Corps unit there. Things are heating up.

Good news: CSM Hunts just returned from his trip to Bucca Prison. Apparently, there were some illegal activities going on with some of his NCOs, and he went to conduct an investigation and cleaning of the house.

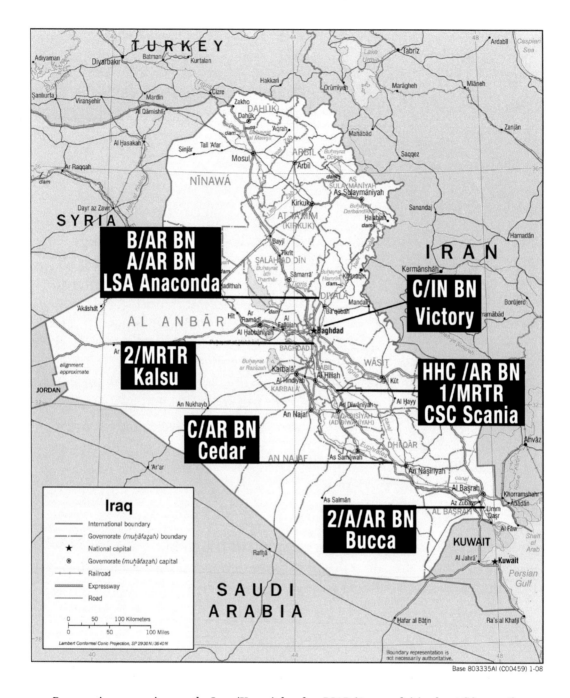

Bucca prison camp is near the Iraq/Kuwait border. BIAP (Anaconda) is about fifteen miles northwest of Baghdad. Map by John J. McBrearty. Source: The World Factbook, CIA Maps.

I got confirmation that Juliana from the Stars & Stripes will be taking a convoy from BIAP (Baghdad International Airport) at 18:00. I arranged to get her a VIP (Very Important Person) trailer.

Today, I also emailed my military biography and next assignment wish list to COL Raskins and the COS back in California. Fuck Slacker, I am not waiting for him to submit anything for us or me. They asked me to send it, and I sent it! Fuck, Slacker! Do we see a trend here?

Further emails from Laylock: what is her problem?

> Major Hillcrest,
>
> Please excuse my previous email to LTC Slacker asking about your whereabouts. I just transferred my email account over to Outlook yesterday and was blocked from sending and receiving emails for most of today, which I didn't know until a few moments ago.
>
> I am in receipt of two emails you sent in regard to my first inquiry – thank you for your timely response.
>
> I have been trying to call you and need to get in contact with you immediately. My main concern is that you contacted the LA Paper reporter directly, and that is not what needed to happen. There are issues I have with what you sent him. Please cease further direct contact with him until we have had a chance to tie off.
>
> My DSN (Defense Service Network) phone number is xxx-xxxx. If you can, try to call me as well. I keep getting a busy signal when I try to call you, but I will continue to try until I get through.
>
> It is 1730hrs, and I am off to dinner and have other projects to follow up on this evening away from the office. I will try to call you first thing in the morning.
>
> Thank you,
>
> CPT Laylock

Fuck me, ladies and gentlemen! Fuck me!

After chow this evening, I signed up for the key to the Distinguished Visitors Quarters for Juliana. She is expected sometime this evening.

Fuck all this stress. I am going to try to finish cleaning my office space. I completed the bookshelves this morning, and now I must clear up my desk. I even took pictures of the area because it was so messy. I got a feeling that it was going to be a long night.

0645 Up and brushed my teeth, dressed, and picked up Juliana at 0730. We dropped off her stuff at my office and went to chow. No eggs to order; too bad. At 08:30, we went with the CA team.

13:00 I spoke with CPT Laylock, and she seemed pretty mellow and not pissed off at all? I don't get this chick?

Discussed a possible golf story with Juliana.

Checked email.

Terribly tired from getting no sleep.

7 Oct 04

Another fast-paced day. I told the reporter Juliana from the Stars & Stripes Newspaper that I make myself so busy that I often work until 10 p.m. Rather than watching DVDs and playing video games, I read about writing, filmmaking, and screenwriting.

After the routine breakfast rituals, I rounded up CPT Rourke from the MTC, CPT Ridges (S2), and Juliana for a trip to our BDOC rooftop for a photo opportunity with our "Philly Three" as Slacker refers to us (because we are all originally from the City of Brotherly Love.) I made sure that Slacker and the boys knew that the photo was for a hometown news release and not the S & S newspaper.

At 10:00, I am taking the reporter out with our roving patrols. It will be exciting. And later this evening, I will take her out with our night patrols. (Like I said earlier, this is going to be a very long day!)

13:30

We returned from our trip with the roving patrol, conducted interviews with the team members, and ate chow. I took the Stars & Stripes reporter out of the Smythe Gate and showed her the site for the future driving range. Went out with the roving patrol SSG Cactus and SPC Hulk, and we witnessed a burning vehicle on the MSR. Apparently, there were problems outside the wire mission this evening; a joint effort with the IPs was conducted, but no traders were arrested.

At 18:30, Juliana and I went with SSG Cactus and his roving patrol for a second time today. This time, it was under the cover of darkness. We borrowed MAJ Rickets NODS for her to use, and she was grateful. It really makes things quite visible at night.

On patrol at night using NODs (Night Observation Devices) near CSC Scania, Iraq.

After driving through the town of Ash Shumali, we headed west on ASR KIEV. Just past MSR TAMPA, we came across an engulfed vehicle. We didn't notice any signs of explosions (IEDs) and nothing too suspicious, so we returned to Ash Shumali and got the Iraqi Police. By this time, the town was packed with people. Thursday evenings are their big night in town, as Friday is the holy day.

8 Oct 04

17:00

Time is flying by! Today, we are wrapping up with the Stars & Stripes Newspaper. I also made headway today on the golf course. CPT Randerson assisted me with measuring off the targets for our driving range. I am putting them at fifty yards, seventy-five yards, one hundred yards, one hundred and fifty yards, and two hundred yards. We pounded stakes into the ground to mark off the measurements and hole locations. It is actually starting to look a bit like a golf course. I telephoned CPT Phillips, the commander of the Engineer Company here at Scania, and asked him to drop gravel where the stakes are marked. He was happy to oblige.

Today, I wrote up a letter of commendation for Juliana, the writer from the Stars & Stripes Newspaper. I also asked CSM Hunts to ask LTC Slacker to give her a coin. We had an informal awards presentation for her, and she was thrilled. Sometimes, it is the little things that we do that can have a high payoff. I am glad that Slacker, Hunts, and the rest saw that this time.

The threat condition is rising. We had intelligence reports that adversarial Iraqis from the KALSU area were going to come down this evening and lay on an extensive mortar attack on us. It is also interesting to note that KALSU was hit hard this week on Thursday, rendering four WIA and one with severe wounds who is in ICU. That follows their TTP (Tactics, Techniques & Procedures) from their devastating attack in May. Following attacking KALSU in the day, they hit us at night. We had sniper teams out and about, as well as MPs assisting with dismounted patrols along the MSR.

Later that evening, CPT Artera stopped by, and we watched a B Movie that I picked up while on leave.

9 Oct 04

The Stars and Stripes article was published on October 9, 2004. It is titled "Major's Dream: A Golf Driving Range in Iraq." It can be found with a Google search.

Today, I had to catch up on BXO duties. I primarily worked on OERs. I also met with CPT Laylock and planned out the PAO schedule for the next two weeks. We are hoping to include the Adjutant General's visit with the LA Paper. I suggested doing a Purple Heart Ceremony when he arrives. I emailed my family the Stars and Stripes article. It kills me because I never asked for this exposure or story. The course is taking shape, and we are just waiting for the Engineers to dump some gravel out on the range. I am taking the PAO to Alie's for dinner tonight, along with a bunch of other

Battalion guys. I am having some computer problems with my Microsoft Outlook, and the computer geeks are doing their magic. Tomorrow is Sunday, and I want to rest. I am looking forward to mass. This week, I thought about my father and how I know he is proud of me for my Catholic Lay Leader duties. I miss him. I heard from my dearest childhood friend, Stew. I told him that it meant more to me to hear from him than anybody else from our High School class. We were quite close in High School and were football teammates.

21:41

I returned to my office to kick it after a Saturday evening dinner at Alie's with Castellano and his crew. My intent was to bring the LA Paper reporter and his photographer with us so he could see our cordial exchange with the local populous. Unfortunately, he got held up in Baghdad, and we had to settle for the Brigade's PAO, CPT Laylock. She had a good time, as I can tell that she isn't too used to dining or interacting with the locals. I gave her a tip: since she is a female, she could get a glimpse at something that we know little about and see nothing of Iraqi females. After dinner, I asked our interpreter to ask Alie if our female (CPT Laylock) could go in and meet the women. He agreed, and she was in. I will ask her what it was like tomorrow, and more importantly (from a PAO perspective), did she get any videos or pictures?

All that I can say about Iraqi food is that I love it. Maybe it is because we are tired of eating every meal in the DFAC (mess hall), which has a rotating twenty-one-day menu. We are hard up for something else to eat, I guess? I don't know, but I love the food! It is all picked from the local fields, and the chicken or beef is usually slaughtered on the same day. That is fresh food! It tastes so much better than the preservative junk that we Americans are so accustomed to.

Iraq cuisine right off the farm. The best!

I have been lacking attention for this book venture of late for a multitude of reasons: my PAO duties, my BXO duties, my golf project, the entertaining of publishing a second book, and the unit video project. I have been referred to as the "busiest man on the camp," and it is of my own doing. I work all day, from the moment I get up in the morning until 10-11 p.m. at night. The other officers watch DVDs and play video games while I am working on my projects. I can't stand still; I must either take advantage of this time to improve myself or produce a product that will outlive all of us. Maybe I am the proverbial closet writer? If so, I should go back to JR College and study some more English grammar. LOL (as the online geeks say).

It is almost 10:00 p.m., and I am listening to the Rolling Stones on a "Hadjie" sound system. I guess this is my Saturday night. Alcohol could be a chapter of this book in its own right. Just wait for when we redeploy; I predict many alcohol-related incidents with the Battalion. The reason why I bring this up is because I overheard an officer this evening say, "Well, we are waiting until Slacker leaves the camp....to buy another shipment of 'Hadjie' whiskey..." As if meaning that Hillcrest will be in charge and that Irish Mother Fucker doesn't care if you are drinking in your 'off duty' time (is there any off duty here?) I honestly look at it as a morale issue. Do I want my soldiers out on patrol drunk? Hell no! No officer or NCO worth their salt would agree to that. However, given our situation and the moderate threat level for the camp, morale is important to me, and morale for the troops is important. I could possibly turn a blind eye as far as booze goes. However, discretion is paramount, and it must be kept out of sight. If it comes out of the tent by way of a fight or something else stupid, I throw the book at you. Lay low, I say. *(These are my innermost thoughts and not my command philosophy by any means. I just believe in giving the soldiers a break from time to time and possibly looking the other way.)*

Perhaps I could go through official channels and ask permission to have a beer party? This is quite customary in military circles, however, not necessarily in the combat zone. In these functions, each soldier is allocated one, two, or maybe three beers each and no more. But what usually happens is that the nondrinkers give their beers to their buddies; you see where this is going?

Girls, we miss them. I guess I have learned that we really are basically all animals. When I took Juliana from the Stars & Stripes magazine into the local large city with our roving patrol, I saw such lust in the eyes of the local Iraqi men. It was even worse with the Pakistani nationals (all men) who worked in the mess hall. Everyone, I mean everyone, EYEBALL FUCKED this poor girl. It was like visiting a prison. I was embarrassed for her! I conclude that we humans are really just animals in a sophisticated form. The academic Ph.D. out there might say, "No shit," to my assertions. Well, professor, reading about it and experiencing it are two different things, and I am experiencing it.

Another example of this is when I had lunch at the local chicken farmer's house several months ago. After lunch, we got to go into the kitchen where the man of the house's wife and two adult daughters were. The two daughters, probably in their late teens or early twenties, "EYEBALL FUCKED" (pardon my French) me like I have never experienced before. I felt like a celebrity. I have deduced this; I was the senior military officer present, and these girls know these things (even though they aren't allowed to dine or interact with us). The Iraqis recognize the hierarchy of the social scale and, of course, military rankings and treat you accordingly. I never had women check me out like that before, and quite frankly, it was quite a turn-on (sorry, Annette, my wife). I think this is how so many American military men end up marrying foreign women. Hell, who wouldn't want to be received like that every day of your life? Just saying!

275

It pains me to admit to this, and I have never told a sole before. That farmer offered up his two daughters to me for marriage. There was a fee involved, of course. I don't remember how much, but by American monetary standards, it wasn't excessive. Multiple wives are totally acceptable in Iraq and a way of life there. All I could say was, good grief! I can barely handle my one headstrong, college-educated career educator of a wife, let alone two sisters as well. Thanks, but no thanks. What man would want all that drama in their life? LOL

UPDATE: Surprisingly enough, I only received a handful of responses to my letter to the High School class of 1978? I guess they are busy?

Herein lies the irony of serving your country. Putting yourself in harm's way, no, not harm's way, THERE ARE MOTHER FUCKERS TRYING TO KILL YOUR ASS!!!!!!!! Excuse me, I get emotional about that topic. By the way, KALSU got heavily mortared two days ago. One of our guys was WIA, and a USMC LTC lost his arm and is in intensive care! It is a matter of time and luck if that could be me?

The irony is that people go on with their lives. The American military does a dirty job that most other Americans don't want to have to deal with. I only wish that America had a better appreciation of our heritage and history so they might be more supportive. An email, a letter, or a package isn't asking for much. I am not worried about myself. I have a good family at home who are holding it together despite the worst conditions that a family could go through. I am more worried about the Specialists and PFCs who are getting the Dear John letters, which is a daily occurrence here. The American public just doesn't want things messy, and we are in a messy situation. Such is the result of my letter to my High School class. Only half a dozen responses from a class of over 666? God bless them all.

AUTHOR'S NOTE FROM AUTHOR: I guess that my High School classmates can buy my books and read about it someday? Just saying.

(UPDATED NOTE FROM AUTHOR): As I edited this manuscript on the dawn of another 9/11 anniversary, ironically, I received an invitation to my high school class's 45th reunion. This afternoon, I was also featured on CBS Los Angeles "Sports Central," which did a piece about my **Children's Golf** *book series and my golf course project in Iraq. I texted one of my old football buddies the streaming info in case he and any of*

our friends wanted to watch the segment. Here is the irony: he asks me if I am going to attend the reunion this year? I almost wanted to laugh. Fly across the country and spend several thousands of dollars in flights, hotels, rent-a-cars, etc., to visit with my High School class who never chose to write me while I was serving in Iraq????

Here is my verbatim reply; "This year, I published four books. I will have 10 published by Christmas. I have been very busy, I do not know." Life is funny sometimes.

10 Oct 04

I slept in a little and missed morning chow (I only need two meals a day anyway). I was the sole staffer at work this morning, excluding the CSM. He even mentioned later to CPT Randerson that if he was considering applying for an AGR job, he needed to get used to the idea of never having days off work.

NOTE FROM AUTHOR: Truer words have never been spoken by the CSM. Although the AGR (Active Guard Reserve) program is a fantastic career with many perks and long-term benefits, it also comes at a price. I have witnessed numerous broken families due to frequent separations. Long hours are an understatement. In my last assignment prior to retirement, I only got one weekend off a month, and that lasted for two years! No joke! I am not complaining about it now by any means, as I wouldn't trade my life and retirement for anything.

Two reporters from the LA Paper, Bronte and Louie, arrived via convoy this afternoon around 12:30-13:00. At 14:30, CPT Laylock brought them by, and it was a joyous reunion. It was particularly nice to see them since I hadn't seen them since the departure ceremony in California. I was excited to show them my screen saver; it is the family photograph that Louie took at our family day in San Bernardino. You could tell that he was touched by seeing the photo. It brought up a lot of memories for us both. Louie said that I looked like I had lost 40 pounds. I said that everyone in the photo has lost weight. Louie asked about my wife and commented that they remembered her being very nervous about the deployment. After dinner, we shot the bull with the LA Paper guys. Bronte is a cool dude; we talked about writing structure over some Cuban cigars.

11 Oct 04

08:15 Slacker and Hunts stopped in. For some reason, Slacker was all buddy, buddy? More than likely, it is because of his upcoming leave. Also, he thinks that he will be hired by the National Guard Bureau as a Title 10 officer. There is a position in Texas that he wants.

Laylock lost the reporters for a while today, but they were later found in the Chapel. (I don't get it; her sole purpose in life as a PAO is to deal with the press. How can you lose track of some reporters visiting from California while here in Iraq?) We ate lunch with them and had small talk. This afternoon, they will go out with the roving patrols.

This afternoon I was pissed because I set up the LA Paper guys to go out with the Roving Patrols, and CPT Laylock didn't go out with them? I would have gone if I knew this. Fucken bitch.

I spent the latter part of the afternoon taking the reporters around the camp to each of our guard towers. They interviewed the troopers and took some good pictures, I am sure.

We ate chow and stopped by the PX. I bought a remnant 3'x5'scatter rug for my tent. I then returned to my office and called my wife. Unfortunately, Annette was teaching, and it was very difficult for her to talk in front of a classroom of youngsters.

Tonight, I am working on my book projects and need to get a shower.

12 Oct 04

In the office by 08:00 to find out that CPT Laylock was sick and couldn't go out with the reporters (how convenient!) Last night, I decided to go out with them to the municipal meeting in Ash Shumali. We met with the mayor and several of his staff. At the meeting, we discussed several issues concerning a contractor at one of our projects not delivering a strong enough water pump as per the contract. We scheduled a luncheon for the IPs to discuss this issue on Thursday. We also talked about the upcoming Ramadan celebration and when it would be appropriate to bring them gifts. They asked for food donations at the start of the thirty-day period, which starts this weekend. We also informed them to get the word out to prospective contractors that the Army's Corps of Engineers will be conducting a seminar for them regarding the procedures for bidding on various projects. The seminar will be this Saturday in Hilla, and we will attend.

We visited the veterinary hospital that we rebuilt, as well as the communication center. This consisted of the telephone company headquarters and post office. I took the opportunity to get some pictures with two of the three postal employees. They told us that one guy delivers all the city's mail on a motorcycle. The LA Paper reporters ate this stuff up. The Iraqis said that they hadn't had a letter in six months? In addition, when I asked the postmaster for the mailing address and zip code, it took them nearly ten minutes to find the zip code? They said that in Iraq, they don't really use zip codes but rather go by the cities. Good grief!

From there, we stopped by the hospital and showed the reporters some electrical improvements that we were making. There was also an additional building being erected for doctor's offices, which was funded through another source of ours.

The city of Ashumali was very busy and crowded. When we left, we saw many schoolchildren headed for home. In the morning, we saw merchants peddling their wares along the main strip of town.

Armor Battalion soldiers on patrol in an Iraqi town.

Following lunch, I took the reporters to our dig sight within the camp. I also made arrangements to have our gravel dropped off on the driving range tomorrow.

13 Oct 04

Another busy day. We saw the LA Paper reporters off. I presented them with Letters of Commendation, and they were very happy with that. Laylock took them down to visit C Co. in Cedar. Today, we dumped the gravel needed for our driving range. I had them dropped at 50 yards, 75 yards, 100 yards, 150 yards, and 200 yards. It now looks like a golfer's driving range. I am very pleased with the outcome.

Driving range being constructed outside of the rear gate of CSC Scania, Iraq.

Earlier, Chrys from our MWR department stopped in. She asked if a shade structure that was placed outside of the Smythe Gate was intended for the golf course. I told her that I had nothing to do with the shade structure and that it wasn't. She was glad to hear that. She said that Earl at KBR was pissed because he thought it was for the golf course and that it wasn't approved for that. She said that it was approved for the LNs (local nationals) use. I told her that, once again, KBR and or the mayor's cell are uptight about this golf course. They just don't want to see it happen. I say Fuck Them ALL!

I also checked on our stash of Astroturf, and it is still there. Tomorrow, I will remove it from the KBR yard, just in case anyone gets any funny ideas; I want to have control of the Astroturf.

A dark night this evening. Talk about dark nights; you have never seen such dark nights as we see here. The moon's illumination is at its lowest point in the month's cycle, and you can't see anything! A little overcast doesn't help. It looks like the ultimate Halloween night or setting for a good horror movie.

I got two cool emails from a cousin who resides in Florida. Her area was recently ravaged by two horrendous hurricanes. Here is a glimpse into some of the family dynamics on my mother's side of the family:

12 Oct 04

> Darby, glad to know you are not bored and that time goes quickly; when do you get to come home? Sherry and the crew are heading to Chattanooga for Thanksgiving. My husband's sister is coming to Florida at the same time. I'm going to see what I can work out. I hate to travel on Thanksgiving; the traffic is horrible.

> You look very thin in your photo. Hope you are well and have just worked and sweated yourself back to your youthful frame. Heard you got to go home recently. Bet it was a shocker to see how much little Junior had grown. Still haven't seen my newborn niece yet, which is another reason to go home at Thanksgiving. All the family members seem to be fine and doing well.

> Love to hear from you. Send more diary stuff.

> Hugs, love, Cousin.

> Hello Cousin,

> Thanks for the email. You should feel privileged, as you are the only family that Sherry still communicates with. I haven't heard from her since my parents died. I don't think that she is supportive

of the war effort. Oh well, such is life. I try to not let it bother me. They also don't communicate with Michael Termagants' brothers? This could be history repeating itself for the Termagant family. (If you would, please don't mention that I said anything to you, thanks.)

I think that Annette is visiting Pennsylvania in November; I hope that my sister will want to see our son, Junior? They have only seen him once and never inquired about him or called.

Enough about family issues. I gave Junior mom's maiden name as his middle name in honor of my mother. I wanted her maiden name in his name as it is in mine so the name could live on. My mom was very happy about that.

I haven't heard from your brother from Chattanooga in a while; tell him that I said hello. Some friends of your parents have written, and I heard from your parents as well. Tell them all that I said thank you for thinking of me.

We are completing our seventh month here and counting the days. I am very sorry to hear about the storms that you had to experience. Mother nature can be tough at times. As for temperatures, in the morning, at around 6:30 a.m., it is a cool 80 degrees, and it still gets up to around 106 in the afternoon.

Did the golf story get through to you?

Tell the family that I was asking for them. And at Thanksgiving, please say a prayer for my soldiers.

Love,

Darby Hillcrest

13 Oct 04

Hello Darby,

Yes, I got the golf story and copied it for my parents. I also shared it with another lady here who has a daughter in Baghdad? Maybe you know her. Her name is Yada-yada-yada, and she is a captain from West Point. Another teacher here also has a son over there; he is an enlisted soldier. Whether we support the war or not, we support our people over there and definitely will say a prayer for your men and women.

My brother's email is out because his wife is moving her legal office computer to her home so she can get some work done while still taking care of the baby. They are out both at home and the office but should be up soon. I will send your regards. Sorry to hear about the Termagants. It is sad, but mum, I will be. Their girls love my parents so much.... that is why they will be visiting Chatt. I don't think that was Michael's choice. You know, I never knew why you named Junior with that middle name, but that's kind of cool and respectful of your parents. My name is derived from my mom and dad, but they just changed the spelling to make it the feminine version. I always thought that was cool. I Hope Junior will, too! How long will you be in Iraq? Do all our soldiers stay the same amount of time?

Got to go for now.

Love/Hugs

Cousin

NOTE FROM AUTHOR: I later found out from other relatives that during Thanksgiving dinner that year, my name never came up at the dinner table. In fact, my name never came up during Sherry and her family's weeklong vacation in Chattanooga, TN. How sad is that? I ask you, is it me? If our founding fathers had this lack of family support at the inception of our republic, there would never have been a United States of America. Hearing this news was like a dagger in my heart.

14 Oct 04

This goes down in my history books as one of the worst days of my life, thanks to loving sister Sherry. (Is there a recurring theme here or what?) Long story short, my lawyer informed Annette and me of some more hurtful information about my sister Sherry.

How can my sister live with herself?

I do not claim to be a saint, but my parents never raised me to be so callous towards others, especially family members. Whatever happened to my sister? We were raised in the same house, but we are such ethically different people? In times like these, I can only turn to the Lord for guidance. I am very upset today.

NOTE FROM AUTHOR: As time passed, I often asked myself how my sister and I could be so different as human beings, particularly having come from the same home and family. It has occurred to me that she never had a job in her life. No career with health benefits or pension. I have all the above and then some. It occurred to me that I have literally been working paying jobs since I was approximately ten years old. As a child, I had paper routes; I cut lawns in the summer months, shoveled snow in the winter, raked leaves in the fall, and carried golf bags in the summer as a caddy. In High School, I bussed tables in restaurants and even worked a summer at Burger King. I have been working my entire life, literally since childhood, and my sister has not. I think that has a lot to do with building character and developing self-responsibility. It absolutely contributes to one's respect for financial responsibility or lack thereof? It is also important for developing dignity and respect for others. (Life according to Hillcrest)! ;-)

My wife wrote me this information, and I could tell that she didn't want to have to do that. Here is what I told her:

> Hi Annette,
>
> I guess that I am numb. All I can think about is staying alive and getting home to you and the kids and playing ball in the backyard with Junior. I can't get into Sherry's issues; I mean that I just can't let it bother me like I would normally. I won't hold up if I do. I know that Sherry turned Mom against me in the end. That hurts more than anything.
>
> All I want in life are the simple things: family, home, golf recreation, a career, to write a book someday, and a healthy romance with my wife.

I am so stupid because there were subtle signs over the years, but when you love someone, you just turn a natural blind eye. Sherry said something years ago, and it always, ALWAYS stuck in the back of my mind. When she introduced me to that famous Disney writer who lived in her neighborhood, and after I had corresponded with the gentleman for a while, Sherry asked me what her "CUT" would be if we did a project together. I was floored and asked her, "What?" She was as serious as a heart attack. She wanted to know what she was going to get monetarily for introducing us if a deal was transacted. She is more Hollywood than Hollywood! I should have seen the signs and known better. As Chaucer and Shakespeare put it, "Love is blind" (For loue is blynd alday and may nat see).

Boy, was I a chump.

Again, all I can do from here in harm's way of Iraq is to say a prayer for Sherry.

I just got interrupted, but I am back now.

I am sorry to have to dump some of this burden on you.

I wish we didn't have all these problems with Sherry; my relationship with her is shattered forever. I only miss her children. F' Sherry and F' her husband Michael, I hope they enjoy all their money and shore homes as they will be enjoying it all without immediate family. Sad.

(Sherry is taking her family to Tennessee for Thanksgiving to visit Mom's relatives if they only knew.)

Keep the faith.

Love,

Darby

I am so sad; I think I am going to throw up. And I can't talk to anyone about this. There are no Priests within 100 miles of this place. Our Combat Stress Ph.D. is cool, but I feel funny since I see her often and we are friends. I feel funny complaining about family stuff. I am one of the leaders here, and the men need guys like me to look up to.

I can email my father-in-law as I have in the past, but I now fear that I might sound like a broken record. I guess that I will have to just suck it up. This sucks.

I have been thinking more and more about mortality lately. I guess that after going to that redeployment conference in Kuwait, I see light at the end of the tunnel. We see that there is an end in sight. We are already talking about who will go on advanced parties, rear parties, etc. I want to play with my son in the backyard so badly. Last night, I stayed up until after midnight, watching photos and videos that I had taken while I was home on leave. I cried, watching my son run around the house and yard. I want to be there for him in the worst way. I also want to be there to see my daughter graduate from college and to walk her down the aisle at her wedding.

So here I am in this situation, and I have only one sister, and that sister hasn't sent me one letter, one email, or one package since I have been here (7 months now). This same sister won't allow her three daughters to email or write to me or my family? I was extremely close to all three and was always considered their "favorite uncle." I am crushed.

Good going, Sherry. All I know in life is that you can always rely on the truth. When you are truthful in your life, you don't have any worries.

I like how Sir Walter Scott set the record straight: "Oh, what a tangled web we weave when we first practice to deceive."

Back to the Iraq situation, today I visited the Iraqi painter who has a small shop on post, next to the Barber Shop. I cut a deal with him to paint five signs for my golf course. I told him that I was paying cash out of my pocket, and it wasn't the Army's money. He said he'd do it for $50.00, and I talked him down to $40.00. I think that is quite a good deal. Wood boards about 1' x 2', painted white with black lettering: 50, 75, 100, 150 and 200. I will nail these to posts at the respective mounds of gravel on the driving range. Later, I plan on cutting up some Astroturf for driving mats.

Awkward. LTC Slacker and CSM Hunts have been coming into my office at 08:00 or so to get a cup of my Starbucks. I enjoy sharing my love of coffee with others. I guess that I am just not used to Slacker being friendly with me, ever! We have had several days of shooting the shit, as friends might do. It is probably good for our relationship, so I should mellow out. Here is the dilemma I have with Slacker; he will piss me off so much, and then he turns around and is nice. He changes like the wind, and you can't predict him. It is hard to like a guy like that. Could he be bipolar? All the signs are there for bipolar, but I am no doctor. I could really use my psychologist father's help now.

This afternoon, I am helping Slacker write his new OER support form and surf the net. I want to start my screenplay about this place, but I am not motivated right now for anything.

The S3 took the Civil Affairs team to Hilla for a bi-monthly meeting. I was really upset with one other thing: SGT Freedom did a bang-up job putting together our battalion's Civil Affairs status report. It had color graphs, before and after photos, budgets, everything. Everything except my name in the credits! He listed all the players, including LTC Slacker and CSM Hunts, but not PAO-MAJ Hillcrest! What pisses me off is that CPT Morehead is getting a lot of credit for stuff that I helped start. I don't normally care to get recognition for anything because this is my job my career, and I ask for nothing in return. However, when your subordinate soldier blatantly discs you in public, it bothers me. Here is my take on SGT Freedom. He has prior service Air Force, which us soldiers and Marines refer to as Air Force pukes. The Air Force is kind of like civilians in uniform, so this guy doesn't know any better. I can overlook this mess for those reasons. He can't help who he is. (Kind of comical if I do say so.)

Just fuck me.

14 Oct 04

19:00

I read every day on the internet headlines that American soldiers are killed at a rate of one soldier a day. Those figures aren't even that accurate. The DOD (Department of Defense) doesn't' add in WIAs (Wounded in Action) who are evacuated out of theater and die of those wounds. They only include those soldiers who are pronounced dead while they are physically in Iraq. So, their number is deceivingly much lower than reality. And the wounded in action figures are quite staggering. Anyway, I see those statistics, and it just wears me out. Most of us agree that a lot of getting hit by a fatal IED (improvised explosive device) or a stray round has much to do with fate and God's big picture. I guess the biggest stress is the fear of the unknown. We are always on edge, 24/7-365. Talk about exhausting. It is worse for those infantry boys in Baghdad, too. Speaking of which, check these recent headlines:

BLASTS KILL FIVE IN BAGHDAD'S GREEN ZONE

TWO AMERICANS DEAD IN BAGHDAD GREEN ZONE BLASTS

BLASTS KILLS SEVEN IN BAGHDAD'S GREEN ZONE

5 KILLED AS 2 BOMBS EXPLODE INSIDE BAGHDAD GREEN ZONE

BOMB KILL AT LEAST 8 IN BAGHDAD'S GREEN ZONE

EXPLOSIONS ROCK GREEN ZONE KILLING SEVEN

SIX U. S. SOLDIERS ARE KILLED IN IRAQ

IRAQ ATTACKS KILL SIX AMERICAN SOLDIERS

Will the killing ever end?

Conclusion:

In **COMBAT JOURNAL,** Part 3 of 4, we witnessed continued decisive combat operations and, unfortunately, more deaths. Major Hillcrest got his long-awaited reprieve from the war effort when he visited home on an R&R trip. However, that was quite a short-lived reprieve as he returned to the "Belly of the Beast" and before you know it, Darby was back in the thick of things.

COMBAT JOURNAL

PART 4 OF 4
Coming Home

John J. McBrearty
Lieutenant Colonel, U.S. Army (Retired)

What is next:

COMBAT JOURNAL

Part 4 of 4

"Coming Home"

In **COMBAT JOURNAL** Part 4 of 4, you will observe the Armor Battalion continue with combat operations. However, at this stage of the deployment, much effort is put forth in civil-military operations. These objectives include hospitals, schools, and even a golf course. The series concludes with the battalion's redeployment home. How will our citizen soldiers be received on the home front? Find out in the forthcoming pages of **COMBAT JOURNAL**, Part 4 of 4.

Glossary of Military Terms

*NOTE FROM AUTHOR: Entire publications have been written concerning military terminology (see references). I will in no way attempt to duplicate such works. This glossary is a partial one that focuses on the military terms that are in the **"American History, a Veteran's Perspective"** and **"COMBATY JOURNAL"** book series.*

15-6 Investigation	This is a formal commander's inquiry into the facts surrounding an incident. An investigating officer is assigned and conducts an investigation.
AAFES	Army & Air Force Exchange Service-stores, restaurants, and shopping malls on military installations.
AAR	After-Action Review
Abayas	Long black long-sleeved robe like dresses worn by Muslim women in Arabic speaking countries, often with a headscarf or veil. It is a symbol of modesty and piety and protects women from unwanted attention.
ADCON	Administrative Control (command relationship).
ADVON	Advanced Party-a small contingent of soldiers who arrive before the main body of soldiers.
AGR	Active Guard Reserve are National Guardsmen/women who work full time in support of their respective units. They receive all the same benefits as active-duty Army personnel as well as an active-duty retirement.
ALCON	All Concerned
ALOC	Army Logistics Operations Center (also sometimes referred to as a rear command post).

Anaconda (LSA Anaconda)	LSA Anaconda: Is a Logistical Support Area, also known as Balad Air Base, is located about 40 miles north of Baghdad. This is a very large facility holding tens of thousands of coalition forces and civilian contractors. Nicked named, "Mortaritaville," a play on the song "Margaritaville," due to its high frequency of incoming mortars. However, this was such a large facility, many of the insurgent's mortar rounds proved ineffective. This location has moderate danger.
AO	Area of Operation (Later Army terminology shifted to the terms battlespace or operational environment.)
AOR	Area of Responsibility
APOD	Air Point of Debarkation
AR	Armor (tanks)
AR BN	Armor Battalion
Article 15	It is part of the Uniform Code of Military Justice and intended for military commanders to use for enforcing standards and discipline within their units. This is used for misconduct. Also known as non-judicial punishment.
ASR	Alternate Supply Route utilized when MSR's Main Supply Routes are destroyed or congested.
AT	Annual Training, or summer camp (two-week training usually conducted in the summer months for reserve component military personnel).
Babylon	Babylon was an ancient Mesopotamian city vast with history located on the lower Euphrates River that dates back to 2,000 B.C.E. (Before Christian Era). Under several millennia it fell under several different empires, it was known as an artistic, architectural, and cultural triumph. Babylon is situated roughly 50 miles south of Baghdad and three miles north of the city of Hillah.
Battle Buddy	Similar to police partners, they do everything together and go everywhere together in order to protect one another in the combat zone.

Battle Rattle	Combat gear that a soldier wears comprising of IB-interceptor body armor, ACH advanced combat helmet, which is made of Kevlar, and our LBE load bearing equipment-ammo pouches with our basic combat load of ammo, canteens, compass, flashlights, etc. This load is approximately 60 pounds of gear. *(See next paragraph please!)*
NOTE FROM AUTHOR:	*And you want to know why the Veteran's Administration has so many Veteran disability claims for back, neck, and shoulder injuries?*
BC	Battalion Commander
BCD	Bad Conduct Discharge (for the different types of discharges from the military refer to references).
BDOC	Base Defense Operations Center
BDU	Battle Dress Uniform
Bed Down or Rack Time	To Sleep
Berm	Artificial Ridge or Embankment
BIAP	Bagdad International Airport -formerly Sadam Hussein Airport, also know as Camp Victory.
Blue Force Tracker	The BFT has a global positioning system in it that reads where you are from a satellite. It has a computer screen much like what you might see in a police car.
BNOC	Basic Noncommissioned Officer Course
Bongo Truck	Bongo trucks have cabs on top of the engine compartment in the front of the vehicle and are quite common in the middle east region.
Boondoggle	Work or activity that is wasteful or pointless but gives the false impression of accomplishment.
BOQ	Bachelor Officer's Quarters
Bucca Prison	The Bucca Prison is located on the Iraq/Kuwait border in Southern Iraq. It has a low threat level outside of the prison, but a high threat level inside of the prison.

BUB	Battle Update Brief
Bunker	A defensive fortification designed to protect soldiers.
Burqa (Burka)	A loose-fitting garment worn by Muslim women that covers their entire body head to toe. The head scarf is referred to as a Hijab.
C2 Linguist	(Category 2 Linguist) A level of linguist proficiency that includes the ability to read, write, speak, and otherwise totally comprehend a foreign language.
CAB (Combat Action Badge	The CAB is awarded to those soldiers who actively engage with the enemy under fire or are engaged by the enemy under fire and perform according to the existing rules of engagement.
Cedar (Camp Cedar, FOB Cedar	Camp Cedar: Located 187 miles south of Scania and 150 miles north of the Kuwaiti border. Cedar also provides fuel for the Iraqi military, the Iraqi civilian population, and coalition forces. Cedar and Scania are stopping points for convoys originating from Kuwait and Saudi Arabia and heading north to major distribution centers. This location is in an agricultural area and has a low threat level.
CERP Funds	Commanders Emergency Response Program is a means of resourcing additional humanitarian and civil assistance for the Iraqis.
CFLCC	Coalition Forces Land Component Command
Chow Hall, Mess Hall, DFAC	Dining facility where soldiers eat.
CIB	Combat Infantry Badge (see CAB for further definition).
CID	Criminal Investigation Department
CJTF-7 OIF	Combined Joint Task Force, Operation Iraqi Freedom

Classes of Supply	Class I – Food, Rations, and Water. Class II – Clothing and Equipment. Class III – Petroleum, Oils, and Lubricants (POL) Class IV – Construction and Barrier Materials. Class V – Ammunition. Class VI – Personal Demand Items. Class VII – Major End Items. Class VIII – Medical Supplies and Equipment.
Classified (documents or information)	Material that the governmental body deems to be highly sensitive in nature and must be protected. Different levels include Top Secret, Secret, Confidential, Restricted, Official, and Unclassified.
Cluster Fuck	Slang for things going horribly wrong.
CMO	Civil Military Operations
CO	Commanding Officer
Combat Arms	These are the soldiers who have direct contact with the enemy on the battlefield. They include Infantry, Armor, Aviation, Artillery, Engineers, Special Forces, and others.
Command Climate	The culture of a unit. How the soldiers feel about their unit and commanders.
Cordon & Search	A military tactic that confines an area for the search for enemy combatants, weapons, etc.
CP	Command Post
Cross Talk	Casual conversation about events.
DCU	Desert Camouflaged Uniform
Dd214	A governmental form or certificate releasing a military member from active duty. It also identifies the veteran's condition of discharge; honorable, other than honorable, dishonorable, etc.
DELTA Force	They are the most highly trained elite units in the US Military. They are the Army's equivalent to the Navy's Seal Team 6. Their missions include counterterrorism, hostage rescue, direct fighting, and sophisticated surveillance often of high-value targets.
DFAC	Dining Facility

Doc	Army Medic, Physician Assistant, or Medical Doctor
DSN	Defense Service Number-Telephones
Ducks in a Row	Squared Away, Done Well (slang term).
Eaches,The Eaches	This is a military slang term referring to minutia or specifics.
EN or ENG	Engineer
ESB	Enhanced Separate Brigade
Fallujah	Fallujah is a large city approximately 64 kilometers west of Baghdad (about a 50-minute drive). The Second Battle of Falluja was the bloodiest battle of OIF with some 95 KIA and 560 WIA.
Fire and Adjust	This is a slang term originating from the artillery community as they will fire a projectile and adjust fire according to where the previous projectile landed.
FOO Money	Field Ordering Officer-finance personnel.
Force Protection	The ability to protect forces, materials, facilities, and equipment from threats or hazards in order to maintain operational effectiveness.
Force Provider Units	Army portable shower facilities.
FORSCOM	U.S. Army Forces Army Command
Frago	Fragmentary Order (changes to an existing OPORD-Operations Order)
Get-Go	Military jargon meaning from the start or beginning.
G.I.	A soldier. This term originated in World War II whereas the government issued equipment was labeled G.I. standing for galvanized iron.
GP Small	A small general-purpose tent.
Green 2 Report	Reporting Sensitive Items (for example weapons).
Green Zone	In the vicinity of central Baghdad, it is heavily guarded which has several former Presidential Palaces. U.S., coalition, and Iraqi authorities live and work. A very dangerous location during the war.

Guard Bum	That is a term we use for someone who does temporary National Guard duty as a primary means of income. This is someone who might not have employment elsewhere.
Gung Ho	Esprit de Corps, Enthusiasm (slang term).
GWOT	Global War on Terrorism
Hajj	Muslim pilgrimage to Mecca. All Muslims are expected to make this journey at least once in their lives.
Haji Mart (or Market) Hadji Mart	Roadside stands or shops that sell small items and touristy products to coalition forces.
Hijab	A head scarf, worn by Muslim women which exposes their face. The Burqa or Burka is the long dress like gown that covers their entire body head to toe.
Hilla	Hillah (also spelled Hilla) is a major city in Central Iraq located some 62 miles south of Baghdad along the Euphrates River. A largely agricultural area due to its proximity to the river.
Hillbilly Armor	Improvised vehicle armor usually salvaged from local trash and landfills for pieces of metal that when attached to military vehicles, provides some protection from hostile fire. Named by the Tennessee National Guard when a Specialist informed Defense Secretary Donald Rumsfeld in December 2004, "Why don't we have up-armored vehicles? We have to get our Hillbilly Armor from the Iraqi trash and landfills?" This made international news.
HMFIC	Head Mother Fucker in Charge (soldier slang).
HMMWV (Humvees)	High Mobility Multipurpose Wheeled Vehicle (colloquial: Humvee)
Hodjie or Hadjiee also spelled Hadji, Hajji or Haji	A slang term used by soldiers meaning an Iraqi person who has made the pilgrimage to Mecca. Also used in a derogatory fashion.
Hooch	Slang for tent.

Hooah	Heard, Understand, and Acknowledge originally HUA. Also, a slang term representing esprit de corps.
HQs	Headquarters
IED	Improvised Explosive Device, a bomb.
IMT	Individual movement technique-infantry types low crawling through the mud as incoming fire is over head-the Marine Corps invented this training.
IN BN	Infantry Battalion
In Country	Military jargon for being in Iraq or other foreign country in combat.
In shaa Allah, inshallah	"God willing" in the Arabic language. This phrase is used by the Iraqis quite frequently.
IP	Iraqi Police
IRR	Individual Ready Reserve. Trained soldiers coming off active duty go into the IRR (or Regular Reserves or National Guard) to complete their military commitment. They can be called upon if needed to replace active-duty service members.
JAG	Judge Advocate General's Corps (lawyers, judges, clerks, etc.)
Joe	A term of endearment for enlisted soldiers. Also slang for coffee.
Kalsu (FOB Kalsu)	FOB Kalsu: Located approximately twenty miles south of Baghdad and on the southern tip of the Sunnie Triangle. This is an extremely dangerous area.
KBR	Kellogg, Brown, & Root, Inc., are civilian contractors who provide maintenance, manpower, and services to the coalition forces in Iraq.
Land Navigation	Traveling and negotiating unfamiliar terrain either by foot or vehicle, utilizing a map, a compass, and other navigational tools to help you find your destination.
LN	Local National (an Iraqi citizen during OIF).
M16	Standard Assault Rifle
M4 Carbine	Smaller and Improved Standard Assault Rifle (shorter in length and easier to maneuver with.)

Mahdi Army or Militia (Mehdi, Madi)	A poorly coordinated militia army comprised of thousands of out-laws led by Muqtada al-Sadr in response to U.S. forces invading Iraq in 2003. A dangerous bunch of militants primarily made up of lower class Shiite Iraqis.
Mayor's cell	A small unit that maintains the day-to-day logistics of a military post. Responsibilities include providing living and eating facilities among other duties.
MCT	Movement Control Team (they execute movement control of the MSR's).
M-Day Soldier	Man Day (a day of military pay) in other words, a weekend warrior.
MDMP	Military Decision-Making Process. This is the U.S. Army's 7-step analytical process for making calculated decisions in tactical and garrison matters. The steps include Receipt of Mission, Mission Analysis, Coarse of Action (COA) Development, COA Analysis, COA Comparison, COA Approval, Orders Production-Dissemination-Transition.
ME	Main Effort
MEDCAP	Medical assistance provided by coalition forces given to local Iraqi citizens.
MEDEVAC	Medical Evacuation
METL	Mission Essential Task Lists
MIA	Missing in Action
Mill Vans	Large military containers that 18-wheeler trucks transport. They contain our equipment or supplies.
MNCI	Multi-National Corps Iraq
MND	Multi-National Division (Southeast, Central South, etc.) Part of coalition forces in Iraq.
MOD II	Individual Combat Skills in Preparation for Iraq.
MOLLE Gear	Modular Lightweight Load-Carrying Equipment

Mosul	Mosul is a large city approximately 400 kilometers north of Baghdad (about a five-hour drive). It is the second largest city in Iraq, second to the capital city Baghdad.
MP	Military Police
MRE	Meal Ready to Eat
MSR	Main Supply Route designated routes for military traffic in areas of operations in combat.
MWR	Moral, Welfare & Recreation
NCO or NONCOM	Non-Commissioned Officer
NCOER	Non-Commissioned Officer Evaluation Report
NCOIC	Non-Commissioned Officer in Charge
NGB	The National Guard Bureau is the headquarters for all the National Guard forces.
Nihilist	A Nihilist is a person who lets the wind out of a sail, that de-motivates others, and sucks the life out of all around him/her.
NODs	Night Observation Device
NOK	Next of Kin
NTC	National Training Center, Fort Irwin, CA
ODP	Officer Development Program (OPD is Officer Professional Development).
OEF	Operation Enduring Freedom (Afghanistan)
OER	Officer Evaluation Report
Offline	This means conducting business (or conversation) in private or away from a group.
OIC	Officer in Charge
OIF	Operation Iraqi Freedom (Iraq)
Old Man	A slang term for the Commanding Officer.
OPCON	Operational Control (command relationship)
OPORD	Operations Order

OTAG	Office of the Adjutant General (the head general of the National Guard of any given state.)
PACT ACT	*Due to burn pit exposure in the Middle Eastern countries during our times of war, Congress passed the PACT Act of 2022 (Promise to Address Comprehensive Toxics). This act ensures that veterans are provided medical treatment from burn pit exposure.* *The resultant PACT Act presumptive conditions covered are numerous and include but are not limited to: Cancer (multiple types-Head, Neck Respiratory, G.I., Kidney, Brain, Melanoma, Reproductive, and Pancreatic Cancers), Sarcoidosis, Bronchitis, Sinusitis, Asthma, and others.*
PAO	Public Affairs Officer
PCIs	Pre-combat Inspections
Plussed up	To Increase
PMCS	Preventive Maintenance Checks and Services
Pogie-bate	Snacks and or junk food.
Port-a-potties	Portable Toilet Facilities
POV	Privately Owned Vehicle
Property Book	A formal set of records for equipment and other government property maintained at the user level.
PT	Physical Training (working out)
PTSD	Post-Traumatic Stress Disorder (a mental condition caused by stress from an injury or psychological shock).
PX	Post Exchange-like a shopping center on a base or post.
Rack time	Sleep (slang term).
Rank	Refer to the provided references for the military rank structure. The list is far too lengthy for this condensed glossary (SGT, SSG, LT, CPT, MAJ, etc.).
RFI	Rapid Fielding Initiative

Right Seat Ride	Also referred to "left seat, right seat" whereas the outgoing unit performs their assigned mission from the left seat and the incoming unit are the observers in the right seat.
Rock Drill or Rock Walk	Setting up terrain models on the ground, literally using rocks and other natural items to resemble actual terrain. Units utilize this method for rehearsing maneuver exercises by placing various units on the terrain model and going through the various phases of the mission. This is a very effective tool for commanders to accurately visualize the battlefield.
ROE	Rules of Engagement
ROK	Republic of Korea (Military members are referred to as ROK or ROKs).
(ROKs)ROWPU	Reverse Osmosis Water Filtration Unit
RPG	Rocket-propelled grenade.
R & R	Rest & Relaxation
S1, S2, S3, S4, etc.	These are primary staff positions at the battalion level, Personnel, Intelligence, Operations, Logistics, etc. For the remainder of the positions refer to the references sited below.
Sabot Round (pronounced saboe)	Tank Ammunition
SAPI Plates	Small Arms Protective Inserts (put inside of a soldier's body armor vest-extremely heavy).
Scania (CSC Scania)	CSC Scania is a Convoy Support Center and does what the name implies, provides fuel, food, water, and other support for American service personnel, coalition forces, Iraqi military, and select Iraq civilians passing through on this main north south transportation corridor of Iraq (MSR-Main Supply Route-Tampa). It is located 25 miles east/southeast of the City of Babylon and approximately 90 miles south of Baghdad. This camp has moderate danger.

SCIF	Sensitive Compartment Information Facility.
SCP	Security Control Point
SEA-TAC Airport	Seattle-Tacoma (Washington) Airport
SGLI	Serviceman's Group Life Insurance
SIPR net	Secure Internet Protocol Router. This is a secret component of the Defense Information System.
Skivvies	Underwear (slang term).
SOP	Standard Operating Procedure
SOS	Shit on the Singles (soldier's slang meaning cream chip beef on toast-a standard in Army cuisine).
SOSO Operations	Stability Operations and Support Operations
SP	Start Point
SPT BTN	Support Battalion
SPT PL	Support Platoon
SQN CDR	Squadron Commander
Squared Away	To have things in order.
SRP	Soldier Readiness Preparation
SSS	Shit, Shower & Shave (slang term).
Stove Pipe Leadership	A Stove Pipe Commander does not allow for information to flow up or down or within their organization. Hinders communication and cooperation with others. Narrow minded thinking *NOTE FROM AUTHOR: This could have been the subtitle for this book series! JM*
Suspense's	Deadlines
SWA	Southwest Asia
TAC	A mobile tactical command center which is usually in the field. The TAC directs combat missions on the battlefield.
TACON	Tactical Control (command relationship)

Tallil (Tallil Airfield)	The Tallil Airfield is located adjacent to Camp Cedar. As the name implies, is an airfield for coalition forces and has a low threat level.
TCN	Third Country National are citizens from a neutral country in Iraq working as a contractor (truck driver, food service, etc.)
TCP	Traffic control point (controls traffic flow).
Termagants	A violent, intimidating, controlling, argumentative, loud shrew of a woman. A turbulent bully with a bad temper. (William Shakespeare)
Terp	Interpreter (slang term).
Theater	Theater or In Theater means Theater of Operations where combat operations occur.
TOC	Tactical Operation Center, most often the center of all planning and operational matters.
TSD	Training support detachment-active-duty Army advisors to enhance a reserve component unit's training. Experts in their respective fields.
TTP	Tactics, Techniques & Procedures
UCMJ	Uniform Code of Military Justice (The military's legal system).
UR (The City of Ur)	In the Bible's Book of Genesis 11:27-32, Ur is referred to as the birthplace of the Profit Abraham around 2166 B.C. Ur is located in Southern Iraq near the city of Nasiriyah. (More information on Ur in my book, **COMBAT ESSAYS**, Chapter 4.)
USPFO	U.S. Property and Fiscal Office
USR	Unit Status Report-a monthly readiness report to the DA-Department of the Army.
UXO	Unexploded Explosive Ordinance
VBIED	Vehicle-borne improvised explosive device, a car bomb.
Victor	A military vehicle.

Victory, Camp Victory	Camp Victory is located in the Green Zone, which is in the heart of the Suni Triangle in Baghdad, Iraq. Camp Victory occupies the surrounding area 3 miles east of BIAP (Baghdad International Airport). This is a very dangerous location.
Warfighting Functions	There are six warfighting functions: leadership, information, command and control, movement and maneuver, intelligence, fires, sustainment, and protection.
Warm and Fuzzy	Having a good feeling about something.
Weapon Status	Weapon Status Amber the weapon is considered substantially safe, loaded magazine in the weapon, bolt forward, and the chamber not loaded which allows the shooter to rapidly transition to black (not safe, ready to fire at a defined target, magazine is in, a round is in the chamber, safety switch is off safe, finger is on the trigger) or red status (marginally safe, the weapon is loaded, magazine is in, but the safety switch is on safe).
Wrecker	A vehicle recovery truck like a civilian tow truck but much larger.
XO	Executive Officer second in command of a unit (company, battalion, brigade, etc.) **(The dude who gets things done!)**

References:

FM 25-100 (Field Manual-Training the Force)
FM 7-0 (Field Manual-Training the Force)
JP 1-02 (Joint Publication-DOD Dictionary of Military and Associated Terms)
FM 6-0 (Field Manual-Command and Staff Organization and Operations)
FM 22-100 (Field Manual-Army Leadership)
FM 6-22 (Field Manual-Developing Leaders)
AR 600-8-22 (Army Regulation-Military Awards)
ADP 5-0 (Army Doctrine Publication-The Operations Process)

Department of Defense Dictionary of Military and Associated Terms. https://www.supremecourt.gov/opinions/URLs_Cited/OT2021/21A477/21A477-1.pdf
Lt. Colonel John J. McBrearty's brain (the primary source of this information).

ACKNOWLEDGMENTS

As in many successful endeavors in life, we quite often didn't get there by ourselves. We had a helping hand along the way. I would like to thank the following individuals for giving me that helping hand along the way.

To my parents and in-laws. To my wife of four decades, my daughter, my son, and my grandsons. To my close friends Dave, Duke, Chris, and Raf. To the Gross family and all the other friends and relatives that wrote to us and sent my unit greatly appreciated care packages while we were in combat. To Callaway Golf. To Stars & Stripes newspaper. To the other news agencies keenly interested in our unit and who covered the deployment.

To Amy Johnson and CBS Los Angeles, "Veterans' Voices" for supporting our veterans.

To Jim Hill, Chris Hayre, Glenn Shimada, and Gordon Allen at CBS Los Angeles, "Sports Central" for supporting our veterans.

To the U.S. Naval Sea Cadet Corps, who gave me my start in uniform when I was just a teen. Thank you, Lt. Commander Stolle and family of Philadelphia, PA.

To Sa Bum Nim (Master Karate Instructor 7th degree black belt) Jung Hung Kim, my Tae Kwon Do instructor in my formative years. The man who instilled in his students respect, discipline, and courage.

To the United States Marine Corps, who gave me my foundation in leadership.

To Valley Forge Military Academy & College, who gave me the academic foundation to become a success in life.

To the Army National Guard for giving me the opportunity to serve my country, state, community, and soldiers.

To all my previous commanders and NCOs who mentored and taught me along the way. They trained me to be firm with my soldiers, but also to be fair.

Assisting me with the writing of this book includes the following:

John Cole, US Marine Corps Veteran of the Vietnam War, author of six novels and a book of poetry, "Giants and Friends," honoring his fellow Vietnam combat Marines. John is a brilliant writer and a good friend and mentor. (Semper-fi Brother!)

Written by Veteran's creative writing group, California State University, San Bernardino. Many members have contributed to my development as an author over the last year and a half. Some of those fellow writers include Cindy Rinne, Pete Schreiber, Fred "Bo" Dunning, and others. They are all published authors and quite an eclectic bunch of patriots.

The Veterans Administration, Loma Linda, CA, and all their wonderful, hardworking, dedicated staff.

Andreas Kossak (the book's editor and mentor extraordinaire!) Andreas founded "Written by Veterans" and is a former adjunct professor at California State University, San Bernardino, CA. This man is truly inspirational, as his selfless service to our veterans is second to none.

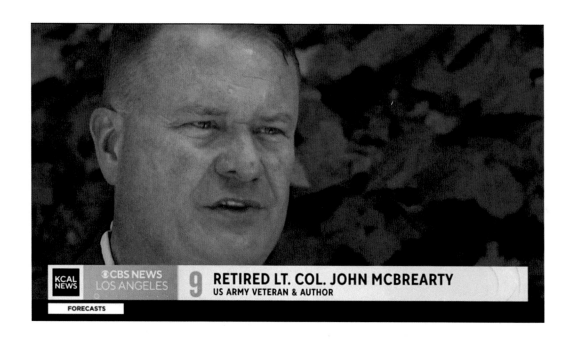

KCAL NEWS | ●CBS NEWS LOS ANGELES | 9 | **RETIRED LT. COL. JOHN MCBREARTY**
US ARMY VETERAN & AUTHOR

FORECASTS

About the Author

Lt. Colonel John J. McBrearty served honorably in our nation's military for 32 years in positions of increasing responsibilities. He has the distinction of serving in both the U.S. Marine Corps and the U. S. Army. His various fields of military training and expertise include Amphibious Assault Vehicles, Infantry, Armor, Cavalry Operations, Operational Planning, Strategic Planning, Public Affairs, and International Relations. His career spanned the globe with operations in Iraq, Kuwait, Japan, Australia, Mexico, and Thailand. His years of dedication and sacrifice are in keeping with the finest traditions of military service.

Upon his retirement, John was recognized for excellence by President Barak Obama.

In 2016 John McBrearty retired as a Lieutenant Colonel.

John J. McBrearty, a member of Phi Beta Kappa, is a magna cum laude graduate of the Valley Forge Military Academy and College, as well as Temple University. He also holds a master's degree in American history from the American Public University. He served as an Assistant Professor of Military Science at California State University, San Bernardino and Claremont McKenna College. His unique multi-service career, increasingly significant military assignments, and combat action give him keen insight into the importance of American history and freedom.

John J. McBrearty is the author of the book series, **American History, a Veteran's Perspective**. **COMBAT ESSAY'S** (Volume II in the series) became an Amazon Best Seller in Iraq War History. **COMBAT JOURNAL'S** 1 of 4 and 2 of 4 were recently published on Amazon. John published his first in a series of children's books, **CHILDREN'S GOLF** (Volume I), which debuted on Amazon as a #1 New Release for physical education. John's children's book series includes **CLAIRE THE MAGICAL DOG,** which is also available on Amazon. Additionally, John contributed to the veteran-written Anthology, **MESSAGES FROM THE BACKROOM**.

John J. McBrearty's other works have been published or featured in Sports Illustrated, Golf Week, Golf Digest, Stars and Stripes, Callaway Magazine, Grizzly Magazine, the Los Angeles Times, the Orange County Register,

Main Line Times, News of Delaware County, Daily Bulletin, San Bernardino Sun, Press-Enterprise, and others.

Having joined the ranks of the "retired," John is active with several Veterans Affairs support groups. John, "COL Mack," is a member of "Written by Veterans" where he serves as a literary mentor and advisor for other veterans. He is a golf instructor and enjoys a friendly game of golf from time to time.

John currently lives with his family in Southern California.

Recently John was featured on segments of CBS Los Angeles:

***"Veterans' Voices"* (American History books)**

and

"Sports Central" (Children's Golf books).

Books by JOHN J. McBREARTY

Books by JOHN J. McBREARTY

COMBAT JOURNAL
Part 1 of 4
"Operation Iraqi Freedom"

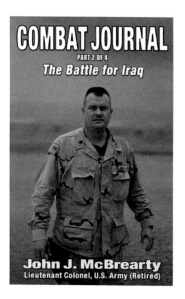

COMBAT JOURNAL
Part 2 of 4
"The Battle for Iraq"

COMBAT JOURNAL
Part 3 of 4
"A Soldier's Journey to Hell"

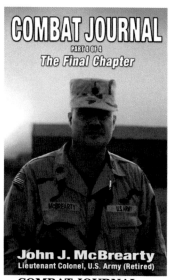

COMBAT JOURNAL
Part 4 of 4,
"Coming Home"

Books by JOHN J. McBREARTY

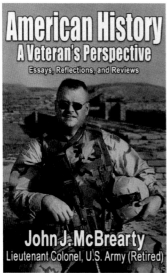

American History
A Veteran's Perspective
Essays, Reflections, and Reviews
VOLUME I

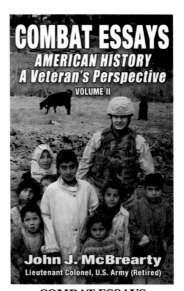

COMBAT ESSAYS
AMERICAN HISTORY
A Veteran's Perspective,
VOLUME II

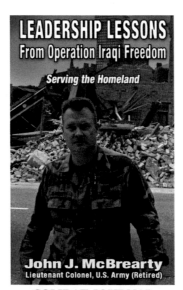

COMBAT JOURNAL
Part V
LEADERSHIP LESSONS
From Operation Iraqi Freedom
"Doing the difficult right and not the easy wrong."

Books By JOHN J. McBREARTY

CHILDREN'S GOLF
*Teach the Golf Swing
in 4 Easy Steps*
VOLUME I

Claire the Magical Dog

Volume I

Claire Introduces Baby to Golf

Claire the Magical Dog

Volume II

Claire Meets Dean & Jacob

Thank you very much for reading my book.

Please feel free to post your thoughts in a review on Amazon.

https://www.amazon.com/stores/John-J.-McBrearty/author/B0BNFDG3VF?

See Lt. Colonel McBrearty on CBS Los Angeles "Sports Central"

https://www.cbsnews.com/losangeles/video/col-john-mcbrearty-using-military-experience-to-teach-golf-to-kids/

Follow John J. McBrearty's other literary works at:

www.johnwriteshistory.com

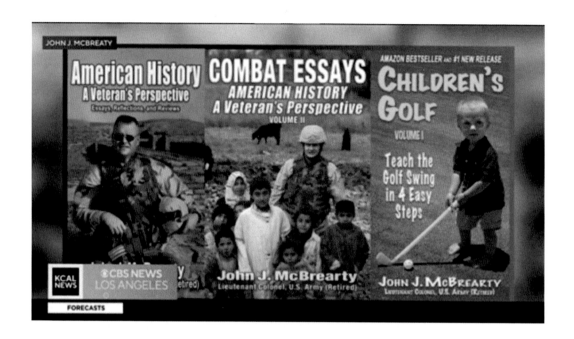

See Lt. Colonel McBrearty on CBS Los Angeles "Veterans' Voices"

https://www.cbsnews.com/losangeles/video/retired-lt-col-john-mcbrearty-u-s-army-veteran-and-author-talks-about-his-books/#x

Legacy

"Our greatest eternal legacy can be judged by our actions here in life."

John J. McBrearty

Veterans Crisis Line
Military Crisis Line

1-800-273-8255 PRESS ❶

Made in the USA
Columbia, SC
04 February 2024

01d311a7-f3c1-4b8c-a9b8-a79852937915R01